HOTELS AND COUNTRY INNS
of Character and Charm
IN PORTUGAL

Hunter Publishing, Inc.
www.hunterpublishing.com

HUNTER PUBLISHING, INC.
130 Campus Drive, Edison NJ 08818
(732) 225 1900, (800) 255 0343; fax (732) 417 0482

IN CANADA
Ulysses Travel Publications
4176 Saint-Denis
Montreal, Quebec H2W 2M5 Canada
(514) 843 9882, ext. 2232; fax 514 843 9448

ISBN 1-55650-904-9
Third Edition

For complete information about the hundreds of other travel guides offered
by Hunter Publishing, visit our website at **www.hunterpublishing.com**

**Hotels and Country Inns
of Character and Charm in Portugal**
Translator: Robin Buss, Derry Hall, and Anne Norris
Front cover photograph: Casa das Torres (Fara-Ponte de Lima, Minho)
Back cover: Casa d'Óbidos (Óbidos, Estremadura)
photos by Fabrice Camoin

Special Sales
Hunter Travel Guides can be purchased in quantity at special discounts. For
more information, contact us at the address above.

Printed in Italy by Litho Service
10 9 8 7 6 5 4 3 2 1

HUNTER RIVAGES

HOTELS AND COUNTRY INNS
of Character and Charm
IN PORTUGAL

Project editor
Michelle Gastaut

Conceived by
Michelle Gastaut
and Fabrice Camoin

Hunter Publishing, Inc.
www.hunterpublishing.com

This new edition details 212 hotels and inns in categories ranging from simple comfort to 'grande luxe.' We have made sure that our readers can always identify the category of each inn or hotel, independent of its star rating.

RURAL TOURISM

This involves lodging in a private home, either in the main house or in other buildiings on the property. You will get to know the family you are staying with, as well as the environment and culture of the country to a degree not possible in a hotel.

Classification:

Turismo de Habitação (TH)

Châteaux, manor houses or residences of recognized architectural value, with quality furniture and decor.

Turismo Rural (TR)

Rustic houses in a small town or nearby, with characteristics fitting their rural location.

Agroturismo (AT)

Houses located on farms, where tourists can take part in the work of the farm.

Booking:

Some of the properties belong to owners' associations, as detailed below. The names of each such property are followed in the text with the symbol for the organization to which it belongs. We recommend that you book in advance, either directly with the owners or through the following associations.

TURIHAB (TH★)

4990 Ponte de Lima, Praça da República
Tel. 00 351/ 58-74 16 72 - 74 28 27 - 74 28 29 — Fax 00 351/ 58-74 14 44
E-mail: turihab@mail.telepac.pt

TURISMO MONTES ALENTEJANOS (TH-MA)

7400 - Ponte de Sôr, Avenida da Libertade 115
Tel. and Fax 00 351/ 204-22 41 02

POUSADAS DE PORTUGAL (★)

Tel. 00351/21-844 20 00/1
Fax 00351/21-844 20 85/7
Web: http://www.pousadas.pt

You should also note that the prices are those quoted to us at the time we went to press and naturally some of them may have changed. Prices are given in Escudos (Esc). At press time, the exchange rate was $1 = 227 Esc.

10, oeu = $45

When making your reservation by phone or fax, you should ask for the latest detailed rates. You should also be aware that rates quoted for half board (one meal) and full board must be added to the room rates given.

In this edition we have also given a selection of restaurants and cafés grouped by the major tourist areas. The prices shown are for a full meal, excluding drinks.

How to use this guide
We have classified hotels by regions in alphabetical order, and within each region by town or locality in alphabetical order. The number of the hotel page corresponds to the hotel number used on the regional maps, in the Contents pages and in the index of hotel names.

Please let us know...
If you are attracted by an inn or hotel not listed in our guide and you think it worthy of selection, please tell us so that we may visit it. In like manner, if you are disappointed by any of our selections, let us know.

Mail can be sent to:

Michelle Gastaut
Editions Rivages
10, rue Fortia
13001 Marseille – FRANCE

You can also contact us on the Guides Rivages' website at:
http://www.guidesdecharme.com

Or get in touch via our US website at
http://www.hunterpublishing.com

Important

CONTENTS LIST

Introduction
Contents list
Restaurants
Essential information
Contents
Map of Portugal
Road maps

RESTAURANTS

Restaurants:

TIME DIFFERENCES

Portugal is 5 hours ahead of EST; same as GMT. Daylight savings is on last Sun, in March (clocks are set 1 hour ahead) and the last Sun. in Sept. (clocks are set 1 hour back).

TELEPHONE/FAX

To call Portugal from the USA, dial 011-351, then the town code and the individual number (omit the first number in brackets from the local number, used only for calls within the country).

AIRPORTS

– **Faro Airport**: Tel. (0)89-242 01 - 7 km from town.
– **Lisbon Airport**: Tel. (0)1-88 91 81 - 8 km from town.
– **Porto – Pedras Rubras Airport**: Tel. (0)2-948 21 44 - 17 km from town.
– **Madeira – Funchal Airport**: Tel. (0)91-52 49 41 - 25 km from town.

WEIGHTS AND MEASURES

1 meter (m) = 1.09 yards
1 kilometer (km) = 0.62 mile
1 gram (g) = 0.04 ounce
1 liter = 1.6 quarts

1 yard = 0.92 m
1 mile = 1.61 km
1 ounce = 25 g
1 quart = 0.94 liter

CONTENTS

A L G A R V E

B   E   I   R   A

D   O   U   R   O

M   I   N   H   O

R I B A T E J O

T R A S - O S - M O N T E S

A Z O R E S

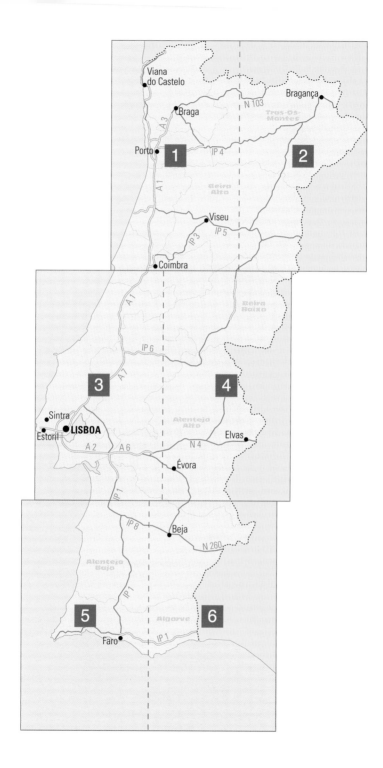

KEY TO THE MAPS

Scale : 1:1,110,000

MOTORWAYS

A9 - L'Océane

Under construction
projected

ROADS

Highway

Dual carriageway

Four lanes road

Major road

Secondary road

TRAFFIC

National

Regional

Local

JUNCTIONS

Complete

Limited

DISTANCES IN KILOMETRES

On motorway   10

On other road   10

BOUNDARIES

National boundary

Region area

Department area

URBAIN AREA

Town   ⊙   ⊙

Big city   ●

Important city   ●

Medium city   •

Little city   •

AIRPORTS   ✈

FORESTS

PARKS

Limit

Center

Created by

90, rue Nationale
75 013 PARIS
01 45 84 30 84

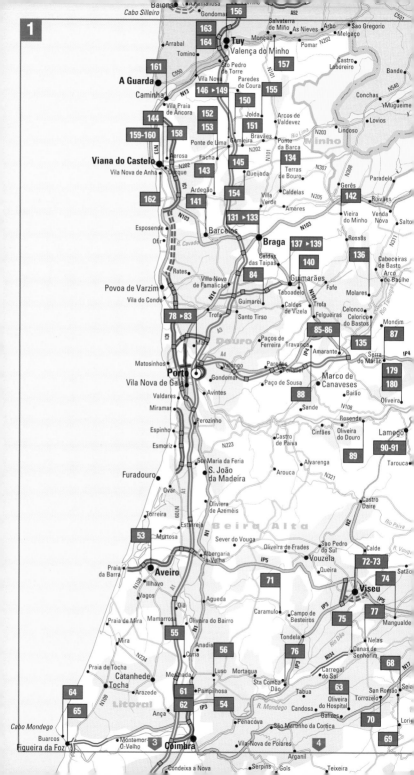

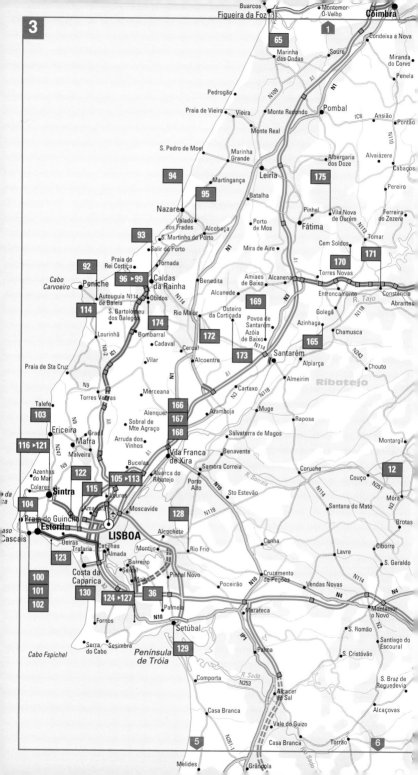

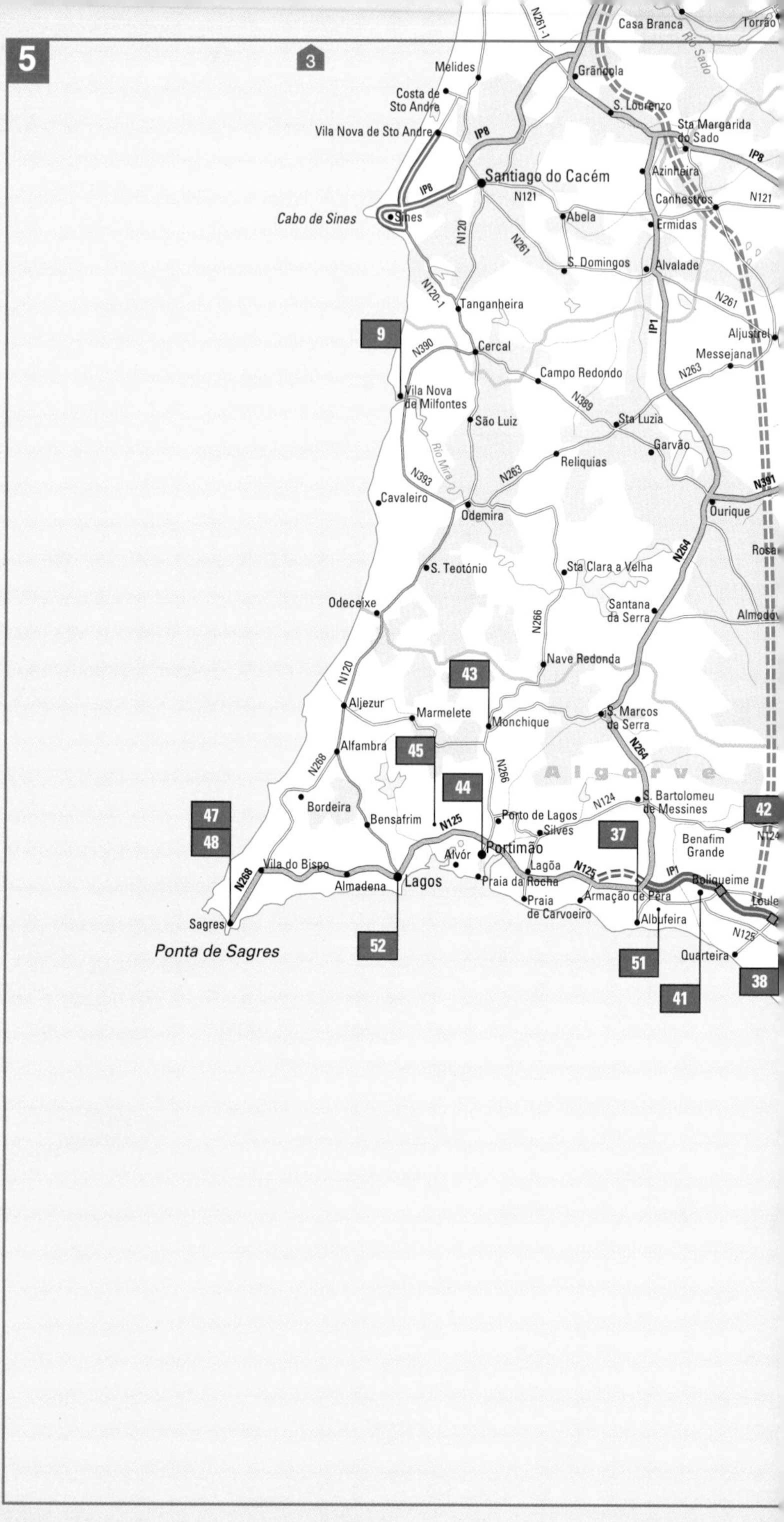

5

3

Casa Branca
Torrão
Rio Sado

Mélides
Grândola
Costa de Sto André
S. Lourenço
Vila Nova de Sto André
IP8
Sta Margarida do Sado
Santiago do Cacém
IP8
Azinheira
N121
Cabo de Sines
N121
Sines
Canhestros
N120
Abela
Ermidas
N261
S. Domingos
Alvalade
N261
N120-1
Tanganheira
IP1

9
N390
Cercal
Campo Redondo
N263
Vila Nova de Milfontes
Sta Luzia
São Luiz
N390
N263
Reliquias
Garvão
Rio Mira
N393
N591
Cavaleiro
Odemira
Ourique
S. Teotónio
Sta Clara a Velha
N264
Rosa
N266
Odeceixe
Santana da Serra
Almodov
N120
Nave Redonda

43
Aljezur
Marmelete
Monchique
S. Marcos da Serra
N264
N268
Alfambra
45
N266
A l g a r v e
42
44
Porto de Lagos
N124
S. Bartolomeu de Messines
N124
47
Bordeira
Bensafrim
N125
Silves
37
Benafim Grande
48
Portimão
Alvor
Lagõa
N125
Vila do Bispo
N258
Almadena
Lagos
Praia da Rocha
Armação de Pera
Algueirão
N268
Praia de Carvoeiro
Albufeira
N125
Sagres
52
51
Quarteira
38
Ponta de Sagres
41

7

CORVO

Corvo

OCÉAN ATLANTIQUE

FLORES

Ponta Delgada
Fajãsinsha
Jajã Grande
Santa Cruz das Flores
Lajes das Flores

GRACIOSA

Santa Cruz da Graciosa
Vitória
Guadalupe
Praia
Luz

196 **195** **194** **193** **192**

Bretanha
Mosteiros
Ginetes
Feteiras
Santo Antonio
Capelas
Fenaes da Luz
Ribeira Grande
Lomba da Maia
Nordestinho
Ponta do Arne
Nordeste
Relva
Ponta Delgada
Lagoa
Fumas
Agua de Pau
Villa franca do Campo
Faial da Terra

SÃO MIGUEL

187 **190 - 191** **188 - 189**

ARCHIPEL DES AÇORES

FAIAL

Praia do N.
Cedros
Salao
Praia
Castelo Branco

186

183 ▸ 185

SÃO JORGE

Rosais
Velas
Calheta
Santo Antão
Topo

Santa Luzia
São Roque do Opici
Horta Madelana
Lajes do Pico
Prainha
Candelaria
São João
Santa Barbara
Ribeiras
Piedale

PICO

TERCEIRA

0   20 km

Quatro Ribeiras
Raminho
Villa Nova
Sanat Barbara
Angra do Heroísmo
Cabo da Praia
São Bartolomeu
Punto Judeu

197 ▸ 199

São Pedro
Santa Barbara
Vila do Porto
Santo Espirito

SANTA MARIA

Royaume-Uni
Irlande
France
Archipel des Açores (Port.)
Portugal
Espagne
Archipel de Madère (Port.)
Maroc
Algérie
Canaries (Esp.)

Camacha
Serra de Dentro
Porto Santo
Ponta

ÎLES DE PORTO SANTO

0   10 km

ARCHIPEL DE MADÈRE

211 **208** **209** **207** **206** **205**

210 **212**

OCÉAN ATLANTIQUE

Ribeira da Janela
Porto Moniz
Ponta do Pargo
Fajã da Ovelha
Seixal
São Vicente
Boa Venrura
Arco de São Jorge
São Jorge
Santana
Faial
São Roque
Porto da Cruz
Prazares
Paúl do Mar
Jardim do Mar
Calheta
Serra da Agua
Curral das Freiras
Ribeiro Frio
Santo Antonio da Serra
Caniça
Machico
Madalena do Mar
Ponta do Sol
Estreito de Camara de Lobos
Monte
Santa Cruz
Ribeira Brava
Santo Antonio
Camacha
Caniço

MADÈRE
Camara de Lobos
Funchal

0   10 km

200 ▸ 204

Monte de Pêro Viegas ᵀᴴ⁻ᴹᴬ

Aldeia Velha 7480 Avis
Tel. 242-41 22 67 - Fax 242-21 41 02
Sr Gonçalo da Cunha e Sà

Rooms 7 with shower. **Price** Single 10,000Esc, double 12,000Esc; extra bed 3,000Esc. **Meals** Breakfast included, served 7.30-10.30. **Restaurant** Reserve 48 hours in advance. **Credit cards** Not accepted. **Pets** Dogs not allowed. **Facilities** Hunting, fishing, riding, parking. **Nearby** Avis (old town, church) - N. Senhora de Entre Águas - Fronteira - Arraiolos - Estremoz. **Open** All year (2 nights min.).

The province of Alentejo is the most beautiful in Portugal, because it is the most unspoilt. Emerging from the historic little town of Avis, you leave the road to start down a small dirt road weaving its way among fields of cork trees. The large house in the distance, apparently isolated, is indeed Monte de Pêro Viegas. The entrance is surprising: you turn into a huge courtyard with palm trees among which peacocks walk freely and casually. Various white farm buildings and the majestic house which has recently been repainted pink, stand around this large patio. Gonçalo Sà occupies the two main floors of the house, but the great drawing room and three bedrooms are open to guests. They are very fine, with views over the courtyard, antique furniture and high ceilings with stucco and moulding. The rooms on the first floor are more independent, comfortable and also with a drawing room, but do not possess the same charm. The situation, on the hunting reserve of Calatrava (9000 ha) and the proximity of the Maranhão dam could provide the opportunity for sporting holidays and interesting trips. A place for lovers of nature – which should, however, be avoided at the height of summer, because of the heat.

How to get there (Map 4): 63km north of Evora.

Monte do Chafariz ^{TH-MA}

Benavilla 7480 Avis
Tel. 242-43 41 37 - 21-354 37 15 - Fax 21-354 37 15
Jorge Moura Neves Fernandes - Vera Lauret Fernandes

Rooms 6 with bath. **Price** Single 8,000Esc, double 12,000Esc. **Meals** Breakfast included, served 8.30-10.30. No restaurant. **Credit cards** Not accepted. **Pets** Dogs not allowed. **Facilities** Swimming pool, boat trips, billiard, hunting, fishing, riding, parking. **Nearby** Avis (old town, church) - N. Senhora de Entre Águas - Fronteira - Arraiolos - Estremoz. **Open** All year (2 nights min.).

Eight kilometers from Avis, which still preserves the memory of its glorious past (the Order of Avis is the oldest Portuguese order of chivalry, from the time of João I), you will find this typically Alentejan house near the Maranhão dam. Long shining white buildings, bordered with ultramarine, surround the paved courtyard. The only prominent feature is the little porch that marks the main entrance. You go directly into the large living room which has kept its original beams and fireplace. The rooms are arranged one after the other, which means that they enjoy the fine proportions of a converted farm. The furniture is rustic, there is a collection of ceramics, and everything is simple, sober and authentic. The rooms are all spacious, decorated with painted furniture, a local craft. The best are those with a sitting room, fireplace and view over the reservoir. For your amusement, the former water trough on the farm has been transformed into a swimming pool and there is a games room. Apart from this, hunting, fishing and riding can be organized for you during your stay.

How to get there *(Map 4): 63km north of Evora. 8km from Avis.*

Monte do Padrão ^{TH-MA}

Figueira e Barros 7480 Avis
Tel. 242-465 153 / 65 250 - Fax 242-465 327
Sr José Godinho de Carvalho

Rooms 6 and 1 suite (4 pers.) with telephone, bath, TV. **Price** Double 15,000Esc, suite 20,000Esc; extra bed 3,000Esc. **Meals** Breakfast included, served 7.30-10.30. **Restaurant** By reservation 48 hours ahead — mealtime specials 2,500Esc. **Credit cards** Not accepted. **Pets** Dogs allowed. **Facilities** Swimming pool, tennis, sauna, hunting, fishing, riding, parking. **Nearby** Avis (old town, church) - N. Senhora de Entre Águas - Fronteira - Arraiolos - Estremoz. **Open** All year (2 nights min.).

You reach Monte do Padrão through woods of cork trees and fields where peaceful bulls graze. Even though the white villages are the tourist curiosity of the Alentejo, the colors highlighting the doors and windows also have an important decorative place in the landscape. The large house has chosen white and yellow on its long frontage, covered by a trellis which thus forms a green, shady gallery. The rooms are in the right wing; they are large, soberly decorated with old-fashioned furniture, as well as being comfortable and very well kept. The main drawing room with its 19th-century furniture, its family photographs and its ceiling painted pink and blue (to match the *azulejos* around the main fireplace), is not without charm either. Here, the guests are offered almost hotel service, which no doubt increases the level of comfort, but also slightly detracts from the charm.

How to get there (Map 4): 63km north of Evora. 8km from Avis.

Pousada de São Francisco *

7800 Beja
Largo D. Nuno Alvares Pereira
Tel. 284-32 84 41 - Fax 284-32 91 43

Rooms 34 and 1 suite with air-conditioning, telephone, bath, WC, satellite TV, minibar; elevator wheelchair access. **Price** Single 18,900-29,000Esc, double 20,300-31,000Esc, suite 38,700-51,300Esc; extra bed +30%. **Meals** Breakfast included, served 8:00-10:30. **Restaurant** Service 8:00AM-10:30PM – mealtime specials 3,650Esc, also à la carte – Specialties: Canja de galinha à Alentejana - Bacalhau conventual - Borreguinhos de Azeite - Doçaria conventual de Beja. **Credit cards** All major. **Pets** Dogs not allowed. **Facilities** Swimming pool, tennis, parking. **Nearby** In Beja: Convent of Nossa Senhora da Conceição. **Open** All year.

Beja, a legendary town, the "white town" of Alentejo, shelters in one of its many beautiful buildings the former monastery of São Francisco, a very attractive *pousada*. You'll see vast rooms such as the refectory, the "conciergerie" and the columned hall, converted into restaurant, lounges and other rooms. The bedrooms are in the former monks' cells which are mostly very large, and with a comfort and luxury not at all monastic! The galleries lining the large cloister have pretty furniture comfortable enough for meditation, or you could retire to the small gothic chapel to contemplate its frescos. Modern needs are catered to in the large garden with swimming pool and tennis court.

How to get there (Map 6): 194km north of Lisboa.

4

Pousada do Castelo de Alvito *

7920 Alvito (Beja)
Largo do Castello
Tel. 284-48 53 43 - Fax 284-48 53 83

Rooms 20 with air-conditioning, telephone, bath, WC, satellite TV; elevator, wheelchair access. **Price** Single 18,000-29,000Esc, double 20,300-31,000Esc, suite 24,300-38,000Esc; extra bed +30 %. **Meals** Breakfast included, served 8:00-10:30. **Restaurant** Service 1:00PM-3:00PM, 7:30PM-10:00PM – mealtime specials 3,650-4,950Esc, also à la carte – Specialties: Bacalhau à Marqués de Alvito. **Credit cards** All major. **Pets** Dogs not allowed. **Facilities** Swimming pool, parking. **Nearby** In Alvito: Church of Matrice, Chapel of Misericórdia, Museum of Sacred Art, chapels of São Sebastião and Santa Luzia - Quinta da Agua do Peixe - Ruins of S. Cucufate - Dam of Odivelas (swimming, fishing) - Vila de Frades. **Open** All year.

The Pousada do Castelo is in the château of this traditional village of Alentejo. It is a robust fortress from the 15th century, flanked by five imposing towers with crenellations, which retain on their walls some traces of their gothic, *mudejar* and "Manuelin" history. The bedrooms are found on two floors and off the long galleries surrounding the main courtyard. This pousada possesses such attractions as a dining room which has preserved its gothic vaulting. The comfort and services are those of a top class hotel, while the garden lacks for nothing: there's a swimming pool for the hottest summer days, and also shady places with a strong scent of orange blossom.

How to get there (Map 6): 30km north of Evora via N254.

Quinta dos Prazeres ^{TR}

7920 Alvito (Beja)
Largo das Alcaçarias
Tel. 284-48 51 70 - Fax 284-48 54 69
Maria Antonia Gois

Rooms 9 with telephone, bath or shower. **Price** Single 11,500Esc, double 12,500Esc, 3 pers. 13,500Esc, 4 pers. 14,500Esc. **Meals** Breakfast included, served 7:30-10:30. **Evenings meals** Service 7:30PM-10:00PM – mealtime specials 2,800Esc. **Credit cards** All major, on request. **Pets** Dogs not allowed. **Facilities** Swimming pool, parking. **Nearby** In Alvito: Church of Matrice, Chapel of Misericórdia, Museum of Sacred Art, chapels of São Sebastião and Santa Luzia - Quinta da Agua do Peixe - Ruins of S. Cucufate - Dam of Odivelas (swimming, fishing) - Vila de Frades. **Open** All year.

This quinta, surrounded by cork and olive trees on the outskirts of a small village, was once a farm house and home to an important producer of olive oil. Today, it is an observatory of game animals and a hunting lodge during the season. The long white building is altogether typical of regional architecture with a friendly living room, cool in the summer and heated in the winter by a superb fireplace. The rooms are not especially spacious but very attractive with their floral decoration. The garden has a duck pond and a swimming pool, very rare in this region, which add to the quality of this place which is best considered a stop-off rather than a place for a longer stay; unless, of course, you plan to do some hunting.

How to get there (Map 6): 30km north of Evora via N254.

Quinta do Barranco da Estrada

7665-880 Santa Clara A Velha (Beja)
Tel. 283-933 901 - Fax 283-933 901 - Sr Franck Mc Clintock
E-mail: lakescape@mail.telepac.pt - Web: www.paradise-in-portugal.com

Room 7 with bath. **Price** Single 12,000-17,500Esc, double 13,250-18,500Esc, with two communicating rooms 25,000-35,000Esc; extra bed 3,000Esc. **Meals** Breakfast included (full breakfast 1,000Esc), served 8:00-10:00. **Evening meals** Service 1:00PM, 8:30PM – mealtime specials 3,000-4,000Esc; mealtime specials for child 1,500-2,000Esc. **Credit cards** Not accepted. **Pets** Dogs not allowed. **Facilities** Canoeing, mountain bikes, jet ski (3,750Esc/15mn), sailing and windsurfing (2,000-4,000Esc/day). **Nearby** Strand des Alentejo - Serra de Monchique. **Open** All year.

Coming from Lisbon, you pass through the wild region of lower Alentejo with its eucalyptus and pine woods. Coming from the Algarve, you cross the Serra de Monchique, a natural barrier to the damp Atlantic winds, favoring vegetation that is dense and luxurious. That is to say that the approach is pleasant in itself. After Santa Clara, the road becomes rather long, giving the impression that one has reached the end of the world. But the reward awaits you: a breathtaking panorama, a veritable oasis overlooking the largest dam in Portugal which has created a micro-climate allowing the cultivation of rare species of plants and meaning that the pure water of the lake can be kept at 28° in summer. Attracted by this spot, Franck, of English origin, decided to create a wild paradise here, part Robinson Crusoe, part Noah's Ark. The garden is full of hibiscus, jasmin, oleanders and fruit trees (you can pick the fruit). The animals also live freely here. As for the humans, they are housed in elegant and comfortable rooms with balconies and views over the lake. Meals, prepared with home produce, are served on the terrace in the shade of the vine. Franck will direct you for all your excursions and offer you an ornithological visit in the migration period.

How to get there (Map 5): 13km from Sta Clara, towards Cortebrique. Do not take the Cortebrique turning, bu follow the road until the sign for the quinta.

Pousada de São Gens *

7830 Serpa (Beja)
Tel. 284-54 47 25 - Fax 284-54 43 37
Sra Maria Amelia Vaz da Silva

Rooms 16 and 2 suites with air-conditioning, telephone, bath, WC, satellite TV, minibar. **Price** Single 14,800-23,100Esc, double 16,300-24,600Esc, suite 20,800-30,500Esc; extra bed +30%. **Meals** Breakfast included, served 7:30-10.30. **Restaurant** Service 12:30PM-3:00PM, 7:30PM-10:00PM – mealtime specials 3,850Esc, also à la carte – Specialties: Migas con carne de porco - Açorda alentejana - Gazpacho alentejano - Ensopado de borrego. **Credit cards** All major. **Pets** Dogs allowed except in restaurant. **Facilities** Swimming pool, parking. **Nearby** Convent of Nossa Senhora da Conceição in Beja. **Open** All year.

This pousada with its rather modern architecture is next to the little chapel of São Gens. One enters Serpa through the Porte de Beja pierced in the old fortress walls surrounding the town. Occupied in turn by the Arabs and Castilians, it has preserved many signs of these different cultures. The two white buildings of the pousada, on top of a small hill a little apart from the town, dominate wide fields of wheat and olives. The interior decoration is sober but the amenities are very comfortable, and there is an appetizing regional cuisine to be sampled. One of the best moments here is when in the evening, from this peaceful countryside the shepherds' voices, the tinkle of bells, and murmurs from the fields rise to your ears. It is one cliché situation you should not miss!

How to get there (Map 6): 29km southeast of Beja via N260.

Castelo de Milfontes

7645 Vila Nove de Milfontes (Beja)
Tel. 283-99 82 31 - Fax 283-99 71 22
Sra Ema da Camara Machado

Rooms 7 with bath and 1 studio in the annex. **Price** With half board 26,000-28,000Esc (2 pers.).
Meals Breakfast included, served 8:30-10:00. **Evening meals** Service 8:00PM, 8:30PM in summer.
Credit cards Not accepted. **Pets** Small dogs allowed on request. **Nearby** In Porto Covo and
Pessegueiro island - Sines - Serra de Monchique. **Open** All year.

If you arrive in Portugal from the south of Spain via Lisbon and the Alentejo coast, you can make a pleasant stop at Castelo de Milfontes, a château with a long history beginning when the Carthaginians first built a fortress here. Repeatedly destroyed and rebuilt over the ages, today it is a place devoted to pure enjoyment. There is a guest house atmosphere and you will be welcomed as friends: the bar is open and all you have to do is note what you drink; if you want to go out for the day, they will make you a picnic... Few of the rooms and reception areas offer anything spectacular, the most attractive of them being those in the tower, but you'll like the sitting room and dining room, both in rustic style, plus an attractive patio giving directly onto the sea. It is worth staying in the region: from Comporta to Sinea the Costa da Galé has fine beaches protected by sand dunes edges with pine woods, while south of Cape Sines, the coast becomes wilder and more rocky.

How to get there (Map 5): 60km north of Lagos, on the Costa Dourada.

Pousada de Nossa Senhora da Assunção *

7040 Arraiolos (Evora)
Quinta dos Loios
Tel. 266-419 340 - Fax 266-419 280 - Luis Abilio

Rooms 30 and 2 suites with air-conditioning, telephone, bath, WC, satellite TV, minibar; elevator. **Price** Single 18,300-29,600Esc, double 20,300-31,600Esc, suite 24,300-38,800Esc; extra bed +30%. **Meals** Breakfast included, served 8:00-10:30. **Restaurant** Service 1:00PM-3:00PM, 7:30PM-10:00PM – mealtime specials 3,650-4,650Esc, also à la carte. **Credit cards** All major. **Pets** Dogs not allowed. **Facilities** Swimming pool, tennis, parking. **Nearby** Arraiolos - Avis - Pavia - Museum of Cristo in Arcos - Evora - Castle of Evoramonte) - Elvas (fortress, aqueduto da Armoreira, Largo Santa Clara, Igreja de Nossa Senhora da Consolação). **Open** All year.

This pousada is the most recent of a series of fine hotels built by this well-known Portuguese chain. A former 16th-century convent, it has been totally renovated and enlarged by José Paulo dos Santos, a leading contemporary Portuguese architect, and is particularly well situated in the midst of the grazing fields and cork trees typical of the Alentejo. Here you find an intelligent and harmonious meeting of two styles as you go from the traditional to the modern through a labyrinth of highly varied shapes where the quality of light plays an important role. The dazzling white of the walls is beautifully set off by brief passages of azure blue, and the exterior decoration as well as the interior are of exemplary sobriety with huge earthen jars on the balconies perfectly in keeping with the authentic rural spirit of the hotel. The rooms enjoy a discreet elegance, the lounges are extremely comfortable, the service is beyond reproach and the welcome you receive is as friendly as you will find anywhere. This is a truly magnificent hotel, one close to Evora and to all the places of interest in the Alentejo.

How to get there *(Map 4): 22km northwest of Evora. 1km north of Arraiolos.*

Monte Velho Da Jordana ^{TR-MA}

7490 Pavia (Evora)
Tel. 266-45 93 40
Rui Nogueira Lopes Aleixo

Apartments 2 (4 pers. and 5 pers.) with bath, 2 or 3 rooms, lounge, kitchenette (2 nights min.). **Price** 18,000Esc (4 pers./days) - 22,500Esc (5 pers./days). **Meals** Breakfast included. No restaurant. **Credit cards** Not accepted. **Pets** Dogs allowed. **Facilities** Parking. **Nearby** Pavia: church, chapel, Casa Museo Manuel Ribeiro de Pavia - Brotas - Arraiolos - Avis - Museum of Cristo in Arcos - Evora - Castle of Evoramonte - Elvas (fortress, aqueduto da Armoreira, Largo Santa Clara, Igreja de Nossa Senhora da Consolação). **Open** All year.

Pavia is a little town in the Alentejo which originates in the neolithic period; the D Dinis chapel occupies a prehistoric dolmen. The environment is bucolic: pastures and woods of cork trees extending to the horizon. The house, typical of local architecture (low, painted white, with yellow along the bottom of the walls) has been restored with a desire to preserve the simplicity, even the rural character of the place and the original building. However, the two apartments, which are in two separate houses, are very well-kept with a high level of comfort and modern bathrooms. The décor is charming: fresh and very pretty. The colors are jolly: each room has its own key color, with painted furniture and fabrics in harmonizing shades. The drawing room with its fireplace is convivial and the kitchen is properly equipped. There are sheep grazing just beneath your windows and, beyond them, the fields stretch away to the horizon. The property is a little isolated, so better suited to those who like the tranquillity of the countryside or hunting and fishing (the Maranhão dam is only five kilometers away).

How to get there (Map 4): 42km northwest of Evora towards Arraiolos, then Pavia. In Pavia, ask the way; it is easy to find.

Monte da Fraga ^{TR-MA}

7490 Mora (Evora)
Herdade do Paço de Baixo
Tel. 266-43 91 25
Teresa and Manuel Caldas de Almeida

Rooms 4 and 2 houses with 1 or 2 rooms, bath, kitchen, sitting room with TV (2 nights min.). **Price** Double 9,200-10,500Esc, apart. with 1 bedroom 12,500Esc, apart. with 2 bedrooms 17,500Esc; extra bed 2,000Esc. **Meals** Breakfast included for bedrooms. No restaurant. **Credit cards** Not accepted. **Pets** Dogs not allowed. **Facilities** Swimming pool, parking. **Nearby** Pavia: church, chapel, Casa Museo Manuel Ribeiro de Pavia - Brotas - Arraiolos - Avis - Museum of Cristo in Arcos - Evora - Castle of Evoramonte - Elvas (fortress, aqueduto da Armoreira, Largo Santa Clara, Igreja de Nossa Senhora da Consolação). **Open** All year.

Mora is a little town on the banks of the River Raia which is famous for the waterfalls of Raia at Fraga. We are still north of Evora in a delightful, resolutely rural part of the country. Monte da Fraga is quite hard to find because nothing is signposted in the center of Mora. It is in fact fifteen kilometers away on a little hill and forms part of the large agricultural estate of Paço de Baixo. The houses rented out to visitors are very charming, painted white and blue, and opening directly on an olive grove and the swimming pool. They are cute, with modernized interiors, visible beams and regional furniture, all thoughtfully and comfortably arranged. A separate communal room is at the disposal of guests, with television, games and a barbecue. The garden is pleasant with a view over the valley, the river and the Furadouro aqueduct. The atmosphere is jolly and sporty: in the three thousand hectares of the estate you can hunt, fish, ride or go out on your mountain bike.

How to get there *(Map 3): 42km northwest of Evora, towards Arraiolos, then Mora.*

Pousada da Rainha Santa Isabel *

7100 Estremoz
Largo D. Diniz - Castelo de Estremoz
Tel. 268-33 20 75 - Fax 268-33 20 79

Rooms 30 and 3 suites with air-conditioning, telephone, bath, WC, satellite TV, minibar; elevator. **Price** Single 24,000-33,000Esc, double 26,500-35,700Esc, "luxe" 34,700-43,400Esc, suite 34,700-52,300Esc; extra bed +30%. **Meals** Breakfast included, served 7:30-10:30. **Restaurant** Service 12:30PM-3:00PM, 7:30PM-10:00PM – mealtime specials 3,650-4,650Esc, also à la carte – Specialties: Carne de porco alentejana - Bacalhao dorado - Agorda alentejana. **Credit cards** All major. **Pets** Dogs not allowed. **Facilities** Swimming pool. **Nearby** Museum of Cristo in Arcos - Castle of Evoramonte - Elvas (fortress, aqueduto da Armoreira, Largo Santa Clara, Igreja de Nossa Senhora da Consolação). **Open** All year.

After having been a barracks and then school, the château of Estremoz was finally converted into a hotel. This is the most luxurious pousada in the country. The interior architecture has grandiose proportions: the monumental staircase of the entry decorated with *azulejos* tiles, the lounges and the long vaulted dining room are majestic. The furnishing includes genuine period pieces, while the rooms have a sober and exquisite luxury. The cuisine is refined and the "cave" well known. This is a high level establishment at reasonable prices.

How to get there *(Map 4): 180km east of Lisboa via A2 then N10 to Athalho, then via N4.*

Monte dos Pensamentos [TR]

7100 Estremoz (Evora)
Estrada da Estacão do Ameixial
Tel. 268-333 166 - Fax 263-332 409 - Sra Leitão

Rooms 1 double and 2 suites (2-3 pers.) with air-conditioning, bath, TV and 2 apartments (2-3 pers.) with kitchen, 1 double room, lounge, bath, TV. **Price** Double 11,000Esc, suite (1-2 pers.) 11,000-13,000Esc, apart. (2-3 pers.) 12,000-14,000Esc; extra bed 2,000Esc. **Meals** Breakfast included in bedroom and suite. **Restaurant** See p. 215. **Credit cards** Not accepted. **Pets** Dogs allowed. **Facilities** Swimming pool, parking. **Nearby** Museum of Cristo in Arcos - Castle of Evoramonte - Elvas (fortress, aqueduto da Armoreira, Largo Santa Clara, Igreja de Nossa Senhora da Consolação). **Open** All year.

Alentejo remains one of the few regions of Portugal where there is still an authentic pastoral spirit. The gentle countryside, alternates green wheatfields, hills of cork-oak trees and green oaks, and meadows with grazing sheep. Estremoz is today known for pottery; and do not miss the picturesque Saturday market. Close by, Monte dos Pensamentos (the house of thought) is a fine traditional white building, in Moorish style, with refreshingly shady arcades all round, with scented eucalyptus and beyond it an olive grove containing a variety of animals: lambs, ducks and hens (whose eggs you will enjoy at breakfast). The few rooms of the hotel are very charming, appointed with a lot of authenticity: painted furniture, pious pictures and everywhere an impressive collection of old plates. Add to this an atmosphere of well-being maintained by Rosemary, who has never forgotten her English origins, nor even the recipe for that bitter orange marmalade she serves at breakfast.

How to get there (Map 4): 180km of Lisboa; at 2km of Estremoz via EN4 towards Lisboa; before "Galp" petrol station take road to the right.

Pousada dos Lóios *

7000-804 Evora
Largo Conde Vila Flor
Tel. 266-704 051/2 - Fax 266-707 248
Sr Frederico Vidal

Rooms 30 and 2 suites with air-conditioning, telephone, bath, WC, minibar, satellite TV. **Price** Single 24,100-32,700Esc, double 26,100-32,700Esc, suite 34,700-52,300Esc; extra bed +30%. **Meals** Breakfast included, served 7:30-10:30. **Restaurant** Service 12:30PM-3:00PM, 7:30PM-10:00PM – mealtime specials 3,650-5,100Esc, also à la carte – Regional cooking. **Credit cards** All major. **Pets** Dogs not allowed. **Facilities** Swimming pool. **Nearby** In Evora: Sé, Roman Temple of Diana, Convento dos Lóios, fortress, Museum of Evora - Convento São Bento de Castris. **Open** All year.

Evora is a fortified town in one of the most beautiful parts of Portugal, and the convent of dos Lóios in which the pousada is installed is part of a delightful group of historic monuments. It is in fact flanked by the famous house of the Dukes of Cadaval on one side, and the palace of the Counts of Basto on the other. Close by are the temple of Diana, cathedral and museum. Inside, the convent has preserved a very attractive gothic-"Manuelin" door, and a small lounge decorated with 18th century furniture and painted walls. The dining room is the convent refectory but in summer meals are served in the shady cloister. The bedrooms are fresh, simple and pleasantly furnished. We recommend the suite with a beautiful painted ceiling and antique Indo-Portuguese furniture.

How to get there (Map 4): 145km east of Lisboa via A2, then N10 to Atalho, then N4 to Montemor and N114.

Albergoria Solar de Monfalim

7000-646 Evora
Largo da Misericórdia, 1
Tel. 266-75 00 00 - Fax 266-74 23 67 - Sra Ramalho Serrabulho
E-mail: reservas@monfalimtur.pt - Web: www.monfalimtur.pt

Category ★★★ **Rooms** 25 and 1 triple with air-conditioning, telephone, bath or shower, WC, TV, minibar, safe. **Price** Single 9,500-11,500Esc, double 11,500-14,000Esc, triple 15250-18,500Esc. **Meals** Breakfast included, served 8:00-10:30. **Restaurant** See p. 215. **Credit cards** Amex, Visa, Eurocard, MasterCard. **Pets** Dogs not allowed. **Nearby** In Evora: Sé, Roman Temple of Diana, Convento dos Lóios, fortress, Museum of Evora - Convento São Bento de Castris. **Open** All year.

Evora is the capital of Upper Alentejo and a very attractive town on which each age has left its traces. Surrounded by walls from the Roman age, it has also preserved its Moorish walls, "Manuelin" palaces, tiled patios and Moorish-Arab balconies, all of which make the town a museum of Portuguese architecture. The Solar Monfalim is an ancient Renaissance palace as testified by the entrance and grand staircase. But it is also a charming house run by Mr. and Mrs. Serrabulho, who have renovated the rooms without having altered its beauty and its atmosphere.

How to get there *(Map 4): 145km east of Lisboa via A2.*

Residencial Policarpo

7000 Evora
Rua da Freiria de Baixo, 16/Rua Conde da Serra
Tel. 266-70 24 24 - Fax 266-70 24 24 - Sra Michèle Policarpo
Web: www.localnet.pt/residencialpolicarpo

Rooms 13 with telephone, bath or shower, WC, TV, 7 without bath. **Price** No private bath 5,000-7,000Esc, with private bath or shower 7,000-10,000Esc. **Meals** Breakfast included, served 8:00-10:30. **Restaurant** See p. 215. **Credit cards** Not accepted. **Pets** Dogs not allowed. **Facilities** Parking (access by Rua Conde da Serra). **Nearby** In Evora: Sé, Roman Temple of Diana, Convento dos Lóios, fortress, Museum of Evora - Convento São Bento de Castris. **Open** All year.

Portugal is a land of *azulejos* and Evora has a most beautiful collection of them. Examples can be found in the church of São João Evangelista, the São Bras hermitage and the Espinheiro convent with even more spectacular ones on the walls of the University. The Residencial Policarpo is a small inn, friendly and unpretentious, simple and inexpensive near the Spanish border. The rooms are rather monastic but very well maintained as is the entire hotel which is impeccably clean and gives off the refreshing fragrance of lavender. Two terraces, one of which allows you a view over the whole valley (though it is not equipped). A valuable address when you want to stay in this unmissable town, even if the service is not always lavish.

How to get there (Map 4): 145km east of Lisboa via A2 exit Evora-West, then N114 towards Evora for 8km.

Casa de Sam Pedro

7000 Evora
Quinta de Sam Pedro
Tel. 266-70 77 31 - Mobile 96-236 20 50 - Fax 266 744 859
Sr Antònio Pestana de Vasconcellos

Room 4, 3 with bath. **Price** Double 12,500Esc. **Meals** Breakfast included, served 7:30-10:30.
Restaurant By reservation – mealtime specials 3,000Esc. **Credit cards** Not accepted. **Pets** Dogs not
allowed. **Nearby** In Evora: Sé, Roman Temple of Diana, Convento dos Lóios, fortress, Museum of Evora
- Convento São Bento de Castris. **Open** All year.

Once outside the walls, you take a little road towards Senhor dos Aflitos. The landscape is wonderful: fields of cork trees and olives, or farms raising bulls, line the road for the five kilometers that take you to Sam Pedro. This is a very fine 18th-century manor belonging to the noble family of Vasconcellos. The interior has been lerft unspoilt with a large drawing room on the first floor which is pleasantly cool in summer. The kitchen is magnificent with its monumental fireplace, its large marble basin, its collection of china plates and moulds, and the impressive copper kitchenware that covers the walls. This is a memorable place to take breakfast. There is one room on the second floor, dark and not very large, so we suggest that you choose the third floor with its view over the garden (one of these rooms has an external bathroom). On the same floor, the little drawing room decorated with Chinese porcelain is an ideal place to take port with the master of the house, who is always happy to give life to his house by sharing it with a few guests.

How to get there (Map 4): 145km east of Lisboa by A2.

Quinta de Espada [TR]

7001 Evora
Estrada de Arroilos, km 4 - Apartado 68
Tel. 266-734 549 - Fax 266-73 64 64
Sra Isabel de Mello Cabral

Rooms 7 with bath. **Price** Single 9,000Esc, double 13,000Esc, triple 16,500Esc. **Meals** Breakfast included, served 7:30-10:30. **Restaurant** By reservation – mealtime specials 3,750Esc. **Credit cards** Not accepted. **Pets** Dogs allowed. **Facilities** Swimming pool, riding, parking. **Nearby** In Evora: Sé, Roman Temple of Diana, Convento dos Lóios, fortress, Museum of Evora - Convento São Bento de Castris. **Closed** Dec 24 - 25.

The name of this quinta, "Farm of the Sword", is a tribute to the brave knight (like du Guesclin, "without fear and beyond reproach", but Portuguese, not French), namely Geral Geraldes who, legend tells us, chose this spot to hide the sword used for the conquest of Evora in 1165. The quinta is four kilometers from this magnificent town (which UNESCO has nominated part of the human patrimony). This is a fine property of the Alentejo region which offers two rooms in the main house and five others in an annexe. All are spacious and pleasantly fitted out with regional wooden furniture painted with floral motifs. The most agreeable are the ones opening on the little French-style garden, which also have more independence. Also at your disposal is the very friendly drawing room, the large, well-equipped kitchen and the swimming pool, a godsend in summer.

How to get there (Map 4): 145km east of Lisboa by A2. At Evora, take the Arroilos road for 4km.

Casa de S. Tiago TH

7000-501 Evora
Lg. Alexandre Herculano, 2
Tel. 266-702 686 - Fax 22-600 0307
Sr Vasconcellos

Room 5 with bath. **Price** Single 10,000-12,250Esc, double 13,000-13,250Esc. **Meals** Breakfast included, served 7:30-10:30. **Restaurant** See p. 215. **Credit cards** All major. **Pets** Dogs allowed. **Facilities** Garage. **Nearby** In Evora: Sé, Roman Temple of Diana, Convento dos Lóios, fortress, Museum of Evora - Convento São Bento de Castris. **Open** All year.

The Casa de S Tiago is a valuable place to know in Evora. Situated right in the center, it offers accommodation in one of the patrician houses of this historic town. The house also belongs to a member of the great family of Vasconcellos, which explains its aristocratic appearance: sculptured porch and an entrance that, in former times, served to admit carriages and hansom cabs, with a decorated floor made of small black-and-white cobbles. The interior is simply done up, leaving the architecture to recall past glories. The two bedrooms on the same level as the great drawing room open on a small patio, where everything is in spotless white, accentuating the elegance of the place. Those on the floor above are also fine-looking, particularly the one at the end of the corridor which has an interesting view over the roofs of the town. Another details, purely practical but important in Evora: you can park a car in the house.

How to get there *(Map 4): 145km east of Lisboa by A2. Near the church.*

Estalagem Monte das Flores

Monte das Flores 7000 Evora
Rua de Alcáçovas
Tel. 266-74 96 80 - Fax 266-74 96 88

Category ★★★ **Rooms** 17 with air-conditioning, telephone, bath, WC. **Price** Single 7,500-12,000Esc, double 7,500-14,000Esc, triple 9,500-14,000Esc. **Meals** Breakfast included, served 8:00-10:30 - half board +3,300Esc, full board +6,600Esc (per pers.). **Restaurant** Service 1:15PM-2:30PM, 8:00PM-10:00PM — mealtime specials 3,550-4,150Esc — Regional cooking. **Credit cards** All major. **Pets** Dogs not allowed. **Facilities** Swimming pool, tennis, parking. **Nearby** In Evora: Sé, Roman Temple of Diana, Convento dos Lóios, fortress, Museum of Evora - Convento São Bento de Castris. **Open** All year.

One leaves Evora in the direction of Alcáçovas, but very soon turning off onto an old still paved road heading into the country, with succeeding fields of olive trees and pastures for bull raising. The long buildings of the farms never rise above two floors allowing one to see the country mile after mile. It is in one of these properties that this inn is installed. The interior is a succession of large rustic rooms with beams and open fireplaces. The bedrooms are not very large but more convivial: flowered fabrics and regional furniture create an old-fashioned but nevertheless warm decor. A tennis court and swimming pool remind one that civilization is not so far away. In course of restoration, all of which should be completed by this summer. Prices may be altered.

How to get there (Map 4): 145km east of Lisboa via A2, then N10 to Atalho, then N4 to Montemor and N114; at 6km from Evora, road for Alcáçovas.

Quinta da Talha TR

7170 Redondo (Evora)
Estrada do Freixo
Tel. 266-99 94 68 - Fax 0(1)-343 30 90
Sra Mafalda-Morais

Rooms 3 with bath, TV and 1 apartment with kitchen, 2 bedrooms, bath, TV. **Price** Double 11,500Esc, apart. 23,000Esc. **Meals** Breakfast included. **Restaurant** See p. 215. **Credit cards** Not accepted. **Pets** Dogs allowed. **Facilities** Swimming pool. **Nearby** Evora - Evoramonte - Estremoz - Elvas. **Open** All year.

One cannot leave Alentejo without going to sample the wine of Redondo, known also for its marble and terra-cotta. Lost in a woodland of palm trees, vines and orange trees, the Quinta da Talha is the ideal stopover. The owners are two attractive and retired Lisboners who have converted the outbuildings into rooms, and the water reservoir into a swimming pool. The bedrooms are charming and bright. Breakfast is taken communally in the main house. Sr Manuel keeps an eye on everything; but be careful! It is not uncommon that after being invited to try his wine, one ends up discussing the world, and drinking two bottles! One leaves delighted.

How to get there *(Map 4): 150km east of Lisboa via A6 to Evora, then N4; 30km east of Evora, 3km of Redondo on Freixo road.*

Hotel Convento de São Paulo

Aldeia da Serra 7170 Redondo (Evora)
Tel. 266-989 160 - Fax 266-99 91 04
E-mail: hotelconvspaulo@mail.telepac.pt

Category ★★★★ **Rooms** 23 with air-conditioning, telephone, bath, WC, satellite TV; elevator, wheelchair access. **Price** Single 16,500-30,000Esc, double 21,500-42,000Esc; extra bed 9,500Esc. **Meals** Breakfast (buffet) included. **Restaurant** Service 12:30PM-2:00PM, 7:30PM-9:00PM – mealtime specials 3,700-5,400Esc, also à la carte – Specialties: Carne de porco alentejano - Burreguinhos em azette. **Credit cards** All major. **Pets** Dogs not allowed. **Facilities** Swimming pool, parking. **Nearby** Evora - Evoramonte - Estremoz - Elvas. **Open** All year.

With its palaces and former convents transformed into pousadas, Alentejo offers many exceptional sites and charming places to stop. Wishing above all to retreat into a peaceful and protected environment, the monks of São Paulo built their monastery in the shelter of the mountains of the Serra d'Ossa. Today it is a superb hotel displaying panoramas of *azulejos* all along the corridors leading to the bedrooms, and also on the ceilings of the refectory - now converted into an elegant restaurant with frescoes. The bedrooms are more sober but also just as traditional in their decor (white walls, regional furniture and wrought-iron beds), and all are extremely comfortable. The monastery is surrounded by 600 hectares of woods with long walks, but the marvel of this place is its patio - an oasis set into the mountain, enclosed by jig-sawed walls surmounted by statues, with a dado of *azulejos*, and a mosaic floor of many-colored marbles, all freshened by mountain waters flowing out of sumptuous baroque fountains. Need one add that this was a royal staging post?

How to get there (Map 4): 180km east of Lisboa via A2 then A6 to Estremoz; towards Redondo for 15km via N381.

23

Casa de Peixinhos TH

7160 Vila Viçosa (Evora)
Tel. 268-98 04 72 - Fax 268-88 13 48
Sr D. José Passanha

Rooms 8 with bath; wheelchair access. **Price** Single 14,000Esc, double 17,500Esc, suite 23,000Esc.
Meals Breakfast included, served 8:30-11:00. **Evening meals** By reservation. **Credit cards** Not
accepted. **Pets** Dogs not allowed. **Facilities** Parking. **Nearby** Evora - Evoramonte - Estremoz - Elvas.
Open All year.

V ila Viçosa, a former royal town but today a museum town, seems to have
fallen asleep in the midst of its citrus groves and marble quarries. To find
the Casa de Peixinhos ("the house of the little fish"), you need only follow the
signs from the town center to arrive in front of a superb 18th-century building,
with all the attraction of a *Mudejar* château. A wrought iron grille, *claustras*,
pebbled paths and a baroque fountain all lead you up to the house, which is
white, as it should be. Inside, there are the same traditional colors: all the
public rooms are yellow with ochre and red shadings, and green shutters. The
marvelously refined bedrooms are in one wing of the house; the breakfast table
is set in the mahogany dining room, where one is served on fine porcelain
monogrammed with the seal of the house. This *casa* is a real find.

How to get there *(Map 4): 200km east of Lisboa via A6 to Estremoz then N4 to
Borba and N255 to Vila Viçosa.*

Posada D. João IV *

7160 Vila Viçosa (Evora)
Terreiro do Paço
Tel. 268-980 742 - Fax 268-980 747
Sra Esmeralda da Costa

Rooms 30 and 6 suites with air-conditioning, telephone, bath, satellite TV, minibar. **Price** Single 18,000-26,500Esc, double 20,300-31,600Esc, suite 24,300-52,300Esc; extra bed +30%. **Meals** Breakfast included, served 7:30-10:30. **Restaurant** Service 12:30PM-3:00PM, 7:30PM-10:00PM – à la carte. **Credit cards** All major. **Pets** Dogs not allowed. **Facilities** Swimming pool, parking. **Nearby** Vila Viçoza: Palate of Ducal, castle - Alandroal - Terena - Borba - Elvas - Evora - Monsaraz. **Open** All year.

The Porta dos Nòs, which owes its name to the great twisted columns on each side of it, welcomes you to the town. You will soon reach the great esplanade of the ducal palace with its equestrian statue of João IV, and it is here too on the terreiro do Paço, that you will find the former convent of Las Chagas, built in the 16th Century and enlarged in the 18th with buildings that have recently been converted into a hotel of luxury and charm. The original architecture is sumptuous and the work of the Portuguese architects who converted it is a great success. The large entrance hall is lit by an impressive well of light. The flooring, in glass blocks, reveals the restored basement. The drawing rooms, decorated in marble and fine paintings on wood, are set round the patio and surmounted by the gallery which opens on the rooms. These are all very lovely, but one must signal out in particular the four described as "special" and the suites: the Professor's Suite, with its 17th-century *azulejos*, the Painter's with a very fine painting by Viajante, the Musician's with musical motifs on its wallpaper, the Astronomer's with its great mural fresco and the Duchessa's, an apartment with a large terrace. Charm, luxury and refinement.

How to get there (Map 4): 18km southeast of Estremoz.

25

Casa de Borba TH

7150 Borba (Estremoz)
Rua da Cruz, 5
Tel. 268-894 528 - Fax 268-841 448
Sr Marie José Tavares Lobo de Vasconcellos

Rooms 5 with bath, TV. **Price** Single 13,000Esc, double 15,000Esc; extra bed 3,500Esc. **Meals** Breakfast included, served 9:00-11:00. **Restaurant** By reservation. **Credit cards** Visa, Eurocard, MasterCard. **Pets** Dogs not allowed. **Facilities** Swimming pool, parking. **Nearby** Borba: Church of São Bartolomeu, Museum of Cristo (2km on Estremoz road) - Vita Viçoza - Estremoz - Elvas - Evoramonte - Evora. **Open** All year.

Some forty kilometers from the frontier at Caia, a stopover at Borba will allow you to discover this interesting town, known for its wine and the marble quarries from which it has richly bedecked itself. The Casa de Borba, right in the center, is surrounded by a fine, lush garden. The entrance door opens on a gigantic hall in which is exhibited a barouche as old as the house itself. A wide double staircase, in marble naturally, leads to the upper floors where you will find the great drawing rooms with a few remaining pieces of family furniture, and the great gallery, which runs along the top of the whole façade overlooking the garden. The rooms are large and comfortable, with furniture of Portuguese 17th-century style. Two of them are on the second floor, including the one with the four-poster bed (our favorite), three are on the top floor. A huge terrace has been created on the roof but in summer we advise you to take the sun near the pool and above all to enjoy the shade in the garden where, on request, you may organize a barbecue.

How to get there (*Map 4*): *14km southeast of Estemoz.*

Pousada Flor da Rosa *

Flor da Rosa 7430 Crato (Portalegre)
Mosteiro de Santa Maria de Flor da Rosa
Tel. 245-99 72 10 - Fax 245-99 72 12

Rooms 24 with air-conditioning, telephone, bath, WC, satellite TV, minibar; elevator. **Price** Single 18,300-29,000Esc, double 20,300-31,000Esc, suite 24,300-38,000Esc; extra bed +30%. **Meals** Breakfast included, served 7:30-10:00. **Restaurant** Service 12:30PM-3:00PM, 7:30PM-10:00PM – mealtime specials 3,650Esc, also à la carte – Regional cooking. **Credit cards** All major. **Pets** Dogs not allowed. **Facilities** Swimming pool, parking. **Nearby** Convento Flor da Rosa - Crato - Portalegre (Fábrica Real, Parque da Corredura) - Dolmen Aldeia da Pedra - Vale do Peso - Monte da Pedra - Gàfete. **Open** All year.

This small village owes its reputation to the ancient monastery of the Order of the Hospitallers and the Order of Malta, which along with its church forms a beautiful fortified structure. Its pottery is also well known, with the traditional *caçoila* still used for cooking. A very modern adjoining building shelters the pousada, but the combination of the two architectural styles is perfect. It was very recently opened, so we were not able to see the bedrooms, but since it is rated in the highest category of pousadas, one can certainly be assured of comfort and excellent services. The region is rich in historical curiosities, which, of course, adds interest to this lodging.

How to get there (Map 4): 23km west of Portalegre.

Monte da Varzea d'Água de Salteiros

Salteiros 7400 Ponte de Sôr (Portalegre)
Tel. 242-283 112 - 242-206 155 - Fax 242-206 235
Luis Miguel Cruz Bucho

Apartments 1 for 3 pers., 2 for 4 pers. **Price** 12,000Esc (3 pers.), 17,500Esc (4 pers.). **Meals** Breakfast included. No restaurant. **Credit cards** Not accepted. **Pets** Dogs not allowed. **Facilities** Swimming pool, parking. **Nearby** Convento Flor da Rosa - Crato - Portalegre (Fábrica Real, Parque da Corredura) - Dolmen Aldeia da Pedra - Vale do Peso - Monte da Pedra - Gàfete. **Open** All year.

Monte de Salteiros, situated in the countryside of Ponte de Sôr and a few kilometers from the Montargil dam, is made up of a charming collection of low houses and agricultural buildings, at the entrance to an estate of 120 hectares. So you are on a real farm with sheep and farmyard animals, orchards and a kitchen garden that the owner will be glad to show you round. The welcome is spontaneously very warm and they ask only one thing: that you should participate or, at least, intake an interest in and benefit from the life on the estate. You have a choice of three houses: the Casa da Eira in front of the area where they put the rice to dry; the Casa do Pastor, which has modern comfort and a very rustic atmosphere; and the Casa do Ganhao. All are charming and comfortable. A magnificent swimming pool surrounded by palm trees is an additional pleasure for your very civilized stay down on the farm.

How to get there (Map 4): 45km west of Portalegre.

Quinta dos Avós [TH]

7370 Campo Maior (Portalegre)
Quinta de S. João
Tel. 268-688 309 - 268-689 622 - Fax 268-688 202
E-mail: turagri@mail.telepac.pt
Sra Maria de Lurdes Gama

Rooms 5 with air-conditioning and 1 apartment with telephone, bath, satellite TV. **Price** Double 10,900Esc. **Meals** Breakfast included, served 7:30-10:30. **Restaurant** Service 12:30PM-2:00PM, 7:30PM-9:00PM — mealtime specials 2,500Esc. **Credit cards** Visa, Eurocard, MasterCard. **Pets** Dogs not allowed. **Facilities** Swimming pool, tennis, riding (14km). **Nearby** Elvas: aqueduct, fortress, cathedral - Ouguela castle - Arronches. **Open** All year.

Campo Major was a little fortified town, of a kind that one often meets in this part of northern Alentejo. But the curious thing about this pretty village is the chapel in the church which is entirely covered in bones, like the capela dos ossos which can be seen in the church of São Francisco in Evora; there is also the astonishing festival which takes place some years in September when the village is entirely covered in colored paper flowers. This is where we fell in love with Quinta dos Avós, which occupies a farm dating from 1640. Once past the porch, the great paved courtyard gives access to the double flight of stairs leading to the main house. The rooms reserved for guests have pretty furniture in the regional style known as Dona Maria and the whole is sober and elegant. Each room opens on a balcony with bougainvillae which add their red color to the white and blue façades. In one of the buildings around the courtyard, there is a very well-equipped apartment and in another of the farm buildings, a little restaurant. The pleasant garden and its refreshing swimming pool, and the owner's kind welcome all add to the harmony of the place.

How to get there (Map 4): 50km southeast of Portalegre. 19km northeast of Elvas.

Pousada Santa Maria *

7330 Marvão (Portalegre)
Tel. 245-99 32 01 - Fax 245-99 34 40
Sra Cristina Andrade

Rooms 29 with air-conditioning, telephone, bath, WC, TV; elevator. **Price** Single 14,800-23,600Esc, double 16,300-25,100Esc, suite 20,800-31,100Esc; extra bed +30%. **Meals** Breakfast included, served 7:30-10:30. **Restaurant** Service 12:30PM-3:00PM, 7:30PM-10:00PM – mealtime specials, also à la carte – Regional cooking. **Credit cards** All major. **Pets** Dogs not allowed. **Nearby** In Marvão: village, castle - Road from Portalegre to Castello de Vide - Convento Flor da Rosa, Crato road - Portalegre (Fàbrica Real, Parque da Corredura). **Open** All year.

Occupying an old whitewashed house in the very pretty medieval village of Marvão, the Pousada Santa Maria is full of charm. This small inn is particularly welcoming in winter when the mists are rising on the Serra de São Mamede. A warm ambiance is provided by the decorated lounges with their painted wooden furniture, very typical of Portuguese popular art. The staff is particularly friendly, and this is a comfortable stopping place, hidden away in the maze of tiny narrow streets. Fortunately there is parking available for clients of the pousada.

How to get there (Map 4): 22km north of Portalegre via N246.

Estalagem Quinta de Sto António

7350 Elvas (Portalegre)
São Srás, Apartado 206
Tel. 268-628 406 - Fax 268-625 050
Sr Jose Telo Abreu

Rooms 29 and 1 suite with air-conditioning, telephone, bath, satellite TV. **Price** Single 10,500-14,500Esc, double 12,500-17,500Esc, suite 18,000-24,000Esc. **Meals** Breakfast included, served 8:30-10:30 - half board +2,500Esc, full board +5,000Esc. **Restaurant** Service 1:00PM-3:00PM, 8:00PM-10:00PM – mealtime specials 3,000Esc, also à la carte – Regional cooking. **Credit cards** All major. **Pets** Dogs not allowed. **Facilities** Swimming pool, tennis, parking. **Nearby** Elvas - Evora - Evoramonte - Estremoz. **Open** All year.

At Quinta de St Antonio, you will find two separate establishments, both belonging to the same owner. The difference is that one is an estalagem, a hotel, the other a quinta de turismo rural, a farm house that receives guests (state which you want when making the reservation). Here, the buildings date from the 18th century and were part of an old country residence in typical Alentejo style with wrought-iron balconies, a water tower crowned by Baroque statues, an open-air patio which has a pool with fountain, as well as a small traditional chapel. This magnificent setting enjoys gardens with superb palm trees and box-woods that are three centuries old. We suggest you stay in one of the older buildings, the villa or the former stables, because those in the annex, in a modern building, have no charm. The rooms are small but possess a pleasant lived-in quality. Each door bears the name of one of the owners and our favorite is marked Luis. To give you a better idea of the surrounding countryside, the management organizes rides on tractors across the fields of the property.

How to get there (Map 4): 8km of Evora, towards Barbacena or via A6 exit number 10, towards Elvas-Center.

31

Monte da Amoreira ᵀᴿ

Quinta de St António
7353 Elvas (Portalegre)
Tel. 268-62 84 06 - Fax 268-62 50 50 - Sr José Telo Abreu
E-mail: santonio@mail.telepac.pt - Web: www.qsantonio.hypermart.net

Rooms 4 and 2 apartments with bath. **Price** With communal bath 5,000-6,000Esc, with bath 7,500-9,000Esc. **Meals** Breakfast included, served 8:30-10:30. **Restaurant** Service 1:00ᴘᴍ-3:00ᴘᴍ, 8:00ᴘᴍ-10:00ᴘᴍ – mealtime specials 3,000Esc – Regional cooking. **Credit cards** Visa, Eurocard, MasterCard. **Pets** Dogs allowed. **Facilities** Swimming pool, tennis. **Nearby** Elvas - Evora - Evoramonte - Estremoz. **Open** All year.

On the Spanish-Portuguese frontier the stronghold of bathajoz (Spanish side) and the fortified town of Elvas (Portuguese side) watch each other and keep guard. A few kilometers from the ramparts, down in the plain, where the corn fields are flowered with poppies and broom, lie the farms of Monte da Amoreira, a property of 800 hectares. The Quinta de Sto Antonio is part of this domain, but to find it you must head into the country: the road grows ever more narrow, paving stones replace the blacktop, and then earth replaces the stones. You then come upon a small jewel. Some long buildings framed in yellow look onto a large pond and a courtyard shaded by palm trees and fresh with fountains. The rooms are however monastic and very rustic, as is the large dining room- drawing room. However, you can enjoy the facilities of the nearby estalagem.

How to get there *(Map 4): 8km of Elvas, towards Barbacena, or on A6, exit 10, towards Elvas-Center.*

Monte Saraz [TH]

7200 Monsaraz
Horta dos Revoredos-Barrada
Tel. 266-55 73 85 - Fax 266-55 74 85 - Monique Dekers
E-mail: monte.saraz@mail.telepac.pt

Rooms 2 (2 nights min.) and 3 suites with kitchenette (3 nights min.). **Price** Double 12,000Esc (with communal bath), 16,000Esc (with bath), suite 19,000Esc; extra bed 6,000Esc (1 pers.), 7,000Esc (2 pers.). **Meals** Breakfast included except in the suite, served 8:00-10:00. No restaurant. **Credit cards** Not accepted. **Pets** Dogs not allowed. **Facilities** Swimming pool. **Nearby** In Monsaraz: rua Direita with the old Tribunal, Misericordia Hospital, castle. **Open** All year.

This is surely one of the most refined hotels in this guide, one that would certainly merit a detour to Monsaraz. In the valley that lies below the Old Town, the farms so typical of the Alentejo region - montes - have mostly been restored. Monte Saraz opens its doors, allowing you to discover the best in country living, Portuguese style. The building materials used in its construction are admirably set off by the interior decoration and nicely-appointed period furniture. The rooms are charming and comfortable with room service available. The lounge is always at your disposal, as is a drink at just the right moment. Breakfast, for guests in rooms without a kitchenette, is served on the terrace as soon as the weather permits or else in the fine drawing room of the house. The swimming pool, surrounded by a set of columns plus a grove of olive trees, is a true oasis, the ideal complement to the ever-present sunshine. A truly rare hotel.

How to get there *(Map 4): 45km southeast of Evora to Reguengoz de Monsaraz, then towards Monsaraz and Barrada*

Casa D. Nuno

Monsaraz 7200 Reguengoz de Monsaraz
Rua do Castelo, 6
Tel. 266-55 71 46 - Fax 266-55 74 00
Sr Isidoro Lores Pinto

Rooms 8 with telephone, bath, satellite TV. **Price** Single 9,000Esc, double 10,000Esc. **Meals** Breakfast included, served 7:30-10:30. No restaurant. **Credit cards** Visa, Eurocard, MasterCard. **Pets** Dogs not allowed. **Nearby** In Monsaraz: rua Direita with the old Tribunal, Misericordia Hospital, castle - Evora. **Open** All year.

Monsaraz is one of the loveliest villages in Alentejo. Enclosed in its walls, it overlooks the whole plain of Evora. Inside the walls, in the main street leading to the church, you will find the charming Casa D Nuno. At the back, the house is a succession of levels that go in stages down to the garden. In this way, they have been able to create a number of drawing rooms in which the architecture itself is an interesting decorative element. The winter room with its fine fireplace, its flooring in black stone, its wooden frame and its collection of popular art around the whitewashed walls, is one of the most welcoming. A larger one opens on the great loggia which overhangs the garden and has a panoramic view of the valley. The comfortable rooms also offer hotel facilities (telephone and television). Beautifully decorated with painted furniture, those with a view over the plain will ensure that you have an unforgettable view when you wake up. A simple little place, full of charm.

How to get there (Map 4): 45km southeast of Evora. In the old town.

Estalagem de Monsaraz

7200 Reguengos de Monsaraz
Arrabalde-Monsaraz
Largo de S. Bartolomeu
Tel. 266-55 71 12 - Fax 266-55 71 01

Rooms 8 and 1 apartment with telephone, bath, TV. **Price** Single 12,500Esc, double 16,000Esc, suite 20,000Esc, apart. 31,500Esc. **Meals** Breakfast included, served 7:30-10:30. **Restaurant** Service 12:30PM-3:00PM, 7:30PM-10:00PM – mealtime specials, also à la carte – Regional cooking. **Credit cards** All major. **Pets** Dogs not allowed. **Facilities** Swimming pool. **Nearby** In Monsaraz: rua Direita with the old Tribunal, Misericordia Hospital, castle. **Open** All year.

Reguengos de Monsaraz is located outside the walls of the old city of Monsaraz, once a highly fortified bastion overlooking the Guadiana Valley and refuge to many during the border wars of the time. The property spreads out over the side of a hill and includes an old house whose exceptional architecture has been preserved. The living room extends into the kitchen with a gigantic traditional fireplace. Rustic decor is everywhere, nicely matching the black flagstones of the floor and the beams stretching across the ceilings. The rooms are all spacious and the most impressive is an apartment with a living room adjacent to a private terrace on the roof overlooking the entire valley. On weekends, a barbecue is held to allow the guests to get to know one another.

How to get there (Map 4): 62km southeast of Evora.

Pousada de Palmela *

2950 Palmela (Setúbal)
Castello de Palmela
Tel. 21-235 12 26/13 95 - Fax 21-233 04 40
Sr Rosa

Rooms 27 and 1 suite with air-conditioning, telephone, bath, WC, satellite TV, minibar; elevator. **Price** Single 17,900-29,000Esc, double 20,300-31,000Esc, suite 22,000-38,000Esc; extra bed +30%. **Meals** Breakfast included, served 8:00-10:30. **Restaurant** Service 12:30PM-3:00PM, 7:30PM-10:00PM – mealtime specials 3,650Esc, also à la carte – Specialties: Sopa do Mar a Costa Azul - Tamboril - Lombo de Porco - Torta de Larania - Doces Conventuais. **Credit cards** All major. **Pets** Dogs not allowed. **Facilities** Parking. **Nearby** In Palmela: Church of São Pedro (azulejos) and castle - Setúbal (church and museum) - Serra de Arrábida - Quinta de Bacalhoa (garden and azulejos) – Torralta Troia golf course (18-hole). **Open** All year.

This inn in the heart of the sierra of Arrábida is within the convent of the château of Palmela, built in 1423 for the knights of Santiago. Very great comfort reigns inside this rather austere building, which has preserved some very beautiful cloisters. Here regular exhibitions are held of the work of Portuguese artists. The rooms are all well appointed and all have a magnificent view, but the best are numbers 22 and 9, where President Mitterand of France stayed during a visit to Portugal. One should also note the attractive swimming pool and the very poetic ruins.

How to get there (Map 3): 43km southeast of Lisboa via A2.

Vila Joya

Praia do Galé
8200 Albufeira (Faro)
Tel. 289-59 17 95 - Fax 289-59 12 01
Sra Fricke

Category ★★★★ **Rooms** 13 and 4 suites (with air conditioning) with telephone, bath, WC, TV, safe, minibar. **Price** With half board per pers.: small double 33,000Esc, double 40,000-43,000Esc, suite 44,000-75,000Esc. **Meals** Breakfast included, served 7:30-11:30. **Restaurant** Service 1:00PM-3:00PM, 7:30PM-9:30PM – mealtime specials 12,900 and 16,500Esc (Thurs.), also à la carte 5,200-8,200Esc – International cooking. **Credit cards** All major. **Pets** Dogs not allowed. **Facilities** Heated swimming pool, sauna, parking. **Nearby** Faro - Praia da Rocha - Peninsula of Sagres. **Closed** Jan 7 – Mar 1 and Nov 11 – Dec 21.

Praia do Galé is one of those seaside resorts recently built in a Neo-Moorish style, and which have become "grand luxe" tourist centers. La Vila Joya is one of the most beautiful hotels around, and it has a superb environment: the ocean at its feet; the shade of the pines, mimosas, orange trees, and a lawn stretching down to meet the waves. All the rooms are treated differently but in a Mediterranean style, with bathrooms in mosaics that recall the luxury of oriental baths. The restaurant and wine cellar meet the highest standards.

How to get there *(Map 5): 40km west of Faro; 6.5km east of Albufeira towards Vale de Parra and Praia do Galé.*

Hotel Dona Filipa

Vale do Lobo 8136 Almancil (Faro)
Tel. 289-35 72 00 - Fax 289-35 72 01
Sr Beverly King

Category ★★★★★ **Rooms** 147 with air-conditioning, telephone, bath, WC, satellite TV, safe, minibar; elevator. **Price** Single 30,000-57,000Esc, double 35,000-57,000Esc, superior with view 42,500-66,000Esc, junior suite and deluxe suite 57,000-160,000Esc; extra bed 15,000Esc. **Meals** Breakfast (buffet) included; half board +7,000Esc (per pers.). **Restaurants** "Primavera", "Dom Quarte" and "Grill São Lorenço": service 7:30PM-11:00PM - Closed Sun - mealtime specials, also à la carte – Portuguese and international cooking. **Credit cards** All major. **Pets** Dogs not allowed. **Facilities** Swimming pool, tennis, San Lorenzo golf course (green fee 7,000Esc), parking. **Nearby** In Almancil: Church of S. Lourenzo - Faro - Praia da Rocha - Peninsula of Sagres – Vale do Lobo golf course (36-hole) - Quinta do Lobo golf course (18-hole). **Open** All year.

It has to said from the start: if you are not a golfer, keep away! This large and modern hotel is very luxurious and very expensive, and it will please those wealthy golfers who come to play on the San Lorenzo course, reputed to be one of the most beautiful in Europe. The location between the ocean and the luxuriant reserve of Ria Formosa is truly superb. The hotel displays the decoration of an international "grand hotel" (with heraldic motifs telling the history of Filippa de Lencastre), but with a few excesses, such as the palm trees with gilded leaves. The rooms are beautiful and very comfortable. The swimming pool is heated or cooled according the weather, and there's floodlit tennis at night, among other luxuries. Weighing it all up, if you are rich even if you are not a golfer, then why not ?

How to get there *(Map 5): 10km west of Faro, take Avenida do mar towards Vale do Lobo.*

La Réserve

Santa Bárbara de Nexe 8000 Faro
Estrada de Esteval
Tel. 289-999 474 - Fax 289-999 402
Sr Fuchs

Category ★★★★★ **Rooms** 12 and 8 apartments (duplex) with air-conditioning, telephone, bath, WC, TV, minibar. **Price** Single 18,000-30,000Esc, double 28,000-40,000Esc, apart. 30,000-40,000Esc. **Meals** Breakfast included, served 8:00-11:00. **Restaurant** (Tel. 289-999 234) Service snacks at noon for the residents, 7:00PM-11:00PM - Closed Tues evening - mealtime specials 7,500Esc, also à la carte – Specialties: Pato assado Vendôme - Codormizes com trufa Don Quijote - Camarão. **Credit cards** All major. **Pets** Dogs not allowed. **Facilities** Swimming pool, tennis, parking. **Nearby** In Faro: Miradouro de San Antonio (visit at sunrise and sunset) - Roman Ruins of Milreu and gardens of the palate of Estói – Vilamoura golf course (18-hole) - Quinta da Lago golf course (9- and 18-hole). **Open** All year.

La Réserve allows you to enjoy, at one and the same time, the peace of a carefully maintained garden, an attractive swimming pool, and a quality table. The hotel owners, of Swiss origin, insist on a more than perfect management, and all personnel respond efficiently to your slightest whim, as appropriate to a grand hotel. The rooms look more like suites, while the latter resemble small apartments. All are decorated with care, and all have a superb view over the countryside with the sea in the distance. All the rooms have individual terraces. In the evening you can try out one of those recipes that have made the reputation of the restaurant.

How to get there (Map 6): 15km north of Faro.

Monte do Casal

Estói 8000 Faro
Estrada de Moncarapacho
Tel. 289-99 15 03 - 289-99 13 41 - Fax 289-99 13 41
Sr M. R. Hawkins

Category ★★★★ **Rooms** 13 with air-conditioning, telephone, bath, WC. **Price** Double 25,200-55,600Esc, double luxe 29,400-61,000Esc, suite 26,400-74,400Esc. **Meals** Breakfast included, served 9:00-10:00; half board on request. **Restaurant** Service 12:00PM-3:00PM, 7:00PM-10:00PM – mealtime specials 6,400-5,600Esc, also à la carte. **Credit cards** Visa, Eurocard, MasterCard. **Pets** Dogs not allowed. **Facilities** Heated swimming pool, parking. **Nearby** In Faro: Miradouro de San Antonio (visit at sunrise and sunset) - Roman Ruins of Milreu and gardens of the palate of Estói – Vilamoura golf course (18-hole) - Quinta da Lago golf course (9- and 18-hole). **Closed** Dec and Jan.

M onte do Casal is a large and beautiful holiday house whose various buildings seem immersed in a superb garden planted with an incredible variety of Mediterranean flora: palm trees, eucalyptus, olive trees, pink oleanders, bougainvillae and begonias invading both terraces and façades with well-controlled abundance. There are only thirteen rooms but all have balconies giving onto the garden (the quieter rooms) or the swimming pool. Some have real private terraces, others have small corner lounges. The decoration is rather commonplace: ship's furniture in the very comfortable bedrooms, a straw-hut style for the bar, rustic for the dining room. In summer activity is centered around the swimming pool, but the garden is large enough to find peaceful little corners. A very convivial ambiance, but children of under 16 are not admitted. At Estoi one should not miss visiting the delightful 18th-century palace.

How to get there *(Map 6): 15km north of Faro; via IP1 exit number 5; 3km of Estoi 5 on the road to Moncaparacho.*

Casa Belaventura ᵀᴿ

Campina de Boliqueime - Alfontes
8100 Loulé (Faro)
Tel. 289-360 633 - Fax 289-366 053 - Sr Carlos Dias
E-mail: belaventur@mail.telepac.pt

Rooms 4 and 1 apartment with bath (communal kitchen and sitting room). **Price** Single 9,000-15,000Esc, double 10,500-17,000Esc, apart. 12,500-17,000Esc. **Meals** Breakfast included in bedrooms, served 8:00-11:00. **Restaurant** In Loulé see p. 217. **Credit cards** Not accepted. **Pets** Dogs not allowed. **Facilities** Swimming pool, Sea (8km), parking. **Nearby** In Faro: Miradouro de San Antonio (visit at sunrise and sunset) - Roman Ruins of Milreu and gardens of the palate of Estói – Vilamoura golf course (18-hole) - Quinta da Lago golf course (9- and 18-hole). **Open** All year.

For those who live in dread of the hordes of oddly-dressed August vacationers, the Casa Belaventura is a true haven, one with a mammoth swimming pool allowing you to choose exactly at what moment you care to take a swim. Not far away, you will find shaded hammocks. This is a lovely country house allowing, for example, the possibility for a family to rent four adjoining rooms. The entire decor is traditional, the lounges being the most colorful in their attractive Mediterranean style. All the rooms open onto gardens and flower beds. The owners are constantly attentive, making sure your stay is a pleasant one, and you needn't hesitate in asking their help, be it for a barbecue in the garden or boat ride on the sea.

How to get there (Map 6): 15km northwest of Faro. 10km of Loulé; 2km before Boliqueime, take the road on the right.

Loulé Jardim Hotel

8100 Loulé (Faro)
Praça Manuel de Arriaga
Tel. 289-413 094 - Fax 289-463 177

Category ★★★ **Rooms** 52 with air-conditioning, telephone, bath, WC, satellite TV; elevator. **Price** Single 5,000-9,000Esc, double 7,000-11,000Esc, triple 9,000-13,000Esc. **Meals** Breakfast included, served 8:00-10:00. **Restaurant** See p. 217. **Credit cards** Visa, Eurocard, MasterCard. **Pets** Dogs allowed. **Facilities** Swimming pool, beaches (10km), garage. **Nearby** Faro - Almancil: Church of S. Lourenço (azulejos) – Vilamoura golf course (18-hole) - Quinta da Lago golf course (9- and 18-hole). **Open** All year.

A recently-built hotel on an attractive square in the center of Loulé, a small and peaceful city surrounded by a delightful countryside. If you cross the Spanish border into southern Portugal, here is a place where you can escape the often feverish seaside resorts. The hotel is very comfortable, its decoration somewhat banal but never in bad taste. The suites are genuinely spacious with comfortable terraces offering a view of the sea. In addition to 100% air-conditioning, you are certain to appreciate the swimming pool and the vast solarium on the roof.

How to get there *(Map 5): 15km northwest of Faro.*

Estalagem Abrigo da Montanha

8550 Monchique (Faro)
Tel. 282-91 21 31 - Fax 282-91 36 60
Sr Fernandes
E-mail: abrigodamontanha@hotmail.com

Category ★★★★ **Rooms** 16 with air-conditioning, telephone, bath, WC. **Price** Double 11,000-16,000Esc, triple 14,700-20,500Esc, suite 15,000-20,000Esc. **Meals** Breakfast included, served 8:00-10:00; half board +3,500Esc, full board +7,000Esc (per pers., 2 days min.). **Restaurant** With air-conditioning. Service 12:00PM-3:30PM, 7:00PM-9:30PM — mealtime specials 3,000-3,200Esc, also à la carte — Specialties: Sopa camponesa - Arroz de lingueirão - Sopa de cacão - Assadura - Frigineco - Cataplana de cabrito - Cabrito no forno - Bebidas - Aguardente de medronho. **Credit cards** All major. **Pets** Dogs not allowed. **Facilities** Swimming pool, parking. **Nearby** Monchique road from Mont Fóia to Nave Redonda - Road from Monchique to Portimão (serra de Monchique). **Open** All year.

This is really one of the best places for a stay on the Algarve, and it's just outside Monchique. One can hardly spot the hotel, built on the flank of a hill and submerged in greenery. Its construction was recent, of cut stone, in simple and attractive proportions. The ambiance is that of a mountain hotel: wood and bare stonework. Now that the furniture and decoration have been restored, all rooms are very agreeable and enjoy the same view over the valley. One can lunch or dine in the large restaurant hall or on the terrace. The young chef offers traditional Portuguese dishes, and the table is excellent though one would recommend the Assadura and the Cataplana. The staff is very friendly and the welcome is warm, making this a perfect place for a stop or for a mountain holiday.

How to get there *(Map 5): 86km northwest of Faro to Portimão via N125, then N266; on the road to Fóia at 2km.*

Hotel Bela Vista

8500 Portimão (Faro)
Avenida Tomás Cabreira
Tel. 282-45 04 80 - Fax 282-41 53 69
Sr Joaquim Ascensão

Rooms 12 and 2 suites with telephone, bath, WC, satellite TV, minibar; elevator. **Price** Single 9,000-22,000Esc, double 10,000-23,000Esc, suite 15,000-34,000Esc; extra bed 2,000-7,000Esc. **Meals** Breakfast included, served 8:30-10:30. **Restaurant** See p. 216. **Credit cards** All major. **Pets** Dogs not allowed. **Facilities** Beach, parking. **Nearby** Praia da Rocha - Lagos - Ponta da Piedade - Praia de Bona Ana - Serra de Monchique – Penina golf course (9- and 18-hole). **Open** All year.

Admirably situated on the cliffs of Praia de Rocha, with the beach at its feet, the Hotel Bela Vista is an attractive refuge for the summer months. Originally a private holiday home, it was converted into a hotel in the 1930's. Recently renovated, with an overall effect in very good taste, it does not have that "almost ready" aspect that one finds so often with hotels beside the sea. Here are wood fittings, comfortable armchairs and leather sofas in the lounges. Things are similar in the bedrooms, and there are numerous scenes in old *azulejos* everywhere. From the large panoramic terrace, where breakfast may be taken, and from Rooms 103 to 107 there's a beautiful view over the beach and sea. The management was right to warn us that from June to September, the terrace throbs every night to the rhythm of live music, so guests can organize their stay and their evenings accordingly.

How to get there *(Map 5): 64km west of Faro via N125 to Portimão then take the small road to Praia da Rocha; the hotel is on the cliffs.*

Casa de Palmerinha TH

8500 Mexilhoeira Grande (Faro)
Rua da Igreja, 1
Tel. 282-969 277 - Fax 282-969 277 - Jose manuel Goncalves Judice gloria
E-mail: josejudice@mail.telepac.pt

Rooms 5 with bath or shower. **Price** Double 7,500-15,000Esc. **Meals** Breakfast included, served 8:30-10:30. **Restaurant** In Portimão see p. 216. **Credit cards** Not accepted. **Pets** Dogs allowed. **Facilities** Swimming pool. **Nearby** Praia da Rocha - Lagos - Ponta da Piedade - Praia de Bona Ana - Serra de Monchique – Penina golf course (9- and 18-hole). **Open** All year.

Mexihoeira is a lovely, all-white village, its color relieved only by the green of its palm trees and blue swimming pools. This house is quite attractive, although the rooms are hardly unforgettable, the best of them being on the third floor, a spacious one with a terrace overlooking the village. All to the credit of the Casa de Palmerinha, there is a lovely swimming pool surrounded by palm trees in an interior courtyard. An additional advantage is the exceptional warmth of the welcome you receive and the service provided by its young owners.

How to get there (Map 5): 65km west of Faro via N125 towards Portimão, then Mexilhoeira Grande. 8km of Portimão.

Pousada de Saõ Brás *

8150 Saõ Brás de Alportel (Faro)
Tel. 289-84 23 06 - Fax 289-84 17 26
Sr Silvio Dias

Rooms 31 and 2 suites with air-conditioning, telephone, bath, WC, satellite TV, minibar; elevator, wheelchair access. **Price** Single 14,500-23,100Esc, double 16,000-24,600Esc, suite 20,400-30,500Esc; extra bed +30%. **Meals** Breakfast included, served 7:30-10:30. **Restaurant** Service 12:30PM-3:00PM, 7:30PM-10:00PM – à la carte – Specialties: Fish. **Credit cards** All major. **Pets** Dogs not allowed. **Facilities** Swimming pool, tennis, parking. **Nearby** Faro - Praia da Rocha - Peninsula of Sagres. **Open** All year.

Its situation and the extraordinary view over the valley and arid mountains of the Algarve made us select this pousada. The restaurant, terrace and swimming pool all look out over this really exceptional setting between sea and mountains. One cannot say as much about the interior decoration, but the refurbishing that's in progress should add more comfort, freshen up everything and make this pousada into a really good stopping place. We shall keep you informed.

How to get there (Map 6): 16km north of Faro; 2km north of São Bras via N2.

Pousada do Infante *

8650-385 Sagres (Faro)
Tel. 282-62 42 22/3 - Fax 282-62 42 25
Sr Falé

Rooms 39 with air-conditioning, telephone, bath, WC, satellite TV, minibar; elevator. **Price** Single 14,800-23,600Esc, double 16,300-25,100Esc, suite 20,800-31,100Esc; extra bed 4,890-7,530Esc. **Meals** Breakfast included, served 8:00-10:30. **Restaurant** Service 1:00PM-3:00PM, 7:30PM-10:00PM – à la carte. **Credit cards** All major. **Pets** Dogs not allowed. **Facilities** Helicopter pad, swimming pool, tennis, parking. **Nearby** Peninsula and fortress of Sagres - Fortaleza - Vila do Bispo and cliffs of Castelejo - Cabo San Vicente - Lagos – Campo de Palmares golf course (18-hole). **Open** All year.

The "infant" who gave his name to this pousada was Henry the Navigator, and the navigation school he founded at Sagres led to the discovery of Maderia and the Azores, among other finds. Situated on this peninsula, the hotel is agreeable in both winter and summer, and one can enjoy a huge view over the Atlantic and the cliffs. Out of season, in such an isolated spot swept by the Atlantic winds, one certainly appreciates the peace and comfort of the rooms. In the holiday period the seawater swimming pool and tennis court may be used by clients, who can also profit from the beaches close by. The restaurant offers an elaborate cuisine, based essentially on seafood.

How to get there *(Map 5): 113km west of Faro via N125; in Sagres follow direction "Pousada".*

Fortaleza do Beliche

8650 Sagres (Faro)
Cabo São Vicente
Tel. 282-62 41 24 - Fax 282-62 42 25

Category ★★★ **Rooms** 4 with air-conditioning, telephone, bath, WC, TV. **Price** Single 10,700-14,800Esc, double 12,200-16,300Esc; extra bed 3,660-4,890Esc. **Meals** Breakfast included, served 9:00-10:30. **Restaurant** Service 1:00PM-3:00PM, 7:30PM-9:30PM – mealtime specials, also à la carte 2,500-4,500Esc – Specialties: Fish. **Credit cards** All major **Pets** Dogs not allowed. **Nearby** Peninsula and fortress of Sagres - Fortaleza - Vila do Bispo and cliffs of Castelejo - Cabo San Vicente - Lagos – Campo de Palmares golf course (18-hole). **Closed** Nov - Feb.

The peninsula of Sagres is an arid region swept by the winds from the open sea, and the Cape Saint Vincent dominates the ocean from its height of 75 meters. It is in this rather impressive environment that one finds the Casa do Beliche, set in a small fortress and situated on one of the cliffs dropping straight into the sea. This miniature hotel with only four rooms, (only one with a view over the sea), is a real oasis in a rather austere area. In the evenings when the gale or storm is blowing, one particularly appreciates all the hotel's comforts !

How to get there *(Map 5): 118km west of Faro via N125; then at Sagres take the road for Cabo São Vicente.*

Quinta do Caracol ᵀᴴ

8800-405 Tavira (Faro)
Bairro de São Pedro
Tel. 281-32 24 75 - Fax 281-32 31 75
Sr Viegas

Apartments 7 (2-7 pers.) with shower, WC, kitchenette. **Price** 1 pers. 10,000-14,000Esc, 2 pers. 12,000-18,000Esc; extra bed 900-3,200Esc. **Meals** Breakfast included, served 7:30-10:30. **Restaurant** See p. 217. **Credit cards** All major. **Pets** Dogs allowed on request. **Facilities** Swimming pool, tennis (1,500Esc/hour), bike rentals, parking. **Nearby** Luz de Tavira - Moncarapacho - Cacela - Manta Rosa and Praia Verde beaches - Vila Real de Santo Antònio - Faro - Loulé - Olhão. **Open** All year.

Tavira, three kilometers from the sea is one of the rare seaside resorts to have been spared the savage urbanization of the Algarve Coast. The Quinta do Caracol is very close to the center; a pretty white and blue property surrounded by a garden. There are no rooms, but ravishing bungalows of different sizes, separated from each other by patios, flowered terraces, shady courtyards or staircases. A large barbecue is available for guests wanting to picnic "at home" or in the garden. This is a spot combining the advantages of town with a small corner of the countryside.

How to get there *(Map 6): 20km east of Faro; 1km of Tavira. 22km from the Spanish frontier.*

Convento do Santo António [TH]

8800-405 Tavira (Faro)
Atalaia, 56
Tel. 281-325 632 - Fax 281-325 632
Isabel Paes

Rooms 7 with bath, WC. **Price** Double 17,000-24,000Esc, suite 28,000-32,000Esc. **Meals** Breakfast included, served 9:00-10:30. **Restaurant** See p. 217. **Credit card** Amex. **Pets** Dogs not allowed. **Facilities** Swimming pool. **Nearby** Luz de Tavira - Moncarapacho - Cacela - Manta Rosa and Praia Verde beaches - Vila Real de Santo Antònio - Faro - Loulé - Olhão. **Closed** Jan.

Tavira is one of those beautiful Alentejo towns, and the Convento do Santo António has been recently converted into a magnificent guesthouse in the upper part of the town. The huge portal of the white chapel besides the entrance announces the majesty of the architecture, and once over the threshold one discovers the attractive garden, the former kitchen garden of the monastery, with its swimming pool. Two types of accommodation are offered: what are called "special" rooms, which are large and well-equipped and decorated to suit the architecture of each; these open directly on to the cloister on the ground floor. Otherwise, you can stay in the smaller, so-called "standard" rooms, which are former monks' cells, attractively decorated, on the first floor. The sitting room with satellite television and a fireplace is also very convivial. Don't hesitate to visit the rest of the convent and admire the view from the large terrace. This has become the place to stay in Tavira.

How to get there (Map 6): 28km east of Faro. 22km of the Spanish frontier.

Estalagem de Cegonha

8125 Vilamoura (Faro)
Tel. 289-302 577 - Fax 289-322 675
Sra José Leiria e Borges

Category ★★★★ **Rooms** 10 with telephone, bath, WC. **Price** Double 13,000-18,000Esc. **Meals** Breakfast included, served 8:00-10:00. **Restaurant** Service 12:00PM-3:00PM, 8:00PM-10:00PM - Closed Tues and Wed – mealtime specials, also à la carte – Specialties: Cabrito assado - Mariscos. **Credit cards** All major. **Pets** Dogs not allowed. **Facilities** Riding. **Nearby** Roman ruins of Cerro da Vila - Albufeira. **Closed** Nov.

This is a good place to escape the crowds on the Algarve coast. Situated in the backcountry, it is still close to the beaches, golf courses, casino and marina of Vilamoura. It will above all attract those who love horses, as a well-known equestrian center is sited on the property. This former baronial mansion has been restored and appointed with a very country feeling: in the lounge, a large open fireplace and leather armchairs make for a rustic and most agreeable ambiance. The spacious dining room looks out over the countryside and riding center. The kitchen forms an integral part of the house, and helps to create that warm climate pervading the hotel.

How to get there (Map 5): 22km west of Faro; in Vilamoura take Albufeira road.

Casa de San Gonzalo

8600 Lagos (Faro)
Rua Candido dos Reis, 73
Tel. 282-76 21 71 - Fax 282-76 39 27
Sra Vieira

Rooms 13 with telephone, bath, WC. **Price** Single 7,500-10,000Esc, double 10,000-14,000Esc, 19,000Esc (4 pers.). **Meals** Breakfast included, served 8:00-10:30. **Restaurant** See p 216. **Credit card** Amex. **Pets** Dogs not allowed. **Nearby** In Lagos: Regional Museum, Church of Santo Antonio - Ponta de Piedade and Praia de Dona Ana - Dam of Bravura – Campo de Palmares golf course (18-hole). **Closed** Mar – Dec.

In a region that has suffered accelerated tourist-based urbanization, where one can find too many rather unattractive dormitory-style hotels, the Caza de San Gonzalo is a genuine refuge of charm: essentially a beautiful old house with attractive antique furniture and rooms in a refined taste. Situated right in the heart of Lagos, the former departure port for the Portuguese expeditions overseas, this hotel makes a good base for discovering the still wild backcountry and the extreme southern point of the Cape Saint Vincent and Sagres, which are also protected. Be sure to book in advance, as the house is often full owing to agreements with travel agencies.

How to get there *(Map 5): 80km west of Faro via N125.*

Hotel Paloma Blanca

3800 Aveiro
Rua Luis Gomes de Carvahlo, 23
Tel. 234-38 19 92 - Fax 234-38 18 44
Sr Bastos

Category ★★★ **Rooms** 52 with air-conditioning, telephone, bath, WC, satellite TV, video recorder; elevator, wheelchair access - no smoking rooms. **Price** Single 10,000-12,000Esc, double 12,000-15,000Esc, triple +3,500Esc. **Meals** Breakfast included. **Restaurant** See p. 218. **Credit cards** All major. **Pets** Dogs not allowed. **Facilities** Parking, garage. **Nearby** In Aveiro: Bairro dos canais, convento de Jésus - Ria d'Aveiro (swimming, boat) - Coímbra - Beaches (8km) - Vouga Valley. **Open** All year.

Aveiro is an industrial town with no great tourist interest but it can make a good starting point for numerous excursions. The hotel is in a charming house in the town center. It has an unexpected, small tropical garden right on the street, planted with bougainvilleas and banana trees; an enormous palm tree reigns supreme. The sombre neo-gothic woodwork of the reception rooms, along with the *azulejos* at the foot of the staircase, all create a cozy atmosphere. But we will stop there, since the new management intends to carry out plans for restoration from spring 2000 to improve the décor, the standard of comfort and the status of the hotel. Professional service, very friendly welcome. A good hotel, ideal for an overnight stop.

How to get there (Map 1): 70km south of Porto.

Palace Hotel do Bussaco

Mata National do Buçaco 3050-261 Luso (Aveiro)
Tel. 231-93 01 01 - Fax 231-93 05 09
Sr João de Castro Ribeiro
E-mail : almeida_hotels@ip.pt

Category ★★★★★ **Rooms** 60 and 4 suites (some with air-conditioning) with telephone, bath, WC, satellite TV; elevator. **Price** Single 19,000-34,000Esc, double 24,000-39,000Esc, suite 70,000-200,000Esc; extra bed 6,000Esc. **Meals** Breakfast (buffet) included, served 8:00-10:00; half board +6,500Esc, full board +12,000Esc (per pers.).**Restaurant** Service 1:00PM-3:00PM, 8:00PM-9:30PM – à la carte 4,100-6,000Esc – Regional cooking. **Credit cards** All major. **Pets** Dogs not allowed. **Facilities** Tennis, garage, parking. **Nearby** Buçaco Forest (Mata: Cruz Alta, obelisco, via sacra) - Coímbra. **Open** All year.

This hotel was formerly the summer palace of the royal family, before it bacme one of the finest tourist hotels in the world in 1917. A majestic palace of "neo-Manuelin" style, it shelters more than one masterpiece: the monumental internal architecture has been made more "habitable" by the carpets and antique furniture that decorate the hotel. The entrance, with the grand staircase, and the breakfast room, decorated with *frescoes* and *azulejos* recounting the adventures of the Portuguese navigators, are particularly outstanding. Surrounded by the magnificent forest of Buçaco which was formerly planted by the Carmelite nuns with rare plants, freshened by the fountains and springs, with the black swans gliding across the ornamental ponds, and the galleries lining the sumptuous park… all help recreate a truly royal ambiance.

How to get there *(Map 1): 31km north of Coimbra via N1 to Mealhada, then N234 for 12km.*

Palace Hotel da Curia

Curia 3780-541 Tamengos
Tel. 231-51 21 31 - Fax 231-51 55 31
Sr Armando Rocha
E-mail: almeida_hotels@ip.pt

Category ★★★ **Rooms** 114 with telephone, bath, WC, satellite TV; elevator. **Price** Single 11,000-14,000Esc, double 14,000-17,000Esc; extra bed 3,600Esc. **Meals** Breakfast (buffet) included, served 8:00-10:00; half board +3300Esc, full board +6,000Esc (per pers.). **Restaurant** Service 12:30PM-3:00PM, 8:00PM-9:30PM – mealtime specials 3,300Esc, also à la carte – Specialties: Leitão assado - Bacalhao. **Credit cards** All major. **Pets** Dogs allowed. **Facilities** Swimming pool, tennis, minigolf, garage, parking. **Nearby** Buçaco Forest (Mata: Cruz Alta, obelisco, via sacra) - Fonte de São João in Luso - Aveiro (convent) - Barra, Mira and Tocha beaches - Ria d'Aveiro (boating) - Coímbra. **Open** Mar 25 - Oct 31.

The Palace Hotel was opened in the 1920's when spas were fashionable and people came in large numbers to take the waters. Its 33-meter swimming pool among the vines, with its surroundings of fine sand, was even then known throughout Europe. Today the place has hardly changed: the dominant white building still extends into the "French garden", while the swimming pool, skillfully architectured with barriers, grilles, steps and diving boards, is still surrounded by its astonishing rotunda. Today the spas have rather lost their attraction but not so the hotel. Today the interior recalls a liner of the "Belle Epoque": the immense reception hall is superb, with its abundance of wrought iron; it opens onto a vast lounge-winter garden; and the just-too-large dining room retains all the memories of many a crazy evening. The bedrooms are also very charming and this is a beautiful hotel in the best Portuguese tradition.

How to get there (Map 1): 27km north of Coímbra.

Villa Duparchy TH*

3050 Luso - Mealhada (Aveiro)
Tel. 231-93 07 90 - Fax 231-93 03 07
Sr Principe Santos

Rooms 6 with bath. **Price** Double 12,500-14,000Esc; extra bed 3,200Esc. **Meals** Breakfast included, served from 9:00. **Evening meals** By reservation or see p. 218. **Credit cards** Amex, Visa, Eurocard, MasterCard. **Pets** Dogs allowed. **Facilities** Swimming pool, parking. **Nearby** Coímbra - Buçaco Forest - Ruins of Conimbriga - Penela. **Open** All year.

Oscar Manuel Principe Santos is a delightful man who will do everything to make your stay at the Villa Duparchy as pleasant as possible. "Residential tourism", as it is called in these parts, sometimes has many advantages. Only six rooms welcome passing guests, a long way from the anonymity of a gigantic hotel complex! All the rooms are large, in particular numbers 2 and 3, and offer a magnificent view of the forest of Buçaco. A special mention for the exceptional quality of the furniture, a mix of Portuguese and British antiques. The lounges and dining room are good for relaxing after long hikes in the forest close by. This is a charming place for a leisurely and family-style holiday.

How to get there *(Map 1): 28km north of Coimbra via A1, exit Mealhada, then C234.*

Casa dos Maias TH

6230 Fundão (Castelo Branco)
Praça do Municipío, 11
Tel. 275-752 123
Sra Maria Emilia Maia Figueira Costa

Rooms 5 (4 with private bath in the room, 1 with private bath out the room). **Price** Single 7,000Esc, double 10,000Esc. **Meals** Breakfast included, served 8:00-10:30. **Restaurant** See p. 217. **Credit cards** Not accepted. **Pets** Dogs allowed. **Facilities** Parking. **Nearby** Serra da Estrela: Zêzere valley from Guarda to Covilhã. **Open** All year.

You may be slightly disappointed on arriving here in Fundão, a city suffering from a serious case of the urban blight common to many frontier cities. The most interesting area is clearly its historical praça velha - old square - and its surroundings, all kept moist by the Zêzere which gives the Serra da Gardunha the look of a vast orchard. The impressive 18th-century façade of la Casa dos Maias dominates this main square with its immense entrance way giving on what were once stables for countless horses. The reception halls are on the upper floors, in perfect condition as each generation has left its indelible mark: silverware, portraits, furniture. The result is an atmosphere evocative of days gone by, adding all the more to the charm of the place. Bedrooms go off a lengthy corridor with appropriate decor: huge beds, vast wardrobes and bathrooms of a more recent vintage which, nonetheless, might do with an overhaul. Your best choice would be the room giving on the street, even if the bathroom, proudly labeled "exclusive", is across the hallway; it is a true treasure. A small verandah overlooks the garden, and not the least of this hotel's attractions is the unfailing smile of Maria Emilia, a descendant of one of the first families of the region.

How to get there (*Map 4*): *44km of Castelo Branco.*

Casa da Comenda TH

6230 Alpedrihna (Castelo Branco)
Tel. 275-56 71 61
Sra Maria Isabel G. Carmona

Rooms 4 (1 with sitting room and private bath, 2 with private bath, 1 with shower). **Price** Single 9,500Esc, double 11,000Esc, 3-4 pers. 14,000Esc; extra bed 2,500Esc. **Meals** Breakfast included, served 8:00-10:30. **Restaurant** In Fundão see p. 217. **Credit cards** Not accepted. **Pets** Dogs allowed. **Facilities** Swimming pool, billiard. **Nearby** Serra da Estrelha: Zêzere valley from Guarda to Covilhã. **Closed** Nov – Apr.

Located on the side of a mountain, the tiny village of Alpedrihna still bears the marks of wars fought along nearby borders. La Casa da Comenda is a vast granite building surrounded by battlements built at the beginning of the 17th century; some of its walls are two meters thick. The owner, a true history buff, will gladly tell you tales of the region and of his house's role in them. The entrance way is quite impressive with its four-meter-high ceiling and imposing granite staircase leading to luxury quarters above. There is regional 19th-century decoration in both the lounges and the rooms which are very spacious, some offering a view of the valley and from which, on a clear day, you can see as far as neighboring Spain.

How to get there *(Map 4): 290km northeast of Lisboa, to Castelo Branco and Alpedrihna (11km of Fundão).*

Casa do Barreiro TH

6230 Alpedrihna (Castelo Branco)
Largo das Escolas
Tel. 275-567 120
Sra Francisca Cabral

Rooms 5 (2 with bath, 2 with shower, 1 without bath). **Price** Double 10,000Esc. **Meals** Breakfast included, served 8:00-10:30. **Restaurant** In Fundão see p. 217. **Credit cards** Not accepted. **Pets** Dogs allowed. **Facilities** Parking. **Nearby** Serra da Estrelha: Zêzere valley from Guarda to Covilhã. **Open** All year.

This Casa do Barreiro should not be confused with one with the same name in Ponte de Lima. Here, you are in the lovely village of La Serra da Estrela - "the Chain of Stars" - now a natural park in a region often unfamiliar to foreign visitors but one which will delight those who enjoy mountainous landscapes. Traditions here have very long lives and in the summer, herds of cattle return to their nearby grazing lands while in winter, wool is still woven on mill-driven looms. This attractive house dating from the beginning of the century offers complex and elegant architecture, its different wings intricately intertwined with charming rooftops and gables. On land that was formerly a quinta, it is surrounded by luxurious vegetation. You will immediately feel at ease in this well-appointed and tasteful interior dating from the end of the 19th century which pleasantly evokes a certain nostalgia for a by-gone era.

How to get there (Map 4): 290km northeast of Lisboa, to Castelo Branco and Alpedrihna (12km of Fundão).

Albergue do Bonjardim ᵀᴴ

Nesperal 61000 Sertã (Castelo Branco)
Cernache do Bonjardim
Tel. 274-80 96 47 - Fax 274-80 96 47
Hubertus Johannes Lenders Biemond

Rooms 4 with bath or shower, WC. **Price** Single 10,000-11,600Esc, double 12,500-14,000Esc; extra bed 3,000-3,200Esc. **Meals** Breakfast included, served 8:00-10:30. No restaurant, but lunch 1,000Esc. Restaurant recommended in Sertã: "Pontavelha". **Credit card** Amex. **Pets** Dogs not allowed. **Facilities** Heated swimming pool, hammam, parking. **Nearby** Lousã - Piedade - Fifueiro dos Vinhos - Penela. **Closed** Nov 15 – Dec 15.

The albergue is a rural house, dating from the 18th Century, standing in an estate of twelve hectares. Nowadays the farm is run by a couple of Dutch farmers who have found here complete freedom to satisfy their desire for nature and local customs. Indeed, as soon as you come in, you will be offered a welcoming glass in the salon lined with large racks and casks. The rooms we prefer are the ones in the main house which are large, bright and perfect for décor and comfort. The two others are in a separate house and can be combined to house a large family. Here, too, a great deal of care has been applied to details, harmonizing the towels and the *azulejos*, for example. The garden is idyllic, with pretty cast-iron furniture and a trellis walkway under which breakfast is served: a real treat – home-made yogurt and honey from the quinta. The produce is all organic: wine from a vineyard "en que só usados tratamentos ancestrais", vegetables, fruit. Tradition, but also modern comfort: after a course in wine appreciation with the owner you can enjoy the covered pool, the sauna or the Turkish bath.

How to get there *(Map 4): 118km southeast of Coimbra. N1 to Pombal, then UC8 to Sertã. 8km west of Sertã.*

Quinta das Lagrimas

Santa Clara 3000 Coímbra
Tel. 239-44 16 15 - Fax 239-44 16 95
Fam. Ozório Cabral de Castro
E-mail: hotelagrimas@mail.telepac.pt - Web: supernet.pt/hotelagrimas

Category ★★★★ **Rooms** 35 and 4 suites with air-conditioning, telephone, bath, WC, TV, minibar; elevator, wheelchair access. **Price** Single 23,000Esc, double 29,000Esc, double luxe 55,000-70,000Esc; extra bed 6,500Esc. **Meals** Breakfast included, served 7:30-10:30; full board +8,000Esc (per pers.). **Restaurant** "Arcadas das Capelas", service 12:30PM-3:00PM, 8:00PM-11:30PM — mealtime specials 4,500Esc, also à la carte. **Credit cards** Amex, Visa, Eurocard, MasterCard. **Pets** Dogs not allowed. **Facilities** Swimming pool, parking. **Nearby** In Coímbra: Old University (the library, the chapel), Museum of Machado de Castro - Buçaco Forest (Cruz Alta, obelisco) - Ruins of Conimbriga - Aveiro - Ria d'Aveiro (boating). **Open** All year.

This quinta is known throughout Portugal as having been the setting of a star-crossed love affair between Prince Don Pedro and Dona Inês de Castro, a lady-in-waiting of the Queen, Constança. Legend has it that the King had her strangled in the garden, and for that reason this "Villa of Tears" has become a site of pilgrimages made by those who gather in front of the fountain and honor the woman known as "The Dead Queen." The manor is superb, its garden an explosion of joyous greenery and cedar trees dating back over centuries and providing shade for the elegant pale yellow façade. The intimate and beautifully appointed interior has already attracted numerous personalities. The salons, the libraries and the royal chamber stand as tributes to the royal family. The rooms are of the quality of a "grand hotel" and regional charm is never absent. In the garden is a less expensive annex allowing the guests to enjoy the setting.

How to get there (Map 1): 118km south of Porto via A3.

Hotel Astória

3000-150 Coímbra
Avenida Emidio Navarro, 21
Tel. 239-82 20 55 - Fax 239-82 20 57
E-mail: almeida_hotels@ip.pt

Category ★★★ **Rooms** 60 with air-conditioning and 2 suites with telephone, bath, WC, TV; elevator. **Price** Single 11,000-15,000Esc, double 14,000-18,000Esc, suite 17,000-22,000Esc. **Meals** Breakfast included, served 8:00-10:00; half board +3,300Esc, full board +6,200Esc (per pers.). **Restaurant** With air-conditioning. Service 1:00PM-3:00PM, 8:00PM-9:30PM – à la carte 3,800Esc – French and Portuguese cooking. **Credit cards** All major. **Pets** Dogs allowed except in restaurant. **Nearby** In Coímbra: Old University (the library, the chapel), Museum of Machado de Castro - Buçaco Forest (Cruz Alta, obelisco) - Ruins of Conimbriga - Aveiro - Ria d'Aveiro (boating). **Open** All year.

Situated close to the university, right in the center of the town on the banks of the Mandego, this hotel has all the charm of an old palace of the 1930's. The interior architecture is interesting, as is the huge lounge with its mezzanine, and the very beautiful rotunda dining room, the "Amphitryon". Fine cuisine with both French and Portuguese specialties is served, along with a very good selection of "grand cru" wines from Buçaco. This is a nostalgic hotel, rather like the town, the former capital of Portugal, whose romantic beauty has inspired more than one poet. The Astoria preserves the memory of writers and painters who stayed here, and in particular of Amalia Rodrigues, who gave her unforgettable *fado* recitals here.

How to get there *(Map 1): 118km south of Porto via A3.*

Pousada Santa Bárbara *

Póvoa das Quartas
3400 Oliveira do Hospital (Coímbra)
Tel. 238-596 52/3 - Fax 238-596 45
Sr João Borges

Rooms 16 with telephone, bath, WC, TV. **Price** Single 12,500-21,000Esc, double 14,300-22,500Esc; extra bed +30%. **Meals** Breakfast included, served 8:00-10:00. **Restaurant** Service 12:30PM-3:00PM, 7:30PM-10:00PM – à la carte 3,650Esc. **Credit cards** All major. **Pets** Dogs not allowed. **Facilities** Swimming pool, tennis, garage, parking. **Nearby** In Oliveira: the church - Church of Lourosa - Mont Torre. **Open** All year.

The rural area of Oliveira do Hospital is most attractive: pine forests following valleys and active farms that supply the hotels with fresh vegetables. The Pousada Santa Barbara is a recent construction, but the fire in the hearth, the objects of popular art, and the view over the prairies all contribute to the agreeable country ambiance that reigns here. Various terraces have been laid out, ideal for drinking a beer or even trying a barbecue. The rooms have balconies, and so from there you can also profit from the local panorama.

How to get there (Map 1): 82km northeast of Coímbra via N17 to Oliveira, then 7km east of Póvoa das Quartas.

Clube de Vale de Leão

Buarcos 3080 Figueira da Foz (Coímbra)
Estrada do Cabo Mondego
Tel. 233-43 30 57 - Fax 233-43 25 71
Sr Armor Cardosso

Category ★★★★ **Studios** 25 with telephone, bath, WC, TV, kitchenette. **Price** 2 pers. 7,250-14,500Esc, 4 pers. 8,900-18,900Esc, 6 pers. 14,200-27,500Esc, 8 pers. 17,300-34,500Esc. **Meals** Breakfast 500-950Esc. **Restaurant** Service 12:00PM-2:00PM, 7:30PM-9:30PM – mealtime specials 3,800Esc, also à la carte – Portuguese and international cooking. **Credit cards** All major. **Pets** Dogs not allowed. **Facilities** Swimming pool, tennis, parking. **Nearby** Serra de Boa Viagem - Figueira da Foz - Montemor-o-Velho - Coímbra. **Closed** Nov – Apr.

Half hotel and half residence, this club offers an ideal base for family holidays with children. It is essentially 25 independent houses, all very well equipped, with a view over the bay of Figueira da Foz. As for leisure activities, everything has been done to provide on-site distractions with a very complete sports complex. For those parents who find that such a formula does not really add up to a holiday, a restaurant has been provided as well as a discotheque. But there is nothing to stop you going out to dinner at Buarcos, which remains an authentic little fishing port, or having a party at Figueira, the fashionable seaside resort.

How to get there (Map 1): 180km north of Lisboa.

Casa de Azenha Velha ᵀᴿ

Caceira de Cima 3080 Figueira da Foz (Coímbra)
Tel. 233-2 50 41
Sra Maria de Lourdes Nogueira

Rooms 6 with air-conditioning and 1 apartment (4 pers.) with telephone, bath, WC, satellite TV, minibar. **Price** Double 13,000Esc, apart. 20,000Esc. **Meals** Breakfast included, served 8:00-10:00. **Restaurant** By reservation. **Credit cards** All majors. **Pets** Dogs not allowed. **Facilities** Swimming pool, tennis, parking. **Nearby** Serra de Boa Viagem - Figueira da Foz - Montemor-o-Velho - Coímbra. **Open** All year.

The road from Coimbra to the ocean at Figueira da Foz is a fine country road, which means that Casa de Azendha, though only four kilometers from the beach, also enjoys a rural setting. The fine, large house, with its daring orange façade, stands in a very beautiful garden with palm trees and eucalyptus. New buildings have recently been constructed adjacent to the old house, with rooms for guests. The whole is harmonious and its modernity means that the lodging is very comfortable: space is not at a premium, the bathrooms are modern and, in summer, the air conditioning is a real asset. The decoration is fresh, with flowered prints, which brightens up otherwise rather dark rooms. In a fine annex, a bar and billiard table are at the disposal of visitors who can take a light meal there, if they ask for it in advance.

How to get there (*Maps 1 and 3): 38km west of Coimbra.*

Quinta da Ponte ^{TH*}

6300 Faia (Guarda)
Tel. 271-926 126 - Fax 271-926 126
Maria Joaquina Trigueiros de Aragão Alvim

Rooms 2 with bath, sitting room area and 5 apartments with bath, kitchenette, sitting room, TV. **Price** 2 pers. 19,000Esc, 4 pers. 26,400Esc; extra bed 2,000Esc. **Meals** Breakfast included, served 8:00-10:00. **Restaurant** In Guarda See p. 218. **Credit card** Amex. **Pets** Dogs not allowed. **Facilities** Swimming pool, tennis, parking. **Nearby** Zêzere Valley via N18 to Covilhã - Poço do Inferno - Mont Torre - Sorthela - Almeida - Linhares. **Open** All year by reservation.

Just as it leaves behind the austere yet lovely city of Guarda - "keeper of the gateway to Portugal" - the road is lined by impressive granite landscapes. A few kilometers further on is Faia in the heart of the Serra de Estrella, renowned for its cloudless skies and owing its name to the beauty of its starry nights. The Quinta da Ponte is ideally located amid attractive sites in this natural park. It is a large property, bordering on a small river and surrounded by woods. The emblazoned portal and small French-style garden are constant reminders that this was a noble residence in the 17th century. The oldest part of the house, once the chapel, now has two rooms, each of which gives on a very attractive central lounge. In addition, there are five well-appointed apartments in an annex adjacent to the swimming pool. The decoration in them doesn't have quite the charm of the others but they open onto the garden which is definitely a plus. This is an excellent place to enjoy nature: fishing, canoeing, hiking.

How to get there (Map 2): 12km north of Guarda, 50km of Spain.

Pousada de São Lourenço *

6260 Penhas Douradas-Manteigas (Guarda)
Estrada da Gouveia
Tel. 275-98 24 50/1 - Fax 275-98 24 53
Sra Marie José

Rooms 21 with telephone, bath, WC, TV, minibar. **Price** Single 14,500-23,100Esc, double 16,300-24,600Esc; extra bed +30%. **Meals** Breakfast included, served 8:00-10:30. **Restaurant** Service 1:00PM-3:00PM, 7:30PM-9:30PM – mealtime specials 3,650Esc, also à la carte – Specialties: Sopa da Beira - Bacalhau a la São Lourenço - Cabrito assado. **Credit cards** All major. **Pets** Dogs not allowed. **Facilities** Parking. **Nearby** Zêzère valley via N18 to Covilhã - Poço do Inferno - Mont Torre. **Open** All year.

At an altitude of 1,290 meters, at the heart of the Serra de Estrela, in the midst of a glorious countryside of mountains and valleys covered with pine trees, the Pousada de São Lourenço is truly hidden away. The wood and stone used in it make it look like a genuine mountain refuge. Inside it is rustic and warm, but well equipped to receive guests at any season: there are large open fireplaces everywhere for the winter months. All the bedrooms have a beautiful view, and numbers 5, 6 and 7 also have small terraces. This will make an agreeable halting site on your journey.

How to get there (Map 2): 133km northeast of Coímbra via N17; 13km of Manteigas on the Gouveia road.

Estalagem da Seia

6270 Seia (Guarda)
Av. Dr Alfonso Costa
Tel. 238-31 58 66 - Fax 238-31 55 38
Sr Luis dos Santos Camelo

Rooms 35 with air-conditioning, telephone, bath, WC, satellite TV; elevator. **Price** Double 11,000-11,500Esc; extra bed for child 2,500Esc. **Meals** Breakfast included, served 8:00-10:30. **Restaurant** Service 12:30PM-2:30PM, 7:30PM-9:30PM – à la carte 2,100-3,150Esc. **Credit card** Visa. **Pets** Dogs not allowed. **Facilities** Swimming pool, parking. **Nearby** Panoramic road from Seia to Covilhã - Poço do Inferno - Viseu. **Closed** Aug 15 – 30.

Seia, gateway to the west of the Serra de Estrella, is a small and friendly tourist village. The Estalagem is located on a mountainside just at the edge of the town. It was a lovely town house in the 17th century that now extends into the garden and its interior has been completely made over, turning it into a traditional hotel, comfortable and nicely furnished. The rooms are all identical but their simplicity has avoided any hint of bad taste. Your best choice would be one of the rooms overlooking the valley. The restaurant and swimming pool enjoy the same view. The reception you get is attentive, offering the latest in sports news plus hints for visitors in the region. This is "the roof of Portugal" with the country's highest mountain range culminating at La Torre - 1,991 meters - only twenty-five kilometers away.

How to get there (Map 1): 45km of Viseu. 90km southwest of Guarda towards Coimbra.

Casa das Tílias

San Romão 6270 Seia (Guarda)
Tel. 238-39 00 55 - Fax 238-39 01 23
Sr José Luis Figueiredo Lopes
Web: www.tilias.com

Rooms 5 and 1 suite with telephone, bath, satellite TV. **Price** Double 10,000-14,000Esc, suite 12,500Esc. **Meals** Breakfast included, served 9:00-11:00. **Restaurant** See p. 218. **Credit cards** Not accepted. **Pets** Dogs not allowed. **Facilities** Swimming pool, parking. **Nearby** Panoramic road from Seia to Covilhã - Poço do Inferno - Viseu. **Open** All year.

On the slopes of the Serra de Estrella, 600 meters above sea level, the Casa das Tílias stands in the village of San Romão, close to Seia. English-style windows, white walls and cast-iron balconies add to the charm of this 19th-century house, so well-restored in the style of the region that it is hard to imagine that José found it in ruins. The reception rooms on the first floor are each more elegant than the next, with polished wood to show off the family silver and china. Do not fail to admire the ceiling, with its cornices decorated with bas-reliefs in stucco showing Isabel, queen and saint. A fine wooden staircase leads to the second floor. There is a cozy atmosphere in the rooms, our preference going to the Mercurio suite with its harmonizing pinks and its painted ceiling with mythological scenes. José is a very welcoming host who will not only insist that you taste his wine, but also his famous aguardente, the local spirit. In the garden, the pool and swimming pool are fed by a spring. As for the region itself, it will delight sports lovers in summer as in winter.

How to get there (Map 1): 45km from Viseu; 90km southwest of Guarda towards Coimbra, San Romão is south of Seia, by N231, towards Loriga.

Quinta da Bela Vista

6270 Torrozelo (Guarda)
Tel. 238-90 22 22 - Fax 238-90 22 22
Sra Maria da Glória Baptipta Simões

Rooms 6 with bath, (5 with TV); wheelchair access. **Price** Double 12,000-13,000Esc. **Meals** Breakfast included, served 8:00:10:30. No restaurant. **Credit cards** Not accepted. **Pets** Dogs allowed. **Facilities** Swimming pool, tennis, parking. **Nearby** Panoramic road from Seia to Covilhã - Poço do Inferno - Viseu. **Open** All year.

Torrozelo is a few kilometers from Seia, at the entrance to the National Park of the Serra de Estrela. Completely integrated with the landscape, this beautiful, renovated mansion will ensure a tranquil and restful stay. Everything has been done to offer the maximum of refined comfort for the guests. Three rooms open below on a garden planted with fruit trees. The quality rustic furniture and the pretty colors chosen for the fabrics create a harmonious ensemble. The three others, more richly furnished (one of them has a magnificent four-poster bed) are on the owners' floor. The communal rooms are pleasant to be in and we particularly liked those with fireplaces where the main element is granite and highly varnished wood. There is a swimming pool and tennis court to add to the sporting activities offered by the long-distance walks in the Serra de Estrella. A lovely spot where you are advised to reserve in advance, since the owner may decide to take a few days holiday.

How to get there (Map 1): 45km from Vieu; 90km southwest of Guarda, towards Coímbra. Torrezelo is 10km southeast of Seia, towards Folhadosa.

Pousada de São Jerónimo *

3475 Caramulo (Viseu)
Tel. 232-86 12 91 - Fax 232-86 16 40

Rooms 6 with air-conditioning, telephone, bath, WC. **Price** Single 12,500-21,000Esc, double 14,300-22,500Esc, extra bed +30%. **Meals** Breakfast included, served 8:00-11:00. **Restaurant** Service 12:30PM-3:00PM, 7:30PM-10:00PM – mealtime specials 3,650Esc, also à la carte – Specialties: Bacalhao dorado - Chanfana - Musela con grelos. **Credit cards** All major. **Pets** Dogs not allowed. **Facilities** Swimming pool, parking. **Nearby** Art Museum of Caramulo - Pinoucas - Caramulinho. **Open** All year.

In the massifs of Caramulo in the midst of a forest of pine trees, one is always happy to find this small and modern pousada, and it is always welcoming. There are no more than six rooms, rustic and simple, but comfort has in no way been neglected. Even if you have not come to fish in the well-stocked Agueda and Criz rivers, you will appreciate the swimming pool, tennis court and hotel park for a few hours. From the rooms, terraces and restaurant you have a superb view over the valleys round about. The small size of the hotel makes for a family ambiance and a warm welcome. Be careful however, as renovations are planned, so be sure to phone in advance.

How to get there (Map 1): 78km northeast of Coimbra via N1 to Mealhada, N234 to Tondela, and then N230 for 11km.

Hotel Grão Vasco

3500-032 Viseu
Rua Gaspar Barreiros
Tel. 232-42 35 11 - Fax 232-42 64 44
Sr Henrique Gonçalves

Category ★★★★ **Rooms** 110 with air-conditioning, telephone, bath, WC, satellite TV; elevator. **Price** Single 11,500-13,500Esc, double 13,500-15,500Esc. **Meals** Breakfast included, served 7:30-10:00; half board +3,500Esc. **Restaurant** Service 12:30PM-3:00PM, 8:00PM-10:00PM – à la carte 3,500-4,100Esc – Specialties: Cabrito assado - Rojões - Vino Dão. **Credit cards** All major. **Pets** Dogs allowed except in restaurant. **Facilities** Swimming pool, parking. **Nearby** In Viseu: old town, cathedral, Museum of Grão Vasco - Church of São Bento (azulejos). **Open** All year.

One cannot visit Portugal without going to Viseu, a city of art of the highest quality. The Old Town is a delight with its famous cathedral and museum that house the essential works of the Viseu School. The hotel bears the name of the most talented of its artists, Grão Vasco. Built in the 1970s, it is the finest hotel in Viseu. An intelligent use of stone provides a graceful transition from the hotel into a large park, providentially sparing a visitor the noise of the surrounding city. The reception area is noteworthy for its elegant antique furniture, while the rooms offer a more regional style plus comfortable surroundings. The restaurant opens out onto the lawn, and the food at the Grão Vasco proudly upholds Viseu's gastronomic reputation.

How to get there (Map 1): 74km east of Aveiro.

Quinta de São Caetano

3500-032 Viseu
Rua Poça das Feiticeiras, 38
Tel. 232-42 39 84 - Fax 232-43 78 27
Sr Julio Vieira de Matos

Rooms 6 (4 with air-conditioning) with bath, WC; wheelchair access. **Price** Single 11,600Esc, double 14,000Esc; extra bed 3,200Esc. **Meals** Breakfast included, served 8:00-10:00. **Evening meals** By reservation – mealtime specials 4,000Esc. **Credit cards** Visa, Eurocard, MasterCard. **Pets** Dogs not allowed. **Facilities** Swimming pool, billiard, parking. **Nearby** In Viseu: old town, cathedral, Museum of Grão Vasco - Church of São Bento (azulejos). **Open** All year.

You will find no sign directing you to the quinta as you come out of Vieu, near the historic center behind the hospital, so you will have to take your bearings on the two giant palm trees on either side of the double stairway leading to the lawn in front of the house. This is an aristocratic house of the 17th Century, elegantly built, whose present owner will tell you tales from history and show you round the little chapel, dated 1680. The rooms are in the main house where there is a drawing room for guests who can also enjoy the billiard room and the dining room, tiled in *azulejos*, where breakfast is served. The rooms are simple and pretty; the flowered bedcovers and the rustic furniture create a pleasant country atmosphere. no. 4 has a direct view of the palm trees and no. 5 a less interrupted view of the swimming pool with the Serra de Estrella and Lousã as a backdrop. The garden, furnished with a fountain, a greenhouse and a pond, has some magnificent trees: including the two palm trees already mentioned, a century-old cedar overlooks the olive trees, figs and vines. A friendly welcome.

How to get there (Map 1): 74km east of Aveiro.

Estalagem Casa d'Azurara

3530-215 Mangualde (Viseu)
Rua Nova, 78
Tel. 232-61 20 10 - Fax 232-62 25 75
Sofia da Costa Cabral

Category ★★★★ **Rooms** 15 with air-conditioning, telephone, bath, WC, TV; elevator. **Price** Double 16,500-21,000Esc. **Meals** Breakfast included, served 8:30-10:30. **Restaurant** Service 12:30PM-2:30PM, 7:30PM-10:30PM – à la carte 4,000-4,500Esc. **Credit cards** All major. **Pets** Dogs allowed. **Facilities** Parking. **Nearby** In mangualde: palácio dos Condes de Anadia (azulejos), Church of Misericórdia - Penalva do Castelo (casa da Insua) - Serra Estrela (Mont Torre, Zêzere Valley). **Open** All year.

Ten kilometers from the lovely city of Viseu, this magnificent little hotel is located in an aristocratic residence with surrounding countryside where flowers are everywhere, a splendid showcase for this attractive white house with windows and a staircase of a pleasant gray. A small shaded garden, some rose bushes and a well-kept lawn stretch out in front of the lounges. These are spacious and impeccably decorated with fine antiques which harmonize nicely with the thick hemp rugs and sofas with bright floral cotton coverings. The restaurant is in what was once the cellar and opens on the lawn, allowing you to eat in the garden, weather permitting. The rooms are upstairs and combine charm with comfort. We prefer those on the front overlooking the garden with a view of the peaks of the Serra d'Estrella. This is a delightful hotel in a region virtually spared of tourist invasion and well worth your visit.

How to get there *(Map 1): 18km east of Viseu towards Guarda; then towards Gouveia to Mangualde.*

Casa de Abreu Madeira TH*

3525 Canas de Senhorim (Viseu)
Largo de Abreu Madeira, 7
Tel. 232-67 11 83
Sr Antonio Alberto de Abreu Madeira

Rooms 3 with (1 with bath, 1 without bath), 1 suite with bath, sitting room, minibar. **Price** Double 14,000Esc. **Meals** Breakfast included. **Restaurant** In Nelas see p. 218. **Credit cards** Not accepted. **Pets** Dogs not allowed. **Facilities** Swimming pool, parking. **Nearby** Dão wineries- Mangualde: palácio dos Condes de Anadia (azulejos), Church of Misericordia - Penalva do Castelo (casa da Insua) - Midões - Serra Estrela (Mont Torre, Zêzere Valley). **Open** All year.

The vineyards surrounding Viseu produce what are reputed to be the best wines in Portugal. It is therefore a region where you will pass through numerous small agricultural communities that offer agreeable strolls along tiny streets lined with old manor houses and baroque churches. It was in this way that we found this noble casa and private chapel on a very calm street, Canas de Senhorim. The owners, members of the Abreu Madeira family, are genuinely friendly and offer a few rooms that we didn't have the opportunity to see. Still, considering what we saw of the house and the historic mementos it contains, there couldn't possibly be any unpleasant surprises. It has no restaurant but you can taste the owner's wine, a delicious "Dão", along with his "Serra" cheese.

How to get there (Map 1): 25km south of Viseu.

Solar da Quinta [TH*]

Póvoa dos Mosqueiros 3440 Santa Comba Dão (Viseu)
Tel. 232-89 17 08 - Fax 232-89 23 82
Fam. António Marques Antunes

Rooms 6 with bath. **Price** 1 pers. 9,000-11,000Esc, double 10,000-14,000Esc. **Meals** Breakfast included, served 8:00-10:00. **Evening meals** On request – mealtime specials 3,000Esc. **Credit cards** Not accepted. **Pets** Dogs allowed. **Facilities** Parking. **Nearby** Dão wineries - Mangualde: palácio dos Condes de Anadia (azulejos), Church of Misericordia - Penalva do Castelo (casa da Insua) - Midões - Serra Estrela (Mont Torre, Zêzere Valley). **Closed** Dec 27 – Jan 4.

After travelling through the pine woods and reservoir-lakes created by the Aguierra dam, you reach Póvoa dos Mosqueiros. The house is in the centre on the village square. This is a noble mansion, more than four hundred years old, which the grandfather of the present owner bought as a ruin. Seven years ago, Antonio decided to restore it and has done so with a love of detail to create a very friendly house. The result has lots of charm: the dining room with its fine wooden ceiling, the drawing room with its billiard table and the library which has the intimate atmosphere suited to reading. The rooms are pretty and snug: cane or brass bedsteads, pretty cotton fabrics, some rooms with a loggia. Only the kitchen, reached down a stone staircase, is modern. Here they prepare and serve good breakfasts with home-made jams and meals based on organic produce, if you reserve them. Your days will be filled with walks and visits.

How to get there *(Map 1): 65km south of Viseu by Ip3, exit Sta Comba Dão.*

Quinta da Fata [AT]

Vilar Seco 3520 Nelas (Viseu)
Rua da Fata
Tel. 232-94 23 32 - Fax 232-94 23 32
Sra Maria Manuela Aires de Abreu

Rooms 5 and 2 apartments with bath. **Price** Double 12,500-14,500Esc. **Meals** Breakfast included. **Restaurant** In Nelas see p. 218. **Credit cards** Not accepted. **Pets** Dogs not allowed. **Facilities** Swimming pool, parking. **Nearby** Dão wineries - Mangualde: palácio dos Condes de Anadia (azulejos), Church of Misericordia - Penalva do Castelo (casa da Insua) - Midões - Serra Estrela (Mont Torre, Zêzere Valley). **Open** All year.

Nelas is known for being the capital of Dão and for housing one on the residences of the Duke of Bragança, possibly the legitimate pretender to the throne of Portugal. The village of Vila Seco is only a few kilometers away and the Quinta da Fata is a vast agricultural and wine-growing property, located between the Dão and the Mondelo rivers, the outer limits of its famous vineyard. The surroundings have great charm, and the small garden with its tall trees, lawns and hydrangea are a delight. The rooms available to guests are in the main building. They are not particularly big, but pleasant and independent. Your best choice would be the suite which bears a slightly higher price. Two apartments have recently been furnished, without much charm but altogether adequate. In addition, Maria Manuela is an adorable hostess.

How to get there (Map 1): 16km south of Viseu.

Hotel Infante de Sagres

4050-259 Porto
Praça Dona Filipa de Lencastre, 62
Tel. 22-339 85 00 - Fax 22-339 85 99
E-mail: his.sales@mail.telepac.pt - Web: www.hotelinfantesagres.pt

Category ★★★★★ **Rooms** 74 with air-conditioning, telephone, bath, WC, satellite TV, minibar; elevator. **Price** Single 28,000Esc, double 30,500Esc, suite 65,000Esc. **Meals** Breakfast included, served 7:30-10:30; half board +5,000Esc, full board +10,000Esc (per pers.). **Restaurant** Service 12:30PM-2:30PM, 7:30PM-10:00PM – à la carte – Regional cooking and fish. **Credit cards** All major. **Pets** Dogs not allowed. **Facilities** Garage. **Nearby** Church of San Francisco - Caves (wine lodges) in Vila Nova de Gaia (Caves Ferreira, rua da Carvalhosa 19; caves Ramos Pinto, av. Ramos Pinto; caves Taylor, rua do Choupelo 250; Fladgatet and Yeatman...) - Convent of Nossa Senhora de Serra do Pilar - Church of Bom Jesus de Matosinhos – Oporto Espinho golf course (18-hole). **Open** All year.

Situated in the heart of the town, close to the town hall and Cordoaria Gardens, the Infante de Sagres is the classy hotel of Porto. The reception area and lounges are richly appointed and the hotel is proud to own some carved furniture of great value. One also finds the same great comfort and luxury in the bedrooms. The dining room has a lot of atmosphere: the wall lamps and center lights in crystal, reflected in the large mirrors, create a very refined ambiance with the pinks and browns of the decoration. The service matches the elegance of the house.

How to get there (Map 1): Take the rua do Almada.

Casa do Marechal

4100-119 Porto
Avenida da Boavista, 2674
Tel. 22-610 47 02 - Fax 22-610 32 41
M. João Paulo Baganha

Rooms 5 with air-conditioning, telephone, bath, WC, satellite TV, minibar. **Price** Single 25,000Esc, double 28,000Esc. **Meals** Breakfast included, served 7:30-10:00. **Restaurant** Service 12:30PM-3:00PM, 7:30PM-10:00PM - Closed weekend except request – à la carte 4,000-6,000Esc – Specialties: Fish, meat from north mountains. **Credit cards** All major. **Pets** Dogs not allowed. **Facilities** Sauna, fitness, parking. **Nearby** Church of San Francisco - Caves (wine lodges) in Vila Nova de Gaia (Caves Ferreira, rua da Carvalhosa 19; caves Ramos Pinto, av. Ramos Pinto; caves Taylor, rua do Choupelo 250; Fladgatet and Yeatman...) - Convent of Nossa Senhora de Serra do Pilar - Church of Bom Jesus de Matosinhos – Oporto Espinho golf course (18-hole). **Closed** Aug and weekends except by reservation.

The Casa do Marechal is the kind of guest house offering the comfort and service of a "grand hotel." Located on one the city's principal arteries and not far from the new center of town, it is an Art-Deco delight. The interior is warm and elegant, with subtle lighting, antique furniture and discreet service that create an intimate atmosphere and a general feeling of well-being so rarely found these days. You are certain to discover in its restaurant all the refinement of Portuguese cuisine. In a word, a hotel in Porto with unfailing charm.

How to get there (Map 1): At the praça Mousinho de Alburquerque-Boavista, take the Avenida da Boavista towards the sea. The Casa do Marechal is on your right, 300 m after the BP filling station.

Hotel Tivoli Porto

4100-020 Porto
Rua Alfonso Lopes Vieira, 66
Tel. 22-609 49 41 - Fax 22-606 74 52
Sr Fernando Rios

Category ★★★★★ **Rooms** 58 and 6 suites with air-conditioning, bath, WC, satellite TV, safe, minibar; elevator. **Price** Single 31,000Esc, double 35,000Esc, suite 62,000Esc. **Meals** Breakfast included, served from 7:00. **Restaurant** Snacks-bar in the hotel or see pp. 218-219. **Credit cards** All major. **Pets** Dogs not allowed. **Facilities** Swimming pool, parking. **Nearby** Church of San Francisco - Caves (wine lodges) in Vila Nova de Gaia (Caves Ferreira, rua da Carvalhosa 19; caves Ramos Pinto, av. Ramos Pinto; caves Taylor, rua do Choupelo 250; Fladgatet and Yeatman...) - Convent of Nossa Senhora de Serra do Pilar - Church of Bom Jesus de Matosinhos – Oporto Espinho golf course (18-hole). **Open** All year.

The cellars of Vila Nova de Gaia, sheltering the famous wines of Porto, have made the reputation of this second city of Portugal. The town has an atmosphere but is not very touristy, and the hotels are the deluxe types of a major commercial port more than hotels of charm. The Tivoli, somewhat of an exception, is situated in a residential quarter of large modern blocks. The hotel has just been fully renovated and provides a warm and refined environment. No two rooms are alike but all have a terrace, most of them looking over the swimming pool. One finds the traditional comfort but also the little thoughtful gestures (coffee, biscuits, dressing gown, umbrella, etc.) that gives a more personal feeling. Also to be noted are the attractive swimming pool, and very efficient service.

How to get there *(Map 1): In the town center, via avenida Boavista.*

Hotel da Bolsa

4050 Porto
Rua Ferreira Borges, 101
Tel. 22-202 67 68/69/70 - Fax 22-205 88 88

Category ★★★ **Rooms** 36 with air-conditioning, bath, WC, satellite TV, minibar; elevator, wheelchair access. **Price** Double 12,500-14,000Esc, double with view 14,500-16,000Esc; extra bed 3,000-3,500Esc. **Meals** Breakfast included, served 7:30-10:30. **Restaurant** See pp. 218-219. **Credit cards** All major. **Pets** Dogs not allowed. **Facilities** Bar D. Nuno, parking (extra charge). **Nearby** Church of San Francisco - Caves (wine lodges) in Vila Nova de Gaia (Caves Ferreira, rua da Carvalhosa 19; caves Ramos Pinto, av. Ramos Pinto; caves Taylor, rua do Choupelo 250; Fladgatet and Yeatman...) - Convent of Nossa Senhora de Serra do Pilar - Church of Bom Jesus de Matosinhos – Oporto Espinho golf course (18-hole). **Open** All year.

With the exception of the truly attractive Infante de Sagres, the Bolsa is the only hotel close to the Ribeira, Porto's seaport. Adjacent to the magnificent Stock Exchange building, it has a special place in this lively and picturesque neighborhood made up of streets leading to the Praça da Ribeira with its countless sidewalk cafés. Here, you find fish vendors lining the piers and small taverns filled with young people. The imposing building that houses the hotel goes back to the 19th century and has been re-designed along more contemporary lines. Apart from their size and location, the rooms are identical. All are comfortable and neatly decorated in pastel colors. The best among them are on the top floor with an incredible view of the activity in the port, the superb arches of the metal bridge designed by Gustave Eiffel plus a delightful rainbow made up of gaily-painted houses stretching along the Douro.

How to get there (Map 1): Near the stock exchange and the port.

Castelo Santa Catarina

4000-457 Porto
Rua Santa Catarina, 1347
Tel. 22-509 55 99 - Fax 22-55 06 613
Sr João Brás

Rooms 25 with telephone, bath, WC, satellite TV. **Price** Single 6,500Esc, double 10,000Esc. **Meals** Breakfast included, served 8:00-10:30. **Restaurant** See pp. 218-219. **Credit cards** Amex, Visa, Eurocard, MasterCard. **Pets** Dogs not allowed. **Facilities** Parking. **Nearby** Church of San Francisco - Caves (wine lodges) in Vila Nova de Gaia (Caves Ferreira, rua da Carvalhosa 19; caves Ramos Pinto, av. Ramos Pinto; caves Taylor, rua do Choupelo 250; Fladgatet and Yeatman...) - Convent of Nossa Senhora de Serra do Pilar - Church of Bom Jesus de Matosinhos – Oporto Espinho golf course (18-hole). **Open** All year.

This beautiful castelo overlooks Porto with proud battlements and lovely façades of *azulejos*, all in perfect harmony with the palm trees in the garden. The main building - the best place to stay - is surrounded by terraces with flowers everywhere. The rooms are exquisitely comfortable with family-owned antique furniture: huge wooden beds, towering wardrobes, and the same comfort is found in the annex, where the rooms have windows opening on the garden (you should note that people may walk by). Here is an interesting hotel offering peace and quiet despite being very close to the center of the city. It has its own parking lot, something extremely rare in Porto.

How to get there (Map 1): Near the trading center.

Pensão Residencial Rex

4050 Porto
Praça da República, 117
Tel. 22-200 45 48 - Fax 22-208 38 82
Sr Paulo Chaves

Rooms 21 with telephone, bath, WC, TV. **Price** Single 7,000Esc, double 8,500Esc, triple 10,000Esc.
Meals No breakfast. **Restaurant** See pp. 218-219. **Credit cards** All major. **Pets** Dogs not allowed.
Facilities Parking **Nearby** Church of San Francisco in Porto - Caves (wine lodges) in Vila Nova de Gaia
(Caves Ferreira, rua da Carvalhosa 19; caves Ramos Pinto, av. Ramos Pinto; caves Taylor, rua do
Choupelo 250; Fladgatet and Yeatman...) - Convent of Nossa Senhora de Serra do Pilar - Church of
Bom Jesus de Matosinhos – Oporto Espinho golf course (18-hole). **Open** All year.

Standing on the edge of the center of Porto, the Pensão is pleasantly situated
opposite the square that occupies part of the Praça de la Repùblica. A
former private house in 1900 style, it retains the *azulejos* and the tall windows
that light the staircases on its four floors. This is a simple and inexpensive
hotel, like many Portuguese guest houses, though without the usual formica
furniture and with large rooms that have often kept the moulding and stucco
from the time when they were built, with sober furniture and impeccable
upkeep. Try however to avoid the rooms on the top floor which have recently
been renovated to increase capacity and which have consequently lost all the
charm that can still be found here. An old-fashioned, but not in any sense dusty
establishment. For those of limited means.

How to get there (Map 1): North of the center of Porto.

Quinta da Picaria ᵀᴴ*

Guimarei 4780 Santo Tirso (Porto)
Tel. 252-89 12 97 - Tel Cell. 0936 705 28 50
Sra Nogueira de Sousa Lopes

Rooms 4 with bath. **Price** Double 12,500-14,000Esc; extra bed 3,200Esc (until 12 year). **Meals** Breakfast included, served from 8:00. **Restaurant** See Santo Tirso p. 220. **Credit cards** Not accepted. **Pets** Dogs not allowed. **Facilities** Pond-swimming pool, parking. **Nearby** Porto - Douro valley - Serra de Marvão. **Open** All year.

Guimarei (not to be confused with Guimarães) is a charming country village some twenty kilometers from Porto, and this farmhouse is a very good alternative if one wants to stay close to town but at little cost. The farm is still active and the owner has fitted out a few rooms in its outbuildings. Such so-called "rural" tourism gives one a more intimate contact with the country, without any constraints. The four rooms offered are very pleasant: independent, comfortable and prettily decorated in the traditional taste. There's an open view over the valley, and one can also enjoy the large kitchen garden and orchard, with its kiwi trees, vegetables and vines. There is no restaurant at the quinta, but two attractive ones that can be easily reached on foot. The surrounding country is rich in Roman and Celtic remains, walks along the rivers with water mills on their banks and local markets. The welcome from Maria is very friendly, like that of a friend who is expecting you for the holidays.

How to get there *(Map 1): 20km northeast of Porto via A3 exit Santo Tirso; then take the N105 to Porto (old road); the Guimarei road is 100 m on the right.*

Casa de Pascoaes TH

São João de Gatão 4600 Amarante (Porto)
Tel. 255-42 25 95 / 42 39 53
Sra Maria Amelia Texeira de Vasconcellos

Rooms 4 with bath. **Price** Double 15,000-18,000Esc. **Meals** Breakfast included. **Evening meals** On request. **Restaurant** In Amarante see p. 218. **Credit cards** Not accepted. **Pets** Dogs not allowed. **Facilities** Parking. **Nearby** In Amarante: Monastery of São Gonçalo, Church of San Pedro - Church of Travanca - Serra de Marvaõ, road from Amarante to Vila Real — Porto wineries in the Douro valley (Peso da Regua, Vila Real, Pinhão) and in Vila Nova de Gaia. **Open** All year.

The Casa de Pascoaes was the home of the Portuguese poet Texeira de Pescoaes, and his library and office are still here, alive with his memory and the love that he had for this northern region. It is a noble manor house of the 18th-century a few kilometers from Amarante, a charming and picturesque little town. Maria Amelia welcomes you to share the refined "savoir vivre" of the Portuguese. Do not be surprised if it is suggested you should lunch in the kitchen; with its monumental granite austerity it is one of the loveliest rooms in the house. The rustic dishes are prepared here, which you sample with the *vinho verde* of Gatão, and here, between culture and tradition, you can best appreciate the soul of Portugal.

How to get there (Map 1): 64km east of Porto via N15. 1.5km north of Amarante towards Gatão.

Zé da Calçada

4600 Amarante (Porto)
Rua 31 de Janeiro
Tel. 255-422 023
Sra Amelia Rosa de Fonseca

Rooms 7 with telephone, bath, WC, TV. **Price** Single 7,500Esc, double 8,500Esc. **Meals** Breakfast included, served 7:00-10:00. **Restaurant** Service 12:00PM-2:00PM, 7:30PM-10:00PM – à la carte 3,500-6,000Esc. **Credit cards** All major. **Pets** Dogs not allowed. **Nearby** In Amarante: Monastery of São Gonçalo, Church of San Pedro - Church of Travanca - Serra de Marvaõ, road from Amarante to Vila Real – Porto wineries in the Douro valley (Peso da Regua, Vila Real, Pinhão) and in Vila Nova de Gaia - Serra do Marvão - Tâmega valley - Guimarães - Lámego - Porto - Vila Real. **Open** All year.

Amarante is one of the most attractive spots in the Douro. Its old fortified bridge, dating from the 18th Century and spanning the River Tâmega, links the two sides of this peaceful town. The restaurant Zé da Calçada is one of those pretty houses with a balcony that are reflected in the waters of the river. It is the highest rated restaurant in town for its cuisine, and also for its situation and the views from its large terrace. On the street side, in the building opposite, the owners have created seven rooms. The décor is faded, but still chic, giving it the charm of a reliable old establishment. The rooms are well-kept and calm, those on the upper floors have the most light. In your trip round northern Portugal, Amarante is an essential stopover for its patisserie, which you can sample with a glass of the local *vinho verde*.

How to get there (Map 1): 57km south of Braga.

Pousada São Gonçalo *

4600 Serra do Marão (Porto)
Curva do Lancete - Ansiães
Tel. 255-46 11 13/23/24 - Fax 255 46 13 53
Sra Calvo Pereira

Rooms 15 with telephone, bath, WC, satellite TV (2 with minibar). **Price** Single 11,100-16,000Esc, double 12,900-17,500Esc; extra bed +30%. **Meals** Breakfast included, served 7:30-10:00. **Restaurant** With air-conditioning; service 12:30PM-3:00PM, 7:30PM-10:00PM – à la carte 3,800Esc. **Credit cards** All major. **Pets** Dogs not allowed. **Facilities** Parking. **Nearby** Serra de Marvão, road from Amarante to Vila Real - Porto wineries in the Douro valley (Peso da Regua, Vila Real, Pinhão) and in Vila Nova de Gaia. **Open** All year.

It is in majestic mountain scenery on the corniche road linking Amarante to Vila Real, hidden in a forest of pine trees, that the Pousada São Gonçalo is to be found. Since it's some 26 kilometers from Amarante, this isolated establishment is better suited for an overnight than a long stay. The hotel is comfortable and welcoming, and its semi-circular design produces the maximum benefit from the fantastic panorama. The rooms are well equipped and the cuisine is good, while the atmosphere is that of a mountain hotel: quiet, calm and warm.

How to get there *(Map 1): 64km east of Porto via N15 to Amarante, then towards Vila Real for 20km.*

Solar de Miragaia TH*

4600 Travanca (Porto)
Tel. 255-688 214 - 22-711 05 00 - Fax 22-510 00 79
Dra Maria Teresa Matos Marta da Cruz

Rooms 4 with bath and 1 apartment. **Price** Single 12,500Esc, double 15,000Esc; extra bed +30% -
Apart 22,400Esc. **Meals** Breakfast included, served 8:00-10:30. **Evening meals** By request. **Credit
cards** Not accepted. **Pets** Dogs not allowed. **Nearby** Swimming pool, parking. **Facilities** Parking.
Nearby Paiva Valley - Monastery of Travanca - Vila Boa de Quires - Penafiel - Paredes - Convent of
Cete - Paço de Sousa - Entre-os-Rios - Marco de Canveses (vinho verde) Amarante. **Closed** Christmas.

The Valley of the Paiva is a lovely region of the douro, famous for its *vinho
verde*, its port and its architectural heritage. Here you can find many
romanesque churches and very fine 17th- and 18th-century domestic
architecture (see Penafiel). Solar de Miragaia is one of those attractive manor
houses that nowadays receive guests. For centuries it was inhabited by
ecclesiastics; the house is splendid and well cared for, for example the stone
kitchen with its collection of old brass, the dining room where breakfast is
served amid the tapestries and the period furniture, and the convivial drawing
room arranged around the old winepress. The rooms are spacious and elegant,
providing exemplary comfort in an old-fashioned setting. The garden, too, is
perfectly maintained: you can relax at the swimming pool/solarium which has
a splendid view over the valley; or, for the more romantic, by the pool with
water lilies. There are many wonderful trips to be had in the surrounding
countryside, the best way to discover the region.

How to get there *(Map 1): 64km east of Porto by A4, exit Penafiel. Then N106
to Entre-os-Rios, cross the river towards Castelo de Paiva, then turn right towards
Nespereira and Travanca. At Travanca follow the signs Turismo d'Habitaçao.
7km from Castelo de Paiva.*

Quinta do Ribeiro ᵀᴴ*

Pedraza 4660 Resende (Porto)
Tel. 254-877 113 - Fax 254-877 129
Maria Augusta Monteiro Dearaújo Gomes

Rooms 4 (3 with bath); wheelchair access. **Price** Single 9,800Esc, double 12,000Esc. **Meals** Breakfast included, served 8:00-10:30. **Evening meals** By request. **Credit cards** Not accepted. **Pets** Dogs not allowed. **Facilities** Swimming pool, parking. **Nearby** Tâmega Valley - Monastery of Travanca - Vila Boa de Quires - Penafiel - Paredes - Convent of Cete - Paço de Sousa - Entre-os-Rios - Marco de Canveses (vinho verde) Amarante - Lamego. **Open** All year.

If you are crossing the Valley of the Douro amid the green hills, the terraced vineyards and the serras, you can make a pleasant stop at the Quinta do Ribeiro. This is a pretty little old rustic house where Maria Augusta makes it a point of honor to introduce her guests to traditional Portuguese hospitality in a typical house of the region. The stone covering of the floor and walls gives it a great deal of charm and the surprising octagonal wood ceiling in the dining room is a real curiosity. In the simple, elegant rooms, linen, the chief material used by the local craft industries, is ever-present: curtains, bed covers, carpets… The double rooms are comfortable, our favorite being the one with a view over the river. On request, they will make dinner for you and let you discover some recipes like the almond cake that Maria Augusta says she learned from the monks. In the orange season, the ones from the garden are delicious. Do not be worried by the bridge that goes over part of the property; it will not bother you at all.

How to get there *(Map 1): 70km east of Porto by A4 exit Marco de Canaveses, then towards Cinfãesa, Penha Longa; cross the bridge of Mosteirõ in Pala. After the bridge, turn left. At Resende, towards Lamego for 2km.*

Quinta da Timpeira ᵀᴿ

5100 Lamego(Viseu)
Penude
Tel. 254-612 811 - Fax 254-615 176
Sr José Francisco Gomes Parente

Rooms 5 with air-conditioning, telephone, bath or shower, TV. **Price** Double 11,000Esc. **Meals** Breakfast included, served 8:00-10:30. **Restaurant** On request or see p. 220. **Credit cards** All major. **Pets** Dogs not allowed. **Facilities** Swimming pool, tennis, parking. **Nearby** Regional museum in Lamego - Church of São João in Tarouca - Porto wineries in the Douro valley (Peso da Regua, Vila Real, Pinhão) and in Vila Nova de Gaia. **Open** All year.

Basking on the bank of the Douro River in the Beira Alta, Lamego offers a countryside where vineyards swiftly give way to cornfields. Its museum is a short course in Portuguese Renaissance painting, and it would be a shame if you were to miss the enchanting staircases decorated with *azulejos* from the Nossa Sehnora dos Remédios sanctuary. While most of the city's hotels are grouped in the center, the Quinta da Timpeira is a good two kilometers away. It is an attractive place, combining modernism and tradition, simplicity and comfort. Here you find an elegant decor with traditional furniture in a sleek and modern architectural setting. The rooms are extremely comfortable and well taken care of, and the surroundings are peaceful and calm with a garden and a very pleasant swimming pool. A truly fine hotel.

How to get there *(Map 1): 70km north of Viseu via N2. In Casto Daire, towards Lamego, 2.5km south of Lamego.*

Casa de Santo António de Britiande ^{TH*}

Britiande 5100-360 (Viseu)
Tel. and Fax 254-699 346
Sr Antonio Carlos Sobral Pinto Ribeiro

Rooms 4 with bath. **Price** Double 16,500-18,500Esc. **Meals** Breakfast included, served 8:00-10:30. **Restaurant** On request or see in Lamego p. 220. **Credit card** Amex. **Pets** Dogs not allowed. **Facilities** Swimming pool, tennis, parking. **Nearby** Regional museum in Lamego - Church of São João in Tarouca - Porto wineries in the Douro valley (Peso da Regua, Vila Real, Pinhão) and in Vila Nova de Gaia. **Open** All year.

This is our last hotel in Lamego area, one exactly five kilometers away in the village of Britiande. While its exterior may appear somewhat foreboding, the interior is nothing but warmth and elegance. There are a limited number of rooms here, each with an independent entrance and proudly presenting its assets: antique furniture, rugs and tables with sprightly tablecloths, each one different. There are small alcoves adding to the intimacy of the hotel, and in the garden, a tennis court and swimming pool are at your disposal, as is the small private chapel with its stunning *azulejos*. The Casa de Santo António is surrounded by delightful natural and historic sites (the Cister wine road, 12th-century monasteries), all contributing to an unforgettable stay in this region. If you want to take home a few souvenirs, you will find wine, local produce and local craft products at la Quinta de Sta Cruz nearby.

How to get there (Map 1): 70km north of Viseu via N2. In Casto Daire, towards Lamego. 5km west of Lamego towards Moimenta da Beira

Casa do Castelo TH

Atouguia da Baleia 2520 Peniche (Leiria)
Tel. 262-750 647 - Fax 262-750 937
Sra Helena Horta Gama Almeida Balthazar

Rooms 7 with bath. **Price** Single 10,700-12,500Esc, double 12,500-14,000Esc. **Meals** Breakfast included, served 9:00-11:00. **Evening meals** By request – mealtime specials 2,500Esc. **Credit cards** Visa, Eurocard, MasterCard. **Pets** Dogs allowed. **Facilities** Swimming pool, parking. **Nearby** Peniche (citadel) - Nossa Senhora dos Remedios - Cabo Carvoeiro (Nau dos Corvos) - Serra del Rei - Ilha Berlenga (50 mn with boat) - In Caldas da Rainha: the park, Museum of Malhóa, Nossa Senhora do Pópulo, Museu Ceramica - Óbidos - Óbidos lagoon (boating) - Monastery of Batalha - Monastery of Alcobaça - Saõ Martinho do Porto. **Open** All year.

Five kilometers from Peniche, the little port of Atougia has real historical interest with its church of S. Leonardo which contains some interesting Romano-Gothic remains. The Casa do Castelo itself was built in the 17th Century on the ruins of an old castle, then enlarged in the 19th Century and recently restored. It backs on the city walls of the Moorish period, the sole vestige of the old Fortress. A large section of this old wall cuts the house into two parts: on one side is the swimming pool, around which are some rooms which have been created out of old outbuildings, while on the other side what was once the main house is hidden by the branches of an imposing dragon tree (classed as a national monument), which contains comfortable, well-lit rooms overlooking the countryside. The whole is surrounded by a citrus orchard, sweet-smelling when in flower. There are many beaches (don't miss the excursion to the Berlenga islands) and historic sites roundabout.

How to get there *(Map 3): 95km north of Lisboa, 5km east of Peniche.*

Quinta da Foz ᵀᴴ

Foz do Arelho
2500 Caldas da Rainha (Leiria)
Tel. 262-97 93 69
Sra Maria Isabel Calado

Rooms 5 and 2 apartments with bath or shower. **Price** Double 20,000Esc, apart. 14,000Esc. **Meals** Breakfast included, served 8:00-10:00. No Restaurant. **Credit cards** Not accepted. **Pets** Dogs not allowed. **Nearby** In Caldas da Rainha: the park, Museum of Malhóa, Nossa Senhora do Pópulo, Museu Ceramica - Óbidos - Óbidos lagoon (boating) - Church of Senhor de Pedra - Monastery of Batalha - Monastery of Alcobaça. **Open** All year.

Few tourists stop in Caldas da Rainha, a small city with hot springs and a thriving ceramic industry with a weekly market on Mondays offering a large choice of quality merchandise. Foz is only a few kilometers away on the saline Óbidos lagoon and enjoys the regular ocean tides. Its landscape is covered with dunes and the inlet is truly a fisherman's paradise. The Quinta da Foz estate hasn't changed since the 16th century and has been very well maintained. Here, you will find excellent lodging and fine service. Apart from the house's historical interest, there is a very attractive riding ring with five horses, a nearby beach - plus the unfailing attention of Madame Calado.

How to get there *(Map 3): 92km north of Lisboa via A1, exit Aveiras, then N366 to Caldas da Rainha; 9km west of Caldas.*

Pensão Restaurante Ribamar

2450-344 Nazaré (Leiria)
Rua Gomes Freire, 9
Tel. 262-55 11 58 - Fax 262-56 22 24
Sr José Amedo

Category ★★ **Rooms** 25 with bath or shower, WC, some with satellite TV; wheelchair access. **Price** Single 10,000Esc, double 18,500Esc. **Meals** Breakfast included, served 8:30-10:00; full board +4,000Esc. **Restaurant** Service 12:30PM-3:00PM, 7:30PM-12:00AM – à la carte 4,150Esc. **Credit cards** All major. **Pets** Dogs not allowed. **Nearby** In Nazaré: belvedere and lighthouse - Castle of Leiria - Monastery of Batalha - Monastery of Alcobaça - São Martinho do Porto. **Closed** Dec 19 - 26.

Situated in Nazaré, the attractive Pensão Restaurante Ribamar has the look of a beach hotel, with its bright yellow woodwork and white façade. Inside, the restaurant, with its dark woods, continues the theme of a charming provincial establishment. The smell of polish hangs in the air as you are led to the small and modest rooms, in which old furniture and flowered curtains create a pleasant atmosphere. The salon-bar with its fireplace is also very convivial. Unfortunately, the inescapable wall-to-wall carpet stains very easily; the best rooms are the ones with a view over the sea: nos. 11, 12, 21 and 22 or suites 13, 23 and 33 which are larger and have views. The hotel has been the most charming place in Nazaré for four generations.

How to get there *(Map 3):85km northwest of Lisbon by A8, exit Caldas da Rainha, then N8 and C242 towards Nazaré (23km). From Portie, A1 exit Leiria, then C242, towards Nazaré (36km).*

Quinta do Campo ᵀᴴ

2450-344 Valado dos Frades - Nazaré (Leiria)
Tel. 262-577 135 - Fax 262-57 75 55
Sr João Pedro Collares Pereira
E-mail: quintadocampo@mail.telepac.pt

Rooms 8, 2 studios with kitchenette and 5 apartments (4 with 1 double room, 1 with 2 double rooms, bath, lounge, terrace). **Price** Single 16,000Esc, double 18,000Esc, studio (2-4 pers.) 22,000Esc, apart. with 1 double room (2-4 pers.) 26,000Esc, apart. with 2 double rooms 30,000Esc. **Meals** Breakfast included for the rooms, served 8:30-10:00. **Restaurant** Snacks available by request, or see p. 225. **Credit cards** All major. **Pets** Dogs not allowed. **Facilities** Swimming pool, tennis, bike. **Nearby** In Nazaré: belvedere and lighthouse - Castle of Leiria - Monastery of Batalha - Monastery of Alcobaça - Saõ Martinho do Porto. **Open** All year.

The Quinta do Campo is one of ten farms that were started in the 12th and 13th centuries by the Cistercian monks, while also constructing their Abbey of Alcobaça. A famous agricultural school as long as the Cistercian influence lasted, the property was then acquired in the 19th century by the forebears of the present owner. Converted into a guesthouse, today you'll find just a few rooms and three apartments. The decor is traditional, with antique furniture and family portraits on the walls. The bedrooms are large and each has a private bathroom. The small but well-equipped apartments are more suitable for a longer stay. The Quinta is well situated: One can enjoy the countryside by using the hotel facilities (swimming pool, tennis courts, and bicycles), and the beaches aren't far away. Nazaré is only five kilometers away and Portugal's largest forest, the Pinhal de Leiria, is less than one kilometer from the hotel.

How to get there (Map 3): 100km north of Lisboa via A8, exit Caldas da Rainha, towards Alcobaça, then Nazaré to Valado dos Frades.

Estalagem do Convento

2510 Óbidos (Leiria)
Rua Dom João d'Ornelas
Tel. 262-959 216 - Fax 262-959 159
Sr De Sousa Garcia

Category ★★★★ **Rooms** 31 with telephone, bath, WC, satellite TV, minibar. **Price** Single 14,000Esc, double 17,000Esc, suite 21,000Esc. **Meals** Breakfast included, served 8:00-10:00; half board +3,200-3,400Esc; full board +4,200-4,500Esc (per pers.). **Restaurant** Service 12:30PM-2:30PM, 7:30PM-9:30PM - Closed Sun and Dec 1 - 15 – mealtime specials 3,200Esc, also à la carte. **Credit cards** Amex, Visa, Eurocard, Mastercard. **Pets** Dogs allowed except in restaurant. **Nearby** In Óbidos: the ramparts - Church of Senhor de Pedra - Laguna of Óbidos (Amoreira, Vau) - Monastery of Alcobaça - Monastery of Bathala. **Open** All year.

Óbidos retains many vestiges of its rich history, and the old house that now lodges the Estalagem was built some 200 years ago as a convent. It later became a school, then a private house, and is now a hotel. The decor has a rustic feel. Rooms are large and appointed with care; their rather dated look is an added charm. Some rooms have balconies with a lovely view over both town and country. The staff are friendly, the service impeccable and the prices reasonable–what more can one say to recommend this inn!

How to get there *(Map 3): 92km north of Lisboa via A1, exit Aveiras, then N366; before reaching Caldas da Rainha, go towards Óbidos.*

Pousada do Castelo *

2510 Óbidos (Leiria)
Paço Real
Tel. 262-95 91 05/46/48 - Fax 262-95 91 48
Sr Nobre Pereira

Rooms 6 and 3 suites with air-conditioning, telephone, bath, WC, TV, (minibar in the suite). **Price** Single 23,000-31,000Esc, double 26,100-34,000Esc, suite 34,700-41,500Esc; extra bed +30%. **Meals** Breakfast included, served 7:30-10:30. **Restaurant** Service 12:00PM-3:30PM, 7:30PM-10:00PM – à la carte 3,650-5,900Esc. **Credit cards** All major. **Pets** Dogs not allowed. **Nearby** In Óbidos: the ramparts - Church of Senhor de Pedra - Laguna of Óbidos (Amoreira, Vau) - Monastery of Alcobaça - Monastery of Bathala. **Open** All year.

Óbidos, surrounded by ramparts, in the midst of a wide plain dominated by one of the most beautiful medieval châteaux in the country, is well worth a visit. Inside the fortifications, the small lanes and white houses create the setting for a slower pace of life. The Castelo is in an ancient 15th century palace that has been faithfully restored. The lounge is warm and inviting, and its sober decor includes some beautiful antique pieces. The dining room has large windows that overlook the courtyard and countryside. The rooms are exceptionally comfortable.

How to get there (Map 3): 92km north of Lisboa via A1, exit Aveiras, then N366; before reaching Caldas da Rainha, go towards Óbidos.

Casal do Pinhão ^{TR}

Bairro Senhora da Luz 2510 Óbidos
Tel. 262-95 90 78 - Fax 262-95 90 78
Sra Maria Adelaide Silveira
E-mail: casalpinhao@mail.pt - Web: www.caldas2000.com/casalpinhao

Rooms 6 and 2 apartments (2-4 pers.) with bath. **Price** Double 12,000-16,000Esc, apart. 15,000Esc (2 pers.), 19,000Esc (4 pers.). **Meals** Breakfast included, served 8:30-10:30. **Restaurant** See p. 224-225. **Credit Cards** Visa, Eurocard, MasterCard. **Pets** Dogs not allowed. **Facilities** Swimming pool, parking. **Nearby** In Óbidos: the ramparts - Church of Senhor de Pedra - Laguna of Óbidos (Amoreira, Vau) - Monastery of Alcobaça - Monastery of Bathala - Caldas da Rainha - Santarem. **Open** All year.

The Casal do Pinhão stands in a wonderful little fortified village. The setting in the midst of pine trees (hence the name) and eucalyptus is especially pleasant. The house, recently enlarged, spread out among the garden trees and the rooms are all on the one level. They are large an open on a loggia which is shared with the other rooms, making it not a truly private space. Breakfast is served in the drawing room among a rather mixed collection of craft objects. The two apartments occupy an independent annex. This is a place to recover your calm, with a swimming pool (plus one for children), after visiting the tourist town of Óbidos.

***How to get there** (Map 3): 100km north of Lisboa; 3km west of Óbidos.*

Casa d'Óbidos TR

Quinta de S. José 2510 Óbidos
Tel. 262-95 09 24 - Cell. 931 96 82 256 - Fax 262-95 99 70
Coronel Fernando do Amaral Campos Sarmento

Rooms 6 and 1 apartment (4 pers.) with bath; wheelchair access. **Price** Single 10,000-14,000Esc, double 14,000-18,000Esc, apart. 250,000Esc (4 pers./week). **Meals** Breakfast included, served 8:30-10:00. **Restaurant** See p. 224-225. **Credit cards** Not accepted. **Pets** Dogs not allowed. **Facilities** Swimming pool, tennis, parking. **Nearby** In Óbidos: the ramparts - Church of Senhor de Pedra - Laguna of Óbidos (Amoreira, Vau) - Prai del Rey - Nazaré - Sintra - Monastery of Alcobaça - Monastery of Bathala - Caldas da Rainha - Tomar. **Open** All year.

Also known as Varzea da Rainha, the Casa d'Óbidos lies in the valley. After passing through forests of pines and eucalyptus, you reach it along a dirt road which you may have to share with sheep. In the background are the town walls, the castle and the white houses of Óbidos. In this peaceful environment, you discover this lovely house, built in the 19th Century by an engineer who worked with Gustave Eiffel and came here to oversee the construction of a railway (hence some architectural similarities with the local grade-crossing keepers' houses). The present owners have done a remarkable job of restoration and the delightful Helena pampers every detail of her home. The drawing room, the dining room and the games room with its billiard table are all furnished with taste and refinement. The bedrooms are very beautiful and very comfortable, each personalized by the care taken with color harmonies; we fell in love with the pink room. A cottage has also been transformed into a pretty, comfortable apartment with a private garden. The garden itself and the swimming pool are equally well kept. A place to note.

How to get there (Map 3): 70km north of Lisboa; 1km west of Óbidos.

Estalagem Senhora da Guia

2750 Cascais (Lisboa)
Estrada do Guincho
Tel. 21-486 92 39 - Fax 21-486 92 27 - Sr Ornellas Monteiro
E-mail: senhora.da.guia@mail.telepac.pt

Category ★★★★★ **Rooms** 39 and 3 suites with air-conditioning, telephone, bath, hairdryer, WC, satellite TV, safe, minibar. **Price** Single 28,000Esc, double 30,000Esc, suite 38,000-48,000Esc; extra bed 1,750-5,000Esc. **Meals** Breakfast (buffet) included, served 7:00-10:30; half board +5,000Esc (per pers.). **Restaurant** Service 1:00PM-3:00PM, 7:30PM-10:00PM – à la carte 5,000Esc – Specialties: Fish. **Credit cards** All major. **Pets** Dogs not allowed. **Facilities** Swimming pool, parking. **Nearby** Boca do Inferno - Praia do Guincho - Estoril - Lisboa – Estoril golf course (9- and 18-hole) - Quinta da Marinha golf course (18-hole). **Open** All year.

More a holiday house than a hotel, this former summer villa faces the ocean, is surrounded by gardens and terraces, and has a superb seawater swimming pool. It is difficult to describe the perfection and intimate ambiance of the lounge, bar, and dining room (in which hang some beautiful still-life paintings). The rooms are just as magnificent. Those in the annex or the duplexes would be most suitable for families; they also have terraces. One can enjoy the sea view at breakfast, served poolside. Set in the countryside, some two kilometers from Cascais, the Estalagem is very close to the golf course and tennis courts at Quinta da Marinha. This is an ideal spot for those wanting to get away in the middle of the year.

How to get there *(Map 3): 35km west of Lisboa via N6; at Cascais take the road towards Guincho via Av. 25 de Abril for 5km.*

Hotel Albatroz

2750 Cascais (Lisboa)
Rua Frederico Arouca, 100
Tel. 21-483 28 21 - Fax 21-484 48 27

Category ★★★★★ **Rooms** 40 with air-conditioning, telephone, bath, WC, TV, radio, minibar; elevator, wheelchair access. **Price** Single 23,500-50,000Esc, double 28,000-55,000Esc, suite 39,000-75,000Esc. **Meals** Breakfast 2,000Esc, served 7:30-10:30. **Restaurant** Service 12:30PM-3:00PM, 7:30PM-10:00PM – mealtime specials, also à la carte from 6,500Esc. **Credit cards** All major. **Pets** Dogs not allowed. **Facilities** Swimming pool. **Nearby** Boca do Inferno - Praia do Gincho - Estoril - Lisboa – Estoril golf course (9- and 18-hole) - Quinta da Marinha golf course (18-hole). **Open** All year.

The summer residence of the royal family in the 19th century, this villa was restored and enlarged to create a luxury hotel. Taste and imagination have integrated contemporary decor with traditional Portuguese style. Many rooms overlook the sea; those in the new building also have balconies. One can swim in the little creek at the foot of the terrace, or in the seawater swimming pool. The restaurant faces the sea, and the cuisine is excellent. It is a pleasure to return to one's room via the old staircase decorated with panels of *azulejos* tiles.

How to get there (Map 3): 30km west of Lisboa via N6.

Casa da Pérgola

2750 Cascais (Lisboa)
Av. Valbom, 13
Tel. 21-484 00 40 - Fax 21-483 47 91
Sra Patricia Gonçalves

Rooms 10 with air-conditioning, bath, WC. **Price** Double 15,500-19,500Esc. **Meals** Breakfast included, served 8:00-10:00. **Restaurant** See p. 223-224. **Credit cards** Not accepted. **Pets** Dogs not allowed. **Nearby** Boca do Inferno - Praia do Gincho - Estoril - Lisboa – Estoril golf course (9- and 18-hole) - Quinta da Marinha golf course (18-hole). **Open** Mar 15 – Nov 15.

The Casa da Pergola has been in the same family for nearly a century; it was built by an English ancestor of the present owners, and despite its façade in *azulejos* tiles, it still has that undeniably snug atmosphere typical of English houses. The interior is tastefully decorated with antique furniture, both Portuguese and British. Maids in uniform, who take extreme care in maintaining the hotel, lend the air of a rather jaded tradition that will appeal to certain among us. The owners will welcome you with exquisite courtesy. For an old-fashioned stay with tea time, complete with scones. This hotel is perfect for those who seek an old fashioned ambiance.

How to get there *(Map 3): 30km west of Lisboa via N6.*

Hotel Vilazul

2655 Ericeira (Lisboa)
Calçada da Baleia, 10
Tel. 261-86 00 00 - Fax 261-86 29 27 - Sr Luis Oliveira
E-mail: vilazul@ip.pt - Web: www.i.am/hotel.vilazul

Category ★★ **Rooms** 21 with air-conditioning, telephone, bath, WC, satellite TV; elevator.
Price Single 6,000-9,000Esc, double 8,500-13,000Esc, triple +30%. **Meals** Breakfast included,
served 8:00-10:00; half board +2,100Esc (per pers.). **Restaurant** "O Poço", service 12:00PM-2:00PM,
7:30PM-9:00PM – à la carte 2,500-4,700Esc. **Credit cards** All major. **Pets** Dogs not allowed. **Nearby**
Lisboa - Cascais - Sintra - Quéluz - Mafra. **Open** All year.

Ericeira is a village which is enjoyed for its authenticity, despite the
urbanization of its surroundings. You should walk through its little street
between pure white houses trimmed in blue to recover a time when only
fisherfolk lived here. The hotel is in the center in the upper part of the village.
This pretty building is occupied on the ground floor by the large restaurant
which serves superb fish and lobster, specialties of the town. The most
exceptional thing about this little hotel is the kindness with which it welcomes
you. Otherwise, the décor is unpretentious, though the rooms are large and
comfortable. The ones overlooking the street are very light, four have a balcony
and the ones on the top floor have views over the sea. The roof terrace has been
fitted out so that you can enjoy a drink and the sun. A simple place in a
charming village.

How to get there (Map 3): 50km north of Lisboa.

Hotel Pálacio

2769-504 Estoril (Lisboa)
Rua do Parque
Tel. 21-464 8000 - Fax 21-468 4867 - Sr Ai Quintas
E-mail: palacioestoril@mail.telepac.pt

Category ★★★★★ **Rooms** 162 with air-conditioning, telephone, bath, WC, satellite TV, minibar; elevator. **Price** Double 35,000-46,000Esc, suite 50,000-60,000Esc. **Meals** Breakfast (buffet) included, served 7:30-10:00. **Restaurant** "Four Seasons" with air-conditioning. Service 1:00PM-3:00PM, 8:00PM-102:00PM – à la carte 5,250-9,000Esc – International cooking. **Credit cards** All major. **Pets** Dogs not allowed. **Facilities** Swimming pool, sauna, parking. **Nearby** Cascais - Boca do Inferno - Praia do Gincho - Lisboa – Estoril golf course (9- and 18-hole). **Open** All year.

Estoril has become an elegant seaside resort area, much appreciated for its mild climate in winter; its well-known golf course and casino attract an international clientele. The Palacio is a very chic hotel offering its clients a full range of facilities: a swimming pool filled with thermal spring water, a sauna, the privilege of using the courts of the Tennis Club, and temporary membership in the Estoril Golf Club. Beautiful gardens surround this "palace" of a hotel, which has a level of comfort, service, and ambiance that does justice to its names. The duplex suites set around the swimming pool deserve a special mention. Dine at least once at the "Four Seasons" restaurant inside the hotel. At 30 minutes from Lisbon and the international airport, Estoril should be remembered for winter holidays.

How to get there *(Map 3): 28km west of Lisboa.*

Lapa Palace

1249-021 Lisboa
Rua do Pau de Bandeira, 4
Tel. 21-395 00 05 - Fax 21-395 40 39
E-mail: reservas@hotelapa.com

Category ★★★★★ **Rooms** 86 and 8 suites with air-conditioning, telephone, bath, WC, satellite TV, safe, minibars; elevator, wheelchair access. **Price** Single 45,000-55,000Esc, double 45,000-60,000Esc, junior-suite 60,000-80,000Esc, suite 75,000-105,000Esc, presidential suite and suite no. 701 100,000-200,000Esc; extra bed 12,000Esc. **Meals** Breakfast (buffet) 2,800Esc. **Restaurant** Service 12:30PM-3:00PM, 7,30PM-10:30PM – à la carte 7,500-10,000Esc – International and Portuguese cooking. **Credit cards** All major. **Pets** Dogs not allowed. **Facilities** Covered swimming pool, swimming pool, fitness club, garage, parking. **Nearby** Palàcio Real and gardens of Queluz - Estoril - Cascais - Sintra – Estoril golf course (9- and 18-hole). **Open** All year.

If luxury is what you want, you'll find it at the Hotel da Lapa, in a historic residential area where palaces neighbor each other. The grand entrance hall recalls the pomp of this former palacete with very little furniture, marble marquetry of the floor, and the grand ceiling frescoes. The rooms are as you would expect: cozy and in good taste. All are individually decorated in styles ranging from classical 18th-century to Art-Deco. The marble bathrooms are very well appointed, and some have whirlpool tubs. The ultimate glory of this hotel is the garden overlooking the Tagus River, with its luxuriant Mediterranean vegetation, waterfalls and fountains. Breakfast on the terrace is an enjoyable way to enjoy the views over the river.

How to get there (*Map 3*): *Near the Museum National de Arte Antiga.*

Hotel Avenida Palace

1200 Lisboa
123, Rua 1er Dezembro
Tel. 21-346 01 51/2/3- Fax 21-342 28 84

Categorie ★★★★★ **Rooms** 82 with air-conditioning, telephone, bath, satellite TV, minibar; elevator. **Price** Single 24,000Esc, double 27,000Esc, suite 45,000-75,000Esc. **Meals** Breakfast included, 7:30-10:30. **Restaurant** Service 12:30PM-3:00PM, 7:30PM-10:30PM – à la carte. **Credit cards** All major. **Pets** Dogs not allowed. **Facilities** Parking. **Nearby** Palàcio Real and gardens of Queluz - Estoril - Cascais - Sintra – Estoril golf course (9- and 18-hole). **Open** All year.

The Avenida Palace, with its imposing classical-style architecture is the best-known hotel in Lisbon. Situated in the center, at the bottom of the busy Avendia de la Libertade, its closeness to the station, under reconstruction up to the time of the Universal Exhibition, meant that we omitted it from the guide. Now that the event has taken place, the hotel has become quieter, despite the bustle of the district. Every capital city has its old palace and the Avenida is Lisbon's. The interior exhibits all the characteristics of the grand hotels of former years: a succession of grand salons, with curtains up to the ceiling, shining with chandeliers. The furniture is classical, inspired by the style of the 18th Century. The same is true of the rooms which have kept their fine proportions and marble bathrooms. Despite this comfort, the whole has an old-fashioned, nostalgic air; but isn't that the atmosphere that one tries to recapture when one stays at these old hotels?

How to get there (Map 3): Near the station.

York House Hotel

1200-690 Lisboa
Rua das Janelas Verdes, 32
Tel. 21-396 25 44 - Fax 21-397 27 93 - Sra Leitão
E-mail: yorkhouse@mail.telepac.pt

Category ★★★★ **Rooms** 34 with telephone, bath, WC, TV. **Price** Double 28,200-33,300Esc. **Meals** Breakfast included, served 7:30-10:00. **Restaurant** Service 12:30PM-3:30PM, 7:30PM-10:00PM – à la carte 5,000Esc – Portuguese cooking. **Credit cards** All major. **Pets** Dogs not allowed. **Nearby** Palàcio Real and gardens of Queluz - Estoril - Cascais - Sintra – Estoril golf course (9- and 18-hole). **Open** All year.

From the moment you enter you'll realize that this hotel is a magical place, with its mysterious staircase, profusion of plants and palm trees in the courtyard, glass window through which one views the dining room, and overall feel of being in the country. Situated off the corridors and passageways are the well-furnished lounges, decorated with faiences and antique objects. The bedrooms are quiet and done in simplicity, comfort, and good taste. This is an excellent base for visiting the Museu National de Arte Antiga. It is imperative to reserve well in advance. The welcome is impersonal.

How to get there (Map 3): Next to the Museum National de Arte Antiga.

Hotel Lisboa Plaza

1269-066 Lisboa
Travessa do Salitre 7 / Avenida Liberdade
Tel. 21-321 82 18 - Fax 21-347 16 30 - Sr Duarte Fernandes
E-mail: plaza.hotels@heritage.pt - Web: www.heritage.pt

Category ★★★★ **Rooms** 94 and 12 suites with air-conditioning, telephone, bath, WC, satellite TV, safe, minibar; elevator. **Price** Single 22,280-31,200Esc, double 23,500-34,600Esc, triple 29,400-43,200Esc, suite 35,000-48,000Esc. **Meals** Breakfast included, served 7:00-10:00; full board +8,800Esc. **Restaurant** Service 12:30PM-3:00PM, 7,30PM-10:00PM – buffet 3,900Esc, à la carte 4,400-5,500Esc – Portuguese cooking. **Credit cards** All major. **Pets** Dogs not allowed. **Facilities** Garage (1,300Esc). **Nearby** Palàcio Real and gardens of Queluz - Estoril - Cascais - Sintra – Estoril golf course (9- and 18-hole). **Open** All year.

The atmosphere at the Lisboa Plaza is at once refined and informal; the hotel was recently renovated by Graça Vitervio, a well known Lisbon decorator. The floors are marble, the furniture is classical in style, and there are green plants and clever flower arrangements throughout. The rooms, as you would expect from this, are large, bright, quiet; and individualized, with comfortable marble bathrooms; some of the rooms overlook the Botanical Gardens. The restaurant, surrounding the patio, is refined and staffed by an attentive and discrete personnel. This oasis in the heart of Lisbon has become one of the classical hotels in the town. A child of under 12 who stays in the parents' room is accepted free.

How to get there (Map 3): Close to the Jardim Botãnico.

As Janelas Verdes

1200-690 Lisboa
Rua das Janelas Verdes, 47
Tel. 21-396 81 43 - Fax 21-396 81 44 - Sr Duarte Fernandes
E-mail: jverdes@heritage.pt - Web: www.heritage.pt

Category ★★★★ **Rooms** 17 with air-conditioning, telephone, bath, WC, TV. **Price** Single 22,280-33,700Esc, double 23,500-37,000Esc, triple 29,400-47,700Esc. **Meals** Breakfast included, served 7:30-11:00. **Restaurant** See pp. 220-223. **Credit cards** All major. **Pets** Dogs not allowed. **Nearby** Palàcio Real and gardens of Queluz - Estoril - Cascais - Sintra – Estoril golf course (9- and 18-hole). **Open** All year.

Situated in the pretty, quiet street which also houses the National Art Museum, this residencia occupies a small 18th-century palace. The charm of the hotel is its Anglo-Portuguese atmosphere. The fin de siècle colonial decor consists of a mixture of objects, souvenirs (Eça de Queiros, who stayed here for a long time, was inspired by the place in one of his stories), furniture, books, and pictures which give a soul to the house. The bedrooms are adorable, especially number 23, which over looks the pretty garden, which has views of the port. The rooms on the top floor are more simple but just as comfortable, and enjoy a better view. Twelve new rooms were to open during the year, as well as a little library with a view over the Tagus. There is no restaurant, but the district has some good ones including Sua Excelência and the restaurant in York House. Here, too, under-12s go free.

How to get there (Map 3): Next to the Museum National de Arte Antiga.

Hotel Metropole

1100-200 Lisboa
Praça do Rossio, 30
Tel. 21-346 91 64 - Fax 21-346 91 66

Category ★★★ **Rooms** 36 with air-conditioning, telephone, bath or shower, WC, satellite TV, safe; elevator. **Price** Single 15,000-22,000Esc, double 17,000-25,000Esc. **Meals** Breakfast (buffet) included, served 7:30-10:00. **Restaurant** See p. 220-223. **Credit cards** All major. **Pets** Small Dogs allowed. **Nearby** Palàcio Real and gardens of Queluz - Estoril - Cascais - Sintra – Estoril golf course (9- and 18-hole). **Open** All year.

The Hotel Metropole is one of the beautiful buildings facing the main square (Rossio) of the "Baixa". This is one of the most lively squares of the capital with its many boutiques, coffee shops, and flower market set around the two baroque fountains that frame the tall column topped by the statue of King Pierre IV. Close to the Chiado (the main shopping district of Lisbon), the Bairro Alto, and the Alfama, the hotel is admirably situated for discovering the city. Recently renovated, the main lounge and bar have been decorated in a 1920's style, and all the bedrooms are very comfortable. Noise insulation and air-conditioning allow one to opt for the rooms overlooking the square without too many risks; they have views over the roofs of the old city and the château. All the bathrooms are well equipped. The staff is very professional. Car rentals, laundry, baby sitting, and other services can be arranged on request.

How to get there (Map 3): In the Rossio.

Hotel Lisboa Tejo

1100 Lisboa
Poço de Borratém, 4
Tel. 21-886-61 82 - Fax 21-886-51 63

Category ★★★ **Rooms** 44 and 7 suites with air-conditioning, telephone, bath, satellite TV, minibar; elevator. **Price** Single 14,000Esc, double 18,000Esc. **Meals** Breakfast included, served 7:30-10:30. **Restaurant** See p. 220-223. **Credit cards** All major. **Pets** Small dogs allowed. **Nearby** Palàcio Real and gardens of Queluz - Estoril - Cascais - Sintra – Estoril golf course (9- and 18-hole). **Open** All year.

The Lisboa Tejo is one of the recently established hotels (1995) in a city that is more and more highly rated for international tourism. A short distance from the Rossio and the Praça da Figueira, in the heart of Lisbon, it is housed in a corner building characteristic of the Pombal architecture of the Baixa. Local decoration in the public rooms on the ground floor where the walls are decorated with panels of *azulejos* illustrating the main towns of Portugal. The rooms are spacious and comfortable without any special decorative effects: furniture designed for the hotel and neutral colors. Try to get one on the corner or overlooking the street (on the Praça da Figueira side), which are better exposed on the west. The Lisboa Tejo is a useful place to know because its amenities have not had time to age too much and its situation brings you at once into the atmosphere of the town.

How to get there (*Map 3*): *Near the Praça da Figueira.*

Albergaria Senhora do Monte

1170 Lisboa
Calçada do Monte, 39
Tel. 21-886 60 02 - Fax 21-887 77 83
Sr Dias

Category ★★★ **Rooms** 24 and 4 suites with air-conditioning, telephone, bath, TV; elevator. **Price** Single 18,000Esc, double 22,000Esc, double with terrace 28,000Esc, triple 28,000Esc, triple with terrasse 30,000Esc. **Meals** Breakfast included, served 7:30-10:00. **Restaurant** See pp. 220-223. **Credit cards** All major. **Pets** Dogs not allowed. **Nearby** Palàcio Real and gardens of Queluz - Cascais - Boca do Inferno - Praia do Gincho - Lisboa – Estoril golf course (9- and 18-hole). **Open** All year.

When you finally arrive at the Albergaria Senhora do Monte, after having had to hunt for it a little, do not be put off by the façade–there are pleasant surprises inside. You'll find a friendly and efficient personnel, and moderate prices for a hotel in the town center. And then there's the view from the rooms: this hotel, built on the side of a hill, has one of the most beautiful views in Lisbon: immediately opposite are the San Jorge Château, the Graça Church, the Tagus and the bridge. The whole town is at your feet. The hotel is at present carrying out a program of gradual renovation. Those rooms already finished are very attractive with their white wood furniture and their shades of pastel; they also have beautiful marble bathrooms. Do not miss having your copious breakfast in the restaurant on the top floor, with its panoramic views.

How to get there (*Map 3*): *In the Graça quarter.*

Casa de San Mamede

1250 Lisboa
Rua da Escola Politécnica, 159
Tel. 21-396 31 66 - Fax 21-395 18 96
Sra Cristina Marques Franco

Category ★★★ **Rooms** 28 with telephone, bath, WC, satellite TV, safe. **Price** Single 10,000-12,000Esc, double 13,000-16,000Esc. **Meals** Breakfast included, served 8:30-10:30. **Restaurant** See pp. 220-223. **Credit cards** Not accepted; Eurochecks. **Pets** Dogs not allowed. **Nearby** Palàcio Real and gardens of Queluz - Estoril - Cascais - Sintra – Estoril golf course (9- and 18-hole). **Open** All year.

This modest little pension has a rather old-fashioned air. For a long time this was home to a magistrate. The sober interior has all the authenticity of an old town house, and has retained its dados of *azuleros* tiles, its white walls, and dark wooden parquet floors and furniture. The bedrooms are simple but comfortable. This little hotel is right next to the Botanical Gardens in what is called the Pombalin area of Lisbon, owing its name to the Marquis de Pombal, the minister at the time of the tremendous earthquake of 1755. The Marquis and the two architects Manuel de Maia and Eugénio do Santos rebuilt Lisbon in a revolutionary way for that time: wide avenues with sober buildings all in the same style. The majestic Avenida da Libertade and the huge Praça Marquês Pombal square both date from that period. Free for children under 12 who sleep in their parents' room.

How to get there (Map 3): Close to the Jardim Botãnico.

Quinta de Santa Catarina TH

2530 Lourinhã (Lisboa)
Rua Visconde Palma de Almeida
Tel. 261-42 23 13 - Fax 261-41 48 75
Sra Teresa Palma d'Almeida

Rooms 5 with bath or shower. **Price** Single 11,600-14,200Esc, double 14,000-17,000Esc; extra bed 4,000Esc. **Meals** Breakfast included, served 8:30-10:00. **Restaurant** Dinner on request or see p. 224. **Credit cards** Not accepted. **Pets** Dogs not allowed. **Facilities** Swimming pool, tennis. **Nearby** In Óbidos: the ramparts - Church of Senhor de Pedra - Laguna of Óbidos (Amoreira, Vau) - Monastery of Alcobaça - Monastery of Bathala – Vimeiro golf course (9-hole) - Praia d'El Rei golf course (18-hole). **Open** All year.

Lourinhãs is well situated, being very close to Lisbon and Óbidos with the Atlantic three kilometers away. This former town house is in the center of the city, and it is a pleasant surprise to discover in back of it a large palm grove, a floral park with bougainvillae and a swimming pool with a well maintained club house offering snacks plus a clay tennis court. The principal lounge, decorated with the family's coats of arms, is open to guests. Most of the rooms give onto the garden and are in different colors, soberly furnished but all very comfortable. We prefer the one at the rear of the building with its small balcony. A fine hotel.

How to get there (Map 3): 60km north of Lisboa via A8.

Pousada Dona Maria I *

2745 Queluz (Lisboa)
Largo do Pálacio
Tel. 21-435 61 58 - Fax 21-435 61 89

Rooms 24 and 2 suites with air-conditioning, telephone, bath, WC, TV, minibar; elevator, wheelchair access. **Price** Single 17,900-29,000Esc, double 20,300-31,000Esc, suite 24,300-38,000Esc; extra bed +30%. **Meals** Breakfast included, served 7:30-10:30. **Restaurant** "Cozinha Velha" – à la carte 7,000Esc. **Credit cards** All major. **Pets** Dogs not allowed. **Facilities** Parking. **Nearby** Palàcio Real and gardens of Queluz - Estoril - Cascais - Sintra - Lisboa – Lisbon Sport Club golf course (18-hole) - Estoril golf course (9- and 18-hole). **Open** All year.

Only twelve kilometers from Lisbon, Queluz is known above all for its Royal Palace and gardens The Palace was the residence of Queen Marie, the official fiancée of Louis XV of France, which may explain the many architectural references to the Château of Versailles. The Pousada Dona Maria was recently opened in some of the buildings where the château personnel were lodged. This is a luxury hotel with all the comforts and services that go with it. The hotel shares its kitchens with the Cozinha Velha restaurant, which is installed in the former kitchens of the palace; here you'll dine in a superb room decorated with gleaming copper objects, and an immense fireplace supported by eight columns. This is a very good spot for lunch or a refreshing drink after visiting the Royal Palace.

How to get there *(Map 3): 12km from Lisboa.*

Pálacio de Seteais

2710 Sintra (Lisboa)
Rua Barbosa do Bocage, 8
Tel. 21-923 32 00 - Fax 21-923 42 77
Sr Francisco Moser

Category ★★★★★ **Rooms** 28 and 1 suite with air-conditioning, telephone, bath, WC, satellite TV; elevator. **Price** Single 28,000-42,000Esc, double 30,000-46,000Esc. **Meals** Breakfast included, served 8:00-11:00; full board +12,500Esc. **Restaurant** Service 12:30PM-2:30PM, 7,30PM-9:30PM – mealtime specials 7,000Esc – French cooking and fish. **Credit cards** All major. **Pets** Dogs not allowed. **Facilities** Heated swimming pool, tennis, riding, parking. **Nearby** Pálacio Real of Sintra - Serra de Sintra (parque da Pena; from Sintra to La Cruz Alta via Castelo dos Mouros (castle); Azenhas do Mar; parque de Monserrate) - Cascais - Estoril - Lisboa – Estoril golf course (9- and 18-hole). **Open** All year.

Is it the gentle climate, or the Portuguese aristocracy that has imbued Sintra with so much charm ? A magnificent example of 18th-century architecture, the palace of Seteais was built for a Dutch consul. Later, the Marquis of Marialva threw fantastic parties here, and also joined the two neo-classical buildings with a triumphal arch to celebrate a visit by the king. Today, the hotel includes a succession of refined lounges: the "noble lounge," the "Pillement lounge," the "lounge-bar," and the "lounge-restaurant" are all decorated with 18th-century furniture and frescoes. The terrace and gardens, which overlook the town, are an additional delight. This is the place for all romantic souls.

How to get there *(Map 3): 29.5km northwest of Lisboa; 1.5km of Sintra on the road from Colares-Monserrate.*

Quinta da Capela [TH]

2710 Sintra (Lisboa)
Monserrate
Tel. 21-929 01 70 - Fax 21-929 34 25 - Sr Pereira

Rooms 7 and 2 apartments with telephone, bath, WC, 3 with TV. **Price** Single 25,000Esc, double 28,000 Esc, suite 34,000 Esc. **Meals** Breakfast included, served 8:30-12:00. **Restaurant** See p. 224. **Credit cards** All major. **Pets** Dogs allowed. **Facilities** Sauna (1,500Esc), swimming pool, parking. **Nearby** Palàcio Real of Sintra - Serra de Sintra (parque da Pena; from Sintra to La Cruz Alta via Castelo dos Mouros (castle); Azenhas do Mar; parque de Monserrate) - Cascais - Estoril - Lisboa – Estoril golf course (9- and 18-hole). **Open** Mar 1 – Oct 30.

The Sintra Serra is a small mountainous massif ending in the Atlantic, and in the villages, caught between sea and mountains, the climate is very mild and the light very soft. Some quintas have been converted into hotels, which are more like guest houses. The Quinta da Capela numbers among then, and shares their indefinable charm. Rebuilt in the 18th century on a hillside, it has a superb view of the hills and châteaux of Pena and Montserrate. The refinement of the house is rather exceptional. There's no bar or restaurant, but you can have a drink or order a light meal in the lounge. The bedrooms are exquisite, with antique furniture, linen sheets, and well-appointed bathrooms. Also very attractive are the two apartments (for two or four people) in the neighboring houses, which have private gardens. For lovers of charm. Building on the success of the quinta, the owners opened the Restaurant Colares Vehla at Colares, which is now counted among the best establishments in Lisbon.

How to get there (Map 3): 28km northwest of Lisboa, 4.5km of Sintra on the Colares road.

Casa Miradouro [TH]

2710 Sintra (Lisboa)
Rua Sotto Mayor, 55 - Apartado 1027
Tel. 21-923 59 00 - Fax 21-924 18 36
Sr Federico Kneubuhl

Rooms 6 with bath. **Price** Single 14,000-18,500Esc, double 16,000-21,000Esc. **Meals** Breakfast included, served 8:30-10:00. **Restaurant** See p. 224. **Credit cards** All major. **Pets** Dogs not allowed. **Nearby** Palàcio Real of Sintra - Serra de Sintra (parque da Pena; from Sintra to La Cruz Alta via Castelo dos Mouros (castle); Azenhas do Mar; parque de Monserrate) - Cascais - Estoril - Lisboa – Estoril golf course (9- and 18-hole). **Closed** Jan 1 - Feb 18.

Sintra attracts people with taste, and the Casa Miradouro, which has just opened, is the town's latest hotel for those who seek charm, simplicity, and refinement. This beautiful two-colored house, which dates from the end of the 19th century, enjoys a sublime site on the side of a mountain, and overlooks the valley and forest with its former royal palace. The delicious breakfast should not be missed. This is the ideal place for enjoying the quiet ways of this royal town.

How to get there (Map 3): 28km northwest of Lisboa.

Quinta das Sequóias ᵀᴴ

2710 Sintra (Lisboa)
Ap. 1004
Tel. 21-924 38 21 - Fax 21-923 03 42 - Sra Maria Candida
Web: www.distrimarketing pt/virtualportugal/quintadassequoias

Rooms 5 with bath, WC. **Price** Double 16,000-24,000Esc. **Meals** Breakfast included. **Restaurant** See p. 224. **Credit cards** All major. **Pets** Dogs not allowed. **Facilities** Swimming pool. **Nearby** Palàcio Real of Sintra - Serra de Sintra (parque da Pena; from Sintra to La Cruz Alta via Castelo dos Mouros (castle); Azenhas do Mar; parque de Monserrate) - Cascais - Estoril - Lisboa – Estoril golf course (9- and 18-hole). **Open** All year.

Acharming town is the setting for a charming hotel, the Quinta das Sequóias. This beautiful house with its white façades framed by pink tiles, rises up out of the woods surrounding Sintra. The drive to the hotel provides marvelous views over the hills, coast, and Palace of La Peña. The house is characteristic of regional architecture, and the refined interior has antique furniture and carpets, and beautiful collector pieces, set in a tasteful decor. The individually decorated rooms are elegant. Start the day with a good breakfast served in the warm and traditional dining room. The billiards room is the ideal spot for a drink, watching the national news on cable TV, or sampling one of the numerous video cassettes. In fine weather the garden offers many quiet and shaded corners, and there's also a swimming pool. The staff is delightful.

How to get there (Map 3): 28km northwest of Lisboa. In Sintra take towards Monserrate. After Setais Hotel turn left. After 1km follow sign.

Villa das Rosas TH

2710 Sintra (Lisboa)
Rua António Cunha, 2/4
Tel. 21-923 42 16 - Fax 21-923 42 16 - Sra Celia Galrão
E-mail: celia@mail.catalao.pt

Rooms 5 and 2 chalets with bath or shower. **Price** Double 16,000-20,000Esc. **Meals** Breakfast included. **Restaurant** See p. 224. **Credit cards** Not accepted. **Pets** Dogs allowed. **Facilities** Swimming pool, tennis, parking. **Nearby** Palàcio Real of Sintra - Serra de Sintra (parque da Pena; from Sintra to La Cruz Alta via Castelo dos Mouros (castle); Azenhas do Mar; parque de Monserrate) - Cascais - Estoril - Lisboa — Estoril golf course (9- and 18-hole). **Open** All year.

An attractive villa with a façade made up of *azulejos* at the entrance to Sintra. It has a garden around it, brimming with bougainvillae and roses, all making you forget that you are in the center of a major city. The rooms are pleasant with private baths and decorated in a style that leans perhaps too heavily on lace and crocheting. There is, in addition, a chalet for family use with two bedrooms and a fully-equipped kitchen. You will also find a barbecue in the garden if you wish to have dinner without leaving the premises.

How to get there (Map 3): 28km northwest of Lisboa.

Casa de Arcada TH

Banzão 2710 Sintra (Lisboa)
Avenida do Atlântico, 161
Tel. 21-929 07 21

Rooms 4 (3 with private bath and WC). **Price** Double 8,500-12,000Esc. **Meals** Breakfast included,
served 7:30-11:00. **Restaurant** See p. 224. **Credit cards** Not accepted. **Pets** Dogs not allowed.
Facilities Parking. **Nearby** Palàcio Real of Sintra - Trips by tram to the coast - Serra de Sintra (parque
da Pena; from Sintra to La Cruz Alta via Castelo dos Mouros (castle); Azenhas do Mar; parque de
Monserrate) - Cascais - Estoril - Lisboa. **Open** All year.

When you leave Sintra, you take the Colares road and follow the route of
the old yellow tram which still takes people down to the beach. The Casa
da Arcada is a white house recently constructed in the Portuguese style with
the arcaded entrance that gives it its name. The welcome is charming and one
is soon enchanted by the place. The main drawing room is light, furnished with
pretty 19th-century furniture. Three of the rooms are in the main building. One
is charming, with a regional feel, but an external bathroom. The largest has a
corner position which makes it very light. The third is more classical, but still
pleasant. The last, with its independent entrance through the garden, called the
"Portuguese room" because of its walls covered in *azulejos* illustrating the
exploits of Christopher Columbus and his three ships, is worth considering.
One drawback: the closeness of the road.

How to get there (Map 3): 35km northwest of Lisbon; 9km from Sintra.

Quinta da Fonta Nova [TH]

Serradas 2735-452 Rio de Mouro (Lisboa)
Tel. 21-916 00 21 - Fax 21-916 11 11
Sr Rogério de Queiroz Soares

Rooms 10 with bath, satellite TV. **Price** Single 15,500Esc, double 17,000Esc, triple 22,000Esc, suite (4 pers.) 25,000Esc. **Meals** Breakfast included. **Restaurant** In Sintra see p. 224. **Credit cards** Not accepted. **Pets** Dogs not allowed. **Facilities** Swimming pool, tennis, parking. **Nearby** Palàcio Real of Sintra - Serra de Sintra (parque da Pena; from Sintra to La Cruz Alta via Castelo dos Mouros (castle); Azenhas do Mar; parque de Monserrate) - Cascais - Estoril - Lisboa – Estoril golf course (9- and 18-hole). **Open** Mar 15 – Oct 31.

A particular favorite among sportsmen with a nearby golf course, plus swimming pool and tennis courts. This is an attractive manor house surrounded by geraniums and bougainvillae with impressive grounds that include trees of almost every description - pines, locusts, cedars and eucalyptus - plus a French-style garden overlooking the countryside. The rooms, independent from the owner's quarters, are of more modern vintage, but of varying quality as some of the bathrooms could use a bit of attention. Some look out on the park, others on the courtyard. Guests here receive an exemplary reception.

How to get there (Map 3): 23km northwest of Lisboa; 5km south of Sintra.

Quinta das Encostas ™

Sassoeiros 2735 Parede (Lisboa)
Largo Vasco d'Orbey
Tel. 21-457 00 56 - Fax 21-458 26 47
Sr Luis Paco d'Arcos

Rooms 4 with bath, TV. **Price** 16,000Esc (1 pers.), 18,000Esc (double). **Meals** Breakfast included. **Restaurant** In Cascais and Sintra see pp. 223-224. **Credit cards** Not accepted. **Pets** Dogs not allowed. **Facilities** Swimming pool, parking. **Nearby** Palàcio Real of Sintra - Serra de Sintra (parque da Pena; from Sintra to La Cruz Alta via Castelo dos Mouros (castle); Azenhas do Mar; parque de Monserrate) - Cascais - Mafra - Queluz - Lisboa – Estoril golf course (9- and 18-hole). **Open** All year.

The Quinta das Encostas is a charming hotel ideally located a mere fifteen kilometers from Lisbon, and ten from both Sintra and Cascais, which is to say very close to the Serra de Sintra. As you enter the courtyard, you discover two guards dressed in *azulejos* standing at attention to welcome you. This is a beautiful house dating from the 17th century and occupied by a descendant of the family who once owned all the surrounding land. It has a very pretty interior, especially the elegant and sun-filled lounges. The upstairs rooms are done in bright pastel colors and have a truly pleasant atmosphere. It would be advisable, however, to reserve the largest of these. The garden is resplendent with roses and bougainvillae, and there is a small French-style garden surrounding the swimming pool.

How to get there (Map 3): 15km west of Lisboa; 10km south of Sintra.

Quinta de Santo Amaro [AT]

Aldeia da Piedade 2925-375 Azeitão
Tel. 21-218 92 30 - Fax 21-218 93 90
Sra Maria da Puresa O'Neill de Mello

Rooms 7 with bath and 1 apartment with 3 bedrooms. **Price** Double 14,500Esc; apart. 216,000Esc/week, 800,000Esc/month. **Meals** Breakfast included for the rooms. No restaurant. **Credit card** Amex. **Pets** Dogs not allowed. **Facilities** Swimming pool. **Nearby** Serra d'Arrábida: Vila Nogueira de Azeitão, Portinho da Arràbida, Miradouro, Outão, quinta de Bacalhaoa, Vila Fresca de Azeitão. **Open** All year.

Scarcely thirty kilometers from Lisbon and very close to the Sierra d'Arrabida are some delightfully discreet places bearing a distinctly Portuguese aspect dating from another era. The Quinta de Santo Amaro plays a big part in keeping alive a subtle feeling of *saudade*, a kind of blues-tinted emotion very dear to the Portuguese and unmistakable when you hear them sing *fados*. This old manor house with white walls of fading crimson and time-worn, moss-covered tiles offers a choice of wings; in the left-hand wing is a two-floor apartment with four rooms and three bathrooms plus a large terrace with roses and lemon trees as well as three very attractive rooms with old furniture and *azulejos*. The right-hand wing has three rooms located in what used to be the cellar and the stables; these rooms can be combined upon request. While breaking up the accommodation this way may prove slightly inconvenient, this is quickly forgotten when you savor the charm of its very spacious lounge. The lush garden is an ideal place for a short stroll leading you through the surrounding trees to a clear blue swimming pool.

How to get there *(Map 3): 30km of Lisboa; 17km west of Setúbal via N10. 4km of Azeitão via R379 towards Sesimbra.*

124

Quinta das Torres

2925 Vila Nogueira de Azeitão (Setúbal)
Tel. 21-218 00 01 - Fax 21-21 90 607
Sr Ayres

Category ★★★★ **Rooms** 8, 2 suites and 2 bungalows with bath, WC. **Price** Double 9,000-16,500Esc, suite and bungalow 14,500-30,000Esc. **Meals** Breakfast included, served 8:00-10:00. **Restaurant** Service 12:00PM-3:00PM, 8:00PM-11:00PM – à la carte. **Credit cards** Visa, Eurocard, MasterCard. **Pets** Dogs not allowed. **Facilities** Parking. **Nearby** Serra d'Arrábida: Vila Nogueira de Azeitão, Portinho da Arrábida, Miradouro, Outão, quinta de Bacalhaoa, Vila Fresca de Azeitão. **Open** By reservation.

Between Setúbal and Lisbon, this ancient 16th-century farm is hidden at the end of an avenue lined with maple trees. In the part occupied by the inn, eight rooms are open to guests; some are more comfortable than others, but all have a personalized and charming decor. Our preference is for the room on the top floor of the tower, which also has a terrace overlooking the courtyard. There is one spacious and attractive suite with a lounge, open fireplace, and an extra room on the mezzanine. The restaurant serves quality cuisine, and from its windows one can view a pretty man-made lake with a small summerhouse on a tiny island in its center. The extensive grounds provide many beautiful country walks. Note that two bungalows are available, set away from the farm near an olive grove.

How to get there (*Map 3*): *27km west of Setúbal via N10. 1km of Azeitão.*

Quinta do Casal do Bispo TH

Aldeia de Piedade 2925 Azeitão (Setúbal)
Estrada dos Romanos
Tel. 21-219 18 12
Sra Maria Inês de Almeida

Rooms 6 with bath or shower. **Price** Double 12,000-14,000Esc. **Meals** Breakfast included, served 8:00-10:00. No restaurant. **Credit cards** Not accepted. **Pets** Dogs not allowed. **Facilities** Parking. **Nearby** Serra d'Arrábida: Vila Nogueira de Azeitão, Portinho da Arràbida, Miradouro, Outão, quinta de Bacalhaoa, Vila Fresca de Azeitão. **Open** All year.

When in Lisbon, it is a treat to visit the Serra da Arràbida, a scant thirty kilometers from the capital. Leaving Azeitão, you first go through olive groves and vineyards, then the fragrant pine forests overlooking the shiny waters of the ocean. The Quinta do Casal do Bispo can be a restful stop-over, even if it has only one room which, as we see it, is wholly up to standard, an attractive place where you are very well received. Nearby is the Quinta das Torres with a restaurant that enjoys an enviable reputation.

How to get there (Map 3): 27km west of Setúbal via N10. 1km of Azeitão.

Quinta de Arrábida [TH]

Casais da Serra 2925 Azeitão
Tel. 21-218 34 33 /21-840 22 69 - Fax 21-840 22 69
Sr Afonso de Miranda Santos Howell
E-mail: howell@mail.telepac.pt

Villas 2 (2 and 4 pers.) with telephone, kitchen, sitting room, 1 or 2 bedrooms, bath, WC, satellite TV.
Price Casa Pinheiro 2 pers./day 12,500-14,000-18,000Esc, Casa do Forno 4 pers./day 16,500-
18,000-24,000Esc. **Meals** Breakfast included. No restaurant. **Credit cards** Not accepted. **Pets** Dogs
not allowed. **Facilities** Swimming pool, parking. **Nearby** Serra d'Arrábida: Vila Nogueira de Azeitão,
Portinho da Arràbida, Miradouro, Outão, quinta de Bacalhaoa, Vila Fresca de Azeitão. **Open** All year.

Along the ocean south of Lisbon, the hills of the low-lying Sierra de
Arrabida serve as a natural barrier against the sea. The large property of
the Quinta de Arrabida stretches out from their inland side with six hectares of
untouched nature and fields, a natural preserve. On it are two attractive little
villas that guests may rent by the day or week. They are called the Casa de
Pinheiro and the Casa do Forno and are spaced far enough apart to be totally
independent. They are built in a traditional and brightly-colored style and
open onto the garden. The kitchen and the amenities are all up to standard, the
furniture is well chosen and each villa has a large terrace. The only difference
lies in the number of rooms. If you wish, everything you may need for your
breakfast can be brought to you. There is a swimming pool shared by the
guests of both villas and there are beaches only six kilometers away via a very
pretty road that goes both through the Sierra and overlooks the ocean.

How to get there (*Map 3*): *13km southwest of Setúbal via N10 and N379-1
towards Arràbida.*

Pálacio de Rio-Frio ᵀᴴ

Rio-Frio 2955 Pinhal Novo (Setúba)
Tel. 21-231 97 01 - Fax 21-231 96 33
Sra Maria de Lourdes d'Orey

Rooms 3 and 1 suite with bath or shower, WC. **Price** Double 16,500Esc, suite 18,500Esc. **Meals** Breakfast included, served 8:00-10:30. No restaurant. **Credit cards** Not accepted. **Pets** Dogs not allowed. **Facilities** Swimming pool, parking. **Nearby** Convento de Jesus in Setúbal - Peninsula of Troia by road (98km) or by ferry (20mn) - Lisboa - Beaches (20km). **Open** All year.

This majestic hotel offers two balconies with exceptional *azulejos* signed Jorge Colaço, in addition to a large lounge lined with spectacular hunting scenes going back to the time of the current owner's grandfather. These ceramics are indeed famous, and if only for that reason you owe it to yourself to visit Rio-Frio, a village halfway between Lisbon and Setúbal. The rooms are in one wing of the building and are at once simple and comfortable. There is a delightful garden, a swimming pool and the possibility to visit the strange landscapes surrounding the estuary of the Tagus River on horseback, all excellent reasons for stopping at Rio-Frio.

How to get there (Map 3): 25km north of Setúbal to Montijo; 10km east of Montijo.

Pousada de São Filipe *

2900 Setúbal
Castelo de São Filipe
Tel. 265-52 38 44 - Fax 265-53 25 38
Sra Carolina Marafusia

Rooms 15 and 1 suite with air-conditioning, telephone, bath, WC, TV. **Price** Single 29,600-32,500Esc, double 31,600-34,500Esc, suite 38,800Esc; extra bed +30%. **Meals** Breakfast included, served 8:00-10:30 - full board +6,600Esc (per pers.). **Restaurant** Service 1:00PM-3:00PM, 7:30PM-10:00PM – à la carte 3,650Esc – Specialties: Fish and shellfish. **Credit cards** All major. **Pets** Dogs not allowed. **Facilities** Parking. **Nearby** Convento de Jesus in Setúbal - Peninsula of Troia by road (98km) or by ferry (20mn) - Lisboa. **Open** All year.

The Pousada is inside the fort of São Filipe, built in 1590 to defend the port of Setúbal. It became a prison in the 18th century but lost all its military attributes in the 19th century. In 1965, part of the citadel–a very good example of military architecture, with its tunnels and hiding places–was converted into a hotel. The decor is in good taste but is rather somber. Its position on the top of a hill gives the Pousada a very beautiful view over the port, bay, and town, especially from its large terrace. The bedrooms are comfortable, but don't accept one without the view. Do not forget to visit the superb chapel entirely decorated with marvelous *azulejos* tiles.

How to get there (*Map 3*): *Near Castelo de São Filipe, 1.5km.*

Quinta dos Medos TH

Fornos (Setúbal)
Tel. 21-268 31 42 - Fax : 21-268 31 42
Sr Manuel Peres

Rooms 2 with bath, TV. **Price** Double 15,000Esc. **Meals** Breakfast included, served 8:00-10:30. **Evening meals** On request. **Credit cards** Not accepted. **Pets** Dogs not allowed. **Facilities** Parking. **Nearby** Lisboa - Serra de Arrábida - Sesimbra - Setúbal. **Open** Jun – Sept.

South of Lisbon between the immense estuary of the Tagus River and the Costa Bela is the national park of Dos Medos where the vegetation is essentially a pine forest spread over hundreds of acres. This area is truly protected and for this reason there are only a few highly privileged constructions in it. Among them is the Quinta dos Medos of recent origin which fits in nicely with the surrounding pines and the only sound is the rustling of their branches. It is a small and well-looked-after house with only two rooms available for guests. It has a garden with large flower pots that add welcome color to a somewhat monotonous landscape. There is a lovely swimming pool where you can cool off while listening to the silence and knowing that Manuel or Christina are never far away when is comes time to share some afternoon watermelon.

How to get there (Map 3): 60km south of Lisboa via A10 Lisboa- Setúbal. Then take the road towards Sesimbra via Lagoa de Albufeira, Alfarim and Fornos (between Alfarim and Caixas).

Hotel do Elévador

4710-455 Braga
Bom Jésus do Monte
Tel. 253-60 34 00 - Fax 253-60 34 09
Sr Albino Viana

Category ★★★★ **Rooms** 22 with air-conditioning, telephone, bath, hairdryer, WC, sattelite TV, minibar; elevator. **Price** Single 10,600-13,600Esc, double 13,300-16,500Esc, suite 18,500-22,700Esc. **Meals** Breakfast included, served from 7:30 - half board +3,100-3,500Esc, full board +6,200-6,400Esc (per pers.). **Restaurant** With air conditioning, service 12:30PM-2:30PM, 7:30PM-9:30PM – à la carte 4,800Esc – Specialties: Papas sarrabulho - Bacalhao a moda Braga - Rojoes a minhota. **Credit cards** All major. **Pets** Dogs not allowed. **Facilities** Parking. **Nearby** In Braga: the cathedral - Monte Sameiro - Church of Santa Maria in Serra de Falperra - Chapel São Frutuoso de Montélios - Parque national da Peneda - Gerês. **Open** All year.

This hotel belongs to the same owner as the Hotel do Parque, situated a few paces away. The rooms all have the same level of comfort, and are decorated in good taste with very pretty furniture. It is best to avoid those in the front, they are a little too noisy because of the tourists. Go for those looking onto the French-style garden at the back of the hotel; they have the additional pleasure of a superb view of the valley. Some rooms have balconies. The restaurant provides panoramic views over the Minho River. This is a pleasant stopping place if you have decided to visit Braga, the capital of the region.

How to get there (Map 1): 50km northeast of Porto via N14 to Braga, then N103.

Hotel Do Parque

4710-455 Braga
Bom Jésus do Monte
Tel. 253-67 65 48 - Fax 253-67 66 79
Sr Albino Viana

Category ★★★★ **Rooms** 45 and 4 suites with air-conditioning, telephone, bath, WC, satellite TV, minibar; elevator. **Price** Single 10,600-13,600Esc, double 13,300-16,500Esc, suite 19,000-24,000Esc. **Meals** Breakfast included, served 7:30-10:30. **Restaurant** "Hotel Elévador". **Credit cards** All major. **Pets** Dogs not allowed. **Facilities** Sitting room, parking. **Nearby** In Braga: the cathedral - Monte Sameiro - Church of Santa Maria in Serra de Falperra - Chapel São Frutuoso de Montélios - Parque national da Peneda - Gerês. **Open** All year.

There is a sanctuary at this major center of pilgrimage, and it has given the name "Bom Jesus" to the small wooded hill where you'll find the Hotel Do Parque. When built in 1890 the hotel was intended to shelter numerous pilgrims, but it was later closed for several years. Now fully renovated, it offers spacious, comfortable, and well-furnished rooms. The proximity of a large park, a horse riding center, and a lake for boating, all add to its charms.

How to get there *(Map 1): 50km northeast of Porto via N14 to Braga, then N103.*

Casa dos Lagos ᵀᴴ

4710 Bom Jésus (Braga)
Monte do Bom Jésus
Tel. 253-67 67 38
Sr and Sra Pinto Barbosa

Rooms 2 and 3 apartments with bath or shower, WC, TV on request **Price** Double and apart. (2 pers.) 12,500-14,000Esc, apart. (4 pers.) 19,500-22,400Esc. **Meals** Breakfast included. **Evening meals** On request. **Restaurant** See p. 225. **Credit card** Amex. **Pets** Dogs not allowed. **Facilities** Swimming pool, parking. **Nearby** In Braga: the cathedral - Monte Sameiro - Church of Santa Maria in Serra de Falperra - Chapel São Frutuoso de Montélios - Parque national da Peneda - Gerês. **Open** All year.

Of the hotels on the well-known Bom Jesus Mountain, you may prefer the charm and simplicity of the Casa dos Lagos as opposed to the style of the two "grand hotels" already mentioned. An aristocratic mansion, formerly residence of the Fraião court, it offers a matchless view of the valley. The room on the first level is immense with very attractive furniture in dark sculpted wood, tapestries and white embroidered bedspreads. The terrace offers a western exposure and the light in the evening is truly exceptional. Next to it is a small room suitable for children. Opposite this is another room which is smaller but most colorful with charming knickknacks plus a large and comfortable bed. It too has a terrace offering the same magical view as the first. A copious breakfast is served in the dining room which opens onto a lovely garden. Here you will be waited on by Andrelina, as discreet as she is attentive to your needs. There will soon be a swimming pool among the lemon trees in the garden. We strongly recommend you discover the Casa dos Lagos for yourself.

How to get there *(Map 1): 50km northeast of Porto via N14 to Braga, then N103.*

Hotel Bela Vista

Caldelas 4720 Amares (Braga)
Tel. 253-36 15 02 - Fax 253-36 11 36
Dr Jose Barbosa
E-mail: hotel.belavista@telepac.pt

Category ★★★ **Rooms** 69 with air-conditioning, telephone, bath or shower, WC, TV; elevator. **Price** Double 10,000-20,000Esc. **Meals** Breakfast included - full board +4,000Esc. **Restaurant** Service 12:30PM-2:30PM, 7:30PM-9:30PM – mealtime specials 2,750Esc – Regional cooking. **Credit cards** All major. **Pets** Dogs not allowed. **Facilities** Swimming pool, tennis, garage, parking. **Nearby** Braga - Bom Jesus - Parque National de Peneda - Gerês. **Open** May 1 – Oct 30.

For a respite during your Portuguese travels, opt for Caldelas, which is located between two rivers. With its thermal spring waters, Caldelas has luxuriant vegetation. The hotel has been adapted to suit the needs of a clientele seeking a quiet holiday, but the facilities aren't lacking: swimming pool, gym, tennis court, and children's garden. The garden is superb, with many attractive shaded corners, while the lawns are just as green as those in England. The service and comfort are those of a traditional hotel.

How to get there *(Map 1): 67km north of Porto to Braga, then towards Vila Verde, Amares is northeast of Braga.*

Casa do Barão de Fermil ᵀᴴ*

Veade - Fermil
4890 Celorico de Basto (Braga)
Tel. 255-36 12 11
D. Fernanda Mourão Correia

Rooms 5 with bath. **Price** Double 14,000Esc; extra bed 3,200Esc. **Meals** Breakfast included, served 8:00-10:30. No restaurant. **Credit cards** Not accepted. **Pets** Dogs not allowed. **Facilities** Swimming pool, parking. **Nearby** Serra de Marão via N15 towards Alto do Espinho - Amarante - Estrada (road) from Vila Real to Amarante - Guimarães - Estrada de Vila Real to Mondim de Basto Guimarães - Vila Real - Lámego - Porto. **Closed** Nov - Feb, Eastern and Sept.

Celorico de Basto is close to Amarante and the Serra do Marão, the natural frontiers separating the regions of Douro and Tras-os-Montes. The valley of the Tamaga River is widely known for both its *vinho verde* and the numerous manor houses offering guest accommodation. The Casa de Fermil is among them, and one is immediately under the spell cast by the mysterious atmosphere produced by its garden with luxurious vegetation and the tall trees that surround the house and its pagoda-like roof. The boxwoods that frame the stairs add an element of humor. In one corner of the property there is a very pleasant swimming pool. We were surprised by our reception here, a mixture of suspicion and lack of cooperation; ordinarily, the Portuguese are well known for their hospitality.

How to get there (Map 1): 100 km west of Porto by A3, Gumarães exit. Take the road towards Fafe, Gandarela. Then towards Celerico de Basto, Mondim, as far as Fermil. The house is on the right on the N304 towards Mondim.

Casa do Campo ^{TH*}

Molares 4890 Celorico de Basto (Braga)
Tel. and fax 255-36 12 31
Sra Maria Armanda Meireles

Rooms 7 and 1 suite with bath. **Price** Single 11,600Esc, double 14,000Esc; extra bed 3,000Esc.
Meals Breakfast included. **Evening meals** On request – mealtime specials 4,000Esc. **Credit cards**
Not accepted. **Pets** Dogs not allowed. **Facilities** Swimming pool. **Nearby** Serra de Marão via N15
towards Alto do Espinho - Amarante - Estrada (road) from Vila Real to Amarante - Guimarães -
Estrada de Vila Real to Mondim de Basto Guimarães - Vila Real - Lámego - Porto. **Open** All year.

Molares is not really on the tourist path and so your best bet is to consult the tourist office if you want the chance of passing through the superb granite gateway of Casa do Campo. This manor house dates from the 17th century, but its real pride is its camelia garden which specialists consider to be one of the oldest in Portugal. Eight rooms are waiting for those wishing to discover this little visited region.

How to get there *(Map 1): 80km east of Porto to Amarante, then towards Mondim de Basto; 4km of Celorico towards Fermil.*

Pousada de Nossa Senhora da Oliveira

4800 Guimarães (Braga)
Rua de Santa Maria
Tel. 253-51 41 57/8/9 - Fax 253-51 42 04
Sra Costa

Rooms 9 and 6 suites with telephone, bath, WC; elevator. **Price** Single 12,900-17,100Esc, double 16,300-24,600Esc, suite 20,800-30,500Esc; extra bed +30%. **Meals** Breakfast included, served 8:00-10:30. **Restaurant** With air-conditioning, service 12:30PM-3:00PM, 7:30PM-10:30PM – mealtime specials 3,650Esc, also à la carte – Specialties: Arroz con frango - Lenguado don Alfonso. **Credit cards** All major. **Pets** Dogs not allowed. **Facilities** Parking **Nearby** In Guimarães: Paço (Palacio) dos Duques de Bragança, Museum of A. Sampaio, Castle and Church of São Francisco (azulejos) - Largo do Toural - Trofa - Braga - Bom Jesus. **Open** All year.

The Pousada is set in the very center of a historic town. Guimarães is a little bit the cradle of Portugal, as Alphonse VI, the sovereign of León and Castille, bequeathed the county of Portucale to his son-in-law, Henry of Burgundy. On the latter's death, his son Alfonso Henriquez rebelled against the regency of his mother, seized power, defeated the Moors, and had himself proclaimed King of Portugal in 1143. The Pousada is in an ancient lordly manor house, and the original style of the house has been preserved and respected. A delightful dining room opens onto a shaded terrace, which overlooks a pretty square. The rooms are all comfortable, but we recommend the suites overlooking the square or the adjacent small lane. The hotel organizes "gourmet weeks" and also has a very good cellar.

How to get there *(Map 1): 49km northeast of Porto via A3.*

Pousada Santa Marinha *

4800 Guimarães (Braga)
Tel. 253-51 44 53/4 - Fax 253-51 44 59
Sr Navega

Rooms 49 and 2 suites with air-conditioning, telephone, bath, WC, minibar, satellite TV; elevator. **Price** Single 17,900-29,000Esc, double 20,300-31,000Esc, suite 39,500-51,300Esc; extra bed +30%. **Meals** Breakfast included, served 7:30-10:00. **Restaurant** Service 12:30PM-2:30PM, 7:30PM-10:30PM – mealtime specials 3,650Esc, also à la carte – Specialties: Toucinho do ceu. **Credit cards** All major. **Pets** Dogs not allowed. **Nearby** In Guimarães: Paço (Palacio) dos Duques de Bragança, Museum of A. Sampaio, Castle and Church of São Francisco (azulejos) - Largo do Toural - Trofa - Braga - Bom Jesus. **Open** All year.

The Santa Marinha could claim to be the most beautiful pousada in the country. It is found in the green hills of Guimarães in an ancient convent founded in 1154 by Don Alfonso Henriquez, the first Portuguese king. The present buildings however date from the period between the 15th and 18th centuries. The architecture is superb, and the sublime *azulejos* tiles are everywhere. From the chapter hall leads off an immense vaulted corridor leads to the rooms. A large terrace called the "Geronimo Balcony", overlooks the garden, itself a marvel. The rooms are appointed with taste, but the suites are even more beautiful. You owe it to yourself to sample the reputed cuisine in one of the three magnificent dining rooms–you will not be disappointed!

How to get there (Map 1): 49km northeast of Porto via A3. On the road for Penha (2.5km).

Casa de Sezim TH*

4800 Guimarães (Braga)
Apartado 410
Tel. 253-52 30 00 - Fax 253-52 31 96
Sr Pinto de Mesquita

Rooms 7 and 2 suites with bath (2 with telephone). **Price** Single 14,600 0Esc, double 18,500Esc; extra bed 3,800Esc. **Meals** Breakfast included. **Evening meals** On request. **Restaurant** See p. 225. **Credit cards** Amex, Visa, Eurocard, MasterCard. **Pets** Small dogs allowed. **Facilities** Swimming pool, riding. **Nearby** In Guimarães: Paço (Palacio) dos Duques de Bragança, Museum of A. Sampaio, Castle and Church of São Francisco (azulejos) - Largo do Toural - Trofa - Braga - Bom Jesus. **Open** All year.

Set in the countryside and close to Guimarães, the first capital of Portugal, the Casa de Sezim is run by Señor Pinto de Mesquita, a former ambassador. The hotel's origins go back to the 16th century and behind the huge façade are thick stone walls. Five suites display an astonishing series of panels by Züber, dating from the 19th century, which relate the discovery of America and the exotic West Indies. Everywhere, family portraits recall the history of this place. In another wing one finds the rooms, all prettily decorated, with matching bedspreads and curtains, and stylish furniture. The suite in the tower, with its two rooms and lounge, is a real jewel, which also profits from a magnificent view. A large shaded terrace overlooks a garden that slowly descends to the swimming pool, which is sheltered by hedges. The wine made on the property is excellent.

How to get there (Map 1): 49km northeast of Porto, towards Santo Tirso. 4.5km south of Guimarães, before entering Guimarães, go towards Santo Amaro.

Paço de São Cipriano ᵀᴴ*

Tabuadelo 4800 Guimarães (Braga)
Tel. and fax 253-56 53 37
D. João Almeida Santiago de Sottomayor

Rooms 7 with bath. **Price** Single 14,600Esc, double 18,500Esc; extra bed 3,800Esc. **Meals** Breakfast included. **Restaurant** See p. 225. **Credit cards** All major. **Pets** Dogs not allowed. **Facilities** Swimming pool, parking. **Nearby** In Guimarães: Paço (Palacio) dos Duques de Bragança, Museum of A. Sampaio, Castle and Church of São Francisco (azulejos) - Largo do Toural - Trofa - Braga - Bom Jesus. **Open** All year.

This noble residence was where pilgrims used to stop on the road to Santiago de Compostela. Today it is a welcoming guesthouse devoted to hospitality. The main part of the house is made up of buildings set around an imposing medieval tower. The bedrooms are all superb in their simplicity and authenticity, with parquet floors of large polished wooden slabs, rather faded colored wallpaper, and family furniture. We particularly liked the "blue room" with its canopied bed of tulle and embroidered drapes. We also liked the granite kitchen, the library, and the marvelous garden where the box hedges, camelias, and other numerous species invite you to a lesson in botany!

How to get there *(Map 1): 49km northeast of Porto, towards Santo Tirso. 6km of Guimarães.*

Quinta de Santa Comba ^{TH*}

S. Bento da Várzea
4750 Barcelos (Braga)
Tel. 253-831 440 - Fax 253-834 540
Sr Carvahlo de Campos

Rooms 5 with bath. **Price** Double 11,000Esc; extra bed 3,000Esc. **Meals** Breakfast included. **Restaurant** See p. 226. **Credit card** Amex. **Pets** Dogs allowed. **Facilities** Swimming pool, riding, parking. **Nearby** Porto - Braga - Viana do Castelo - Beaches (15km). **Open** May 1 - Oct 15.

L ess than fifty kilometers from Lisbon, fields of maize and vines of the famous *vinho verde* wine surround this superb historic residence. It is a very beautiful example of 18th-century rural architecture, built of granite and chestnut wood. The same rustic comfort and elegance is found inside. An advance reservation is indispensable to stay here.

How to get there (Map 1): 42km north of Porto to Familição, then towards Barcelos (5km before arriving at Barcelos).

Pousada de São Bento

Caniçada 4850 Vieira do Minho (Braga)
Tel. 253-64 71 90/1 - Fax 253-64 78 67
Sr Amaral

Rooms 29 with air-conditioning, telephone, bath, WC, satellite TV, minibar. **Price** Single 12,900-20,200Esc, double 16,300-24,600Esc; extra bed +30%. **Meals** Breakfast included, served 8:00-10:30. **Restaurant** Service 12:30PM-2:30PM, 7:30PM-9:30PM – à la carte 3,650Esc – Specialties: Bacalhao - Rojoes - Trout. **Credit cards** All major. **Pets** Dogs not allowed. **Facilities** Swimming pool, tennis, parking. **Nearby** Parque National de Peneda-Gerès (road from Rio Cavado to Leonte, Serra do Gerès, excursion to Fraga Negra) - Cathedral of Braga - Bom Jesus. **Open** All year.

The Pousada de São Bento is found in the Peneda-Gerês National Park, which protects some archeological remains, as well as flora and fauna of great interest. The hotel has a magnificent location above the River Caldo and its wooded banks. It is an attractive building of stone and wood covered by Virginia creeper. Inside, the lounge and dining room open wide onto the surrounding natural beauty. The rooms are rustic but very comfortable; numbers 4, 6, and 8 have a beautiful view. The swimming pool is an extra attraction to ensure you'll have a pleasant stay.

How to get there *(Map 1): 87km northeast of Porto via N14 to Braga, then N103. 7km northwest of Caniçada via N304*

Quinta de Vermil ᵀᴴ*

Ardegão 4990 S. Julião do Freixo (Ponte de Lima)
Tel. 258-76 15 95 - Fax 258-76 18 01
Sra Torres Fernandes Westebbe

Rooms 8 and 4 apartments (2-4 pers.) with bath. **Price** Single 11,600Esc, double 14,000Esc, apart. 14,000-22,400Esc. **Meals** Breakfast included for bedrooms, served 9:00-11:00. **Evening meals** On request. **Credit cards** Not accepted. **Pets** Dogs allowed. **Facilities** Swimming pool, tennis, parking. **Nearby** In Barcelos: market - Viana do Castelo: Church and Celtic ruins of Santa Luzia, Municipal museum- Bravães - Lindoso - Ponte de Lima (Church and Museum of São Francisco) – Braga – Estela golf course (18-hole) - Barca do Lago golf course (9-hole) - Ponte de Lima golf course (18-hole). **Open** All year.

The backcountry is a beautiful hilly region of pine trees and eucalyptus, small rivers, pastures, and vineyards, and is where you'll find the Quinta de Vermil. This house belonged to several aristocratic families before being completely restored. It has acquired the charm of its new owners, who have decorated the rooms with the same comfort as in their own private quarters. Rooms have antique furniture and are reached via a private entrance. The garden is luxuriant, and fresh spring water supplies the artificial ponds and swimming pool. The terrace shade is inviting for a siesta or reading or, if you're feeling more active, the tennis court is not far away. In the evening you can dine at the guests' table, or prepare your own barbecue in a corner of the garden made available for this. The Quinta is a lovely place with a charming staff.

How to get there (Map 1): 22km northwest of Braga; via A3, exit number 10, RN308 towards Freixo, Ardegão.

Casa do Ameal TH*

Meadela 4900 Viana do Castelo
Rua do Ameal, 119
Tel. 258-82 24 03
Sra Dona Maria Elisa Faria de Araújo

Rooms 1 and 7 apartments (2-4 pers.) with bath, TV. **Price** Double 14,000Esc, apart. 14,000-22,400Esc. (3 nights min.); extra bed 3,200Esc. **Meals** Breakfast included. **Evening meals** On request. **Restaurant** In Viana do Campo see p. 225. **Credit cards** Not accepted. **Pets** Dogs not allowed. **Facilities** Swimming pool, ping pong, parking. **Nearby** Viana do Castelo: Church and Celtic ruins of Santa Luzia, Municipal museum - Bravães - Lindoso - Ponte de Lima (Church and Museum of São Francisco) - Braga — Povoa de Varzim golf course (9-hole). **Open** All year.

Only five kilometers from Viana do Castelo, the Casa do Ameal was built in the 16th century and then acquired by the ancestors of the present owner. Rebuilt over the centuries, tradition has been preserved. Here, hospitality is a quality handed down from generation to generation, and for this reason Doña Maria Elisa opened her guesthouse. A courtyard in front of the large granite ornamental basin fringed with box hedges. The bedrooms, in newly built outbuildings, are decorated with taste, comfortable, and have private bathrooms. You'll admire the sizeable collection of clothing and costumes that belonged to the family, and appreciate the delightful hospitality of Madame Faria de Araujo, who speaks excellent French and English.

How to get there *(Map 1): 2km from Viana do Castelo.*

Casa das Pereiras TH

4990 Ponte de Lima (Viana do Castelo)
Largo das Pereiras
Tel. 258-94 29 39 - Fax 258-94 29 39
Sra D. Maria Filomena Reynolds de Abreú Coutinho

Rooms 3 with bath or shower. **Price** Single 9,000Esc, double 12,000Esc. **Meals** Breakfast included.
Restaurant See p. 225-226. **Credit cards** Not accepted. **Pets** Dogs not allowed. **Facilities** Swimming
pool. **Nearby** Ponte de Lima (Church and Museum of São Francisco); market (Mon every 2 weeks) -
Viana do Castelo: Church and Celtic ruins of Santa Luzia, Municipal museum - Bravães - Lindoso -
Braga – Ponte de Lima golf course (18-hole). **Open** All year.

Despite its being located in the center of Ponte de Lima, the Casa das
Pereiras is a lovely country house that, behind a beautiful 18th-century
wall, hides a superb terraced garden with a stunning collection of camellias.
The old stables have been converted into a lounge and dining room where
breakfast is served. The rooms are upstairs and although somewhat small, each
has a distinct charm. What we liked most about this place was its surroundings
in which a swimming pool is nicely integrated.

How to get there *(Map 1): 100km north of Porto via A3 (Braga/Valença), exit*
Ponte da Barca/Ponte de Lima.

Quinta de Sabadão ^{TH*}

Arcozelo
4990 Ponte de Lima (Viana do Castelo)
Tel. 258-94 19 63
Sra M. Abreu Lima e Fonseca

Rooms 3 and 1 apartment (4 pers.) with telephone, bath, WC. **Price** Double 14,000Esc, apart. 22,400Esc. **Meals** Breakfast included. **Restaurant** See p. 225-226. **Credit cards** Not accepted. **Pets** Dogs allowed. **Facilities** Parking. **Nearby** Ponte de Lima (Church and Museum of São Francisco); market (Mon every 2 weeks) - Viana do Castelo: Church and Celtic ruins of Santa Luzia, Municipal museum - Bravães - Lindoso - Braga — Ponte de Lima golf course (18-hole). **Open** All year.

The Council of Europe voted Ponte de Lima a model town for the conservation of European heritage; it combines Roman, gothic, and baroque architecture. Two kilometers away in the surrounding countryside, the Casa de Sabadão is a beautiful residence with a great courtyard and vine-covered bowers. The house has many attractive rooms, each with its own private entrance, but our real favorite is in the small mill, just a hundred meters away, that has been converted into a four-person apartment. There are two rooms, a bathroom, and lounge on two levels, all prettily decorated. The site is enchanting, with its murmuring waters, and greenery. One could stay here a very long time and quite forget the rest of the world !

How to get there *(Map 1): 100km north of Porto via A3 (Braga/Valenca), exit Ponte da Barca/Ponte de Lima; 2km (north of Ponte de Lima) on the Arcos de Valdevez road.*

Casa do Arrabalde ^{TH*}

Arcozelo
4990 Ponte de Lima (Viana do Castelo)
Tel. 258-74 24 42
Dr Francisco Maia e Castro

Rooms 3 with bath or shower and 2 apartments (4 pers.). **Price** Double 14,000Esc, apart. 22,400Esc. **Meals** Breakfast included. **Restaurant** See p. 225-226. **Credit cards** Not accepted. **Pets** Dogs not allowed. **Facilities** Swimming pool, parking. **Nearby** Ponte de Lima (Church and Museum of São Francisco); market (Mon every 2 weeks) - Viana do Castelo: Church and Celtic ruins of Santa Luzia, Municipal museum - Bravães - Lindoso - Braga – Ponte de Lima golf course (18-hole). **Open** Apr - Oct 15.

You will find the Casa do Arrabalde not far away from a large, beautiful bridge, with sixteen arches alternating with openwork-design pillars. This historic house, built in 1729, remains a refuge of tranquility near the town center. It includes a chapel, an astonishing music lounge–which has a ceiling decorated with a sculptured violin, and antique furnishing throughout.

How to get there (Map 1): 100km north of Porto via A3 (Braga/Valenca), exit Ponte da Barca/Ponte de Lima; 1km of Ponte de Lima.

Casa do Outeiro ^{TH*}

Arcozelo
4990 Ponte de Lima (Viana do Castelo)
Tel. 258-941 206
Dr João Gomes d'Abreu e Lima

Rooms 3 and 1 apartment (2 pers.) with bath or shower. **Price** Double and apart 14,000Esc. **Meals** Breakfast included. **Restaurant** See p. 225-226. **Credit cards** Not accepted. **Pets** Dogs not allowed. **Facilities** Swimming pool, parking. **Nearby** Ponte de Lima (Church and Museum of São Francisco); market (Mon every 2 weeks) - Viana do Castelo: Church and Celtic ruins of Santa Luzia, Municipal museum - Bravães - Lindoso - Braga – Ponte de Lima golf course (18-hole). **Open** All year.

Hidden away in the leafy chestnut woods some two kilometers from Ponte de Lima, the Casa do Outeiro was the first private residence in the area to open its doors to tourists. The owners were very concerned about preserving their traditions, and thought that the best way to do this was to share them. On arrival one can admire the handsome entrance gate with its coat of arms, and in the house itself the traditional granite kitchen. Three rooms and a small independent apartment (for two people) are some five hundred meters from the main house. The atmosphere is very peaceful; install yourself on the veranda and enjoy the view over the ancient bridge bestriding the Outeiro river.

How to get there *(Map 1): 100km north of Porto via A3 (Braga/Valença), exit Ponte da Barca/Ponte de Lima; 2km of Ponte de Lima towards Calheiros.*

Convento Val de Pereiras ᵀᴴ

Arcozelo
4990 Ponte de Lima (Viana do Castelo)
Tel. 258-74 21 61 - Fax 258-74 20 47

Rooms 9 and 1 suite with bath. **Price** Single 10,000Esc, double 11,000Esc, suite 13,000Esc. **Meals** Breakfast included. **Restaurant** See p. 225-226. **Credit cards** Not accepted. **Pets** Dogs not allowed. **Facilities** Parking. **Nearby** Ponte de Lima (Church and Museum of São Francisco); market (Mon every 2 weeks) - Viana do Castelo: Church and Celtic ruins of Santa Luzia, Municipal museum - Bravães - Lindoso - Braga — Ponte de Lima golf course (18-hole). **Open** All year.

Virtually nothing remains of the 16th-century convent that once stood on this site except the delightful French-style garden and the magnificent view of the vineyards. The owners live in the old house, and you go down a long trellis-covered walk to a recently-constructed building in regional style where the upstairs rooms, tasteful and traditional, overlook the countryside. On the ground floor, guests may gather in a bright and cheerful living room giving on a very pleasant terrace. If you chose to eat at the hotel, there is a fine dining room as well as excellent room service - withal, an excellent combination.

How to get there (Map 1): 100km north of Porto via A3 (Braga/Valenca), exit Ponte da Barca/Ponte de Lima; 2km of Ponte de Lima towards Calheiros.

Paço de Calheiros ^{TH*}

Calheiros 4990 Ponte de Lima (Viana do Castelo)
Tel. 258-94 71 64 - Fax 258-94 72 94
Sr Conde de Calheiros
E-mail: paco_calheiros@nortenet.pt

Rooms 9 and 6 apartments (2, 4 and 6 pers.) with bath. **Price** Double 18,500Esc, apart. 18,500-
26,400-31,200Esc; extra bed 3,800Esc. **Meals** Breakfast included, served 8:00-10:00. **Evening meals**
On request – mealtime specials 5,000Esc (per pers.). **Credit cards** Not accepted. **Pets** Dogs allowed.
Facilities Swimming pool, tennis, riding (1,700Esc/hr), parking. **Nearby** Ponte de Lima (Church and
Museum of São Francisco); market (Mon every 2 weeks) - Viana do Castelo: Church and Celtic ruins
of Santa Luzia, Municipal museum - Bravães - Lindoso - Braga – Ponte de Lima golf course (18-hole).
Open All year.

The Paço de Calheiros is inextricably linked with the history of the region,
and its owner, the Count of Calheiros, remains mayor of the village. He is
very keen that visitors should discover his region. An avenue lined with plane
trees, leads to a superb mansion, which has a chapel for its central section. The
most agreeable rooms are on the ground floor and look onto the beautiful
18th-century garden. A more recent building shelters the two-person
apartments. Perfectly situated on higher ground, the swimming pool and tennis
court dominate the surroundings. Elegance, refinement, and relaxation are all
to be found here at Calheiros.

How to get there *(Map 1): 100km north of Porto via A3 (Braga/Valenca), exit
Ponte da Barca/Ponte de Lima; 5km (north of Ponte de Lima) on the Arcos
road, Calheiros road.*

Casa do Barreiro TH*

S. Tiago da Gemieira
4990 Ponte de Lima (Viana do Castelo)
Tel. 258-94 81 37 - Fax 258-94 86 65
Maria Teresa Meneses Malheiro de Faria Barbosa

Rooms 6 and 1 apartment (4 pers.) with bath or shower. **Price** Double 14,000Esc, apart. 22,400Esc; extra bed 3,200Esc. **Meals** Breakfast included. **Restaurant** See p. 225-226. **Credit cards** Not accepted. **Pets** Dogs not allowed. **Facilities** Swimming pool, parking. **Nearby** Ponte de Lima (Church and Museum of São Francisco); market (Mon every 2 weeks) - Viana do Castelo: Church and Celtic ruins of Santa Luzia, Municipal museum - Bravães - Lindoso - Braga – Ponte de Lima golf course (18-hole). **Open** All year.

If many historic houses have recently opened their doors to tourism, it is often to save a patrimony held by the same family for many generations, which has become difficult to maintain. One can see the colonial, African, Indian, or Brazilian influences in many of these houses. The Casa do Barreiro dates from 1652. The patio here maintains the elegant architecture of that era. The swimming pool has been treated as an artificial pond, and is found in a recess of the terraced garden, which enjoys a wide view over the valley, and is filled with the delightful scent of eucalyptus.

How to get there (Map 1): 100km north of Porto towards Viana do Castelo; 5km east of Ponte de Lima, towards Barca.

Casa das Torres ^{TH*}

Facha 4990 Ponte de Lima (Viana do Castelo)
Tel. 258-94 13 69 - 258-82 37 79
Manuel Correia Malheiro

Rooms 3 and 1 cottage-apartment (4 pers.) with bath; wheelchair access. **Price** Single 11,600Esc, double 14,000Esc, apart. 22,400Esc; extra bed 3,200Esc. **Meals** Breakfast included, 8:00-10:00. **Restaurant** See p. 225-226. **Credit cards** Not accepted. **Pets** Dogs not allowed. **Facilities** Swimming pool, parking. **Nearby** Ponte de Lima (Church and Museum of São Francisco); market (Mon every 2 weeks) - Viana do Castelo: Church and Celtic ruins of Santa Luzia, Municipal museum - Bravães - Lindoso - Braga – Ponte de Lima golf course (18-hole). **Open** All year.

The Casa das Torres, preceded by a great porch with a coat of arms (from the bridge of Ponte de Lima and the palm tree, symbol of victory over the Spaniards), is quite easy to find from the center of Ponte de Lima. It is a fine manor house constructed in 1751 by the Italian architect Nazoni and still inhabited by the sixth generation of the same family. The rooms reserved for guests are on a level with the garden. All are spacious, not very light, with fine painted ceilings, prettily furnished in the old style. Our preference is for the twin room with its lovely bathroom in stone and porcelain, and its little drawing room. Several rooms are at the disposal of guests whether they want to take breakfast, play billiards or watch television. On the second floor are the private apartments with adjoining drawings rooms, and the dining room gleaming with chandeliers and the family silver. There is an extensive view over the green hills. In one of the buildings opening on the paved courtyard, there is a very well-appointed apartment for four people who can live here more independently, the atmosphere in the mainhouse being rather austere.

How to get there *(Map 1): 6km south of Ponte de Lima towards Barcelos on N204.*

Casa de Várzea ^{TH*}

Beiral do Lima 4990 Ponte de Lima (Viana do Castelo)
Tel. 258-94 86 03 - Fax 258-94 84 12
Ana Maria and Inácio Barreto Caldas da Costa
E-mail: casa.varzea@netc.pt

Rooms 6 with bath, WC. **Price** Single 10,000-16,000Esc, double 12,500-14,000Esc, apart. 22,400Esc; extra bed 3,200Esc. **Meals** Breakfast included, served 8:00-9:00. **Evening meals** On request – mealtime specials 2,500Esc. **Restaurant** See p. 225-226. **Credit cards** Not accepted. **Pets** Dogs not allowed. **Facilities** Swimming pool, parking. **Nearby** Ponte de Lima (Church and Museum of São Francisco); market (Mon every 2 weeks) - Viana do Castelo: Church and Celtic ruins of Santa Luzia, Municipal museum - Bravães - Lindoso - Braga – Ponte de Lima golf course (18-hole). **Open** All year.

You can see the house above the terraced vineyards that surround it as you come into the village of Beiral. A path under a trellis leads you to the entrance. This is another old family house, where the present owner was born and which he has decided to restore to keep up the old family tradition of hospitality. While the architecture is that of an 18th-century house, the period furniture has not survived, even though the rooms are furnished with old-style piece, including a dressing-table with secret drawers. This means that the atmosphere is less strait-laced and more convivial. The bedrooms are on the ground floor or the second floor. They are simple, but comfortable, our own preference being for the one with the bell, because of its fine view. The kindness of Inácio and his willingness to help contribute greatly to the well-being of the house: he will invite you to sample his *vinho verde*, his aguardente and his home-made jams. If you wish, you can order a dinner to taste some regional specialties. A very pleasant and friendly place to stay.

How to get there (Map 1): 10km from Ponte de Lima, towards Ponte de Barca as far as Martinho da Gandra where you turn right for Beiral.

Quinta do Baganheiro ^{TH*}

Queijada
4990 Ponte de Lima (Viana do Castelo)
Tel. 258-94 16 12 - Fax 258-74 90 16

Rooms 2 with bath and 2 apartments (4-6 pers.) with bath, WC, TV. **Price** Double 14,000Esc, apart. 14,000-28,800Esc; extra bed 3,200Esc. **Meals** Breakfast included. **Restaurant** In Ponte de Lima see pp. 225-226. **Credit cards** Not accepted. **Pets** Dogs not allowed. **Facilities** Swimming pool, parking. **Nearby** Ponte de Lima (Church and Museum of São Francisco); market (Mon every 2 weeks) - Viana do Castelo: Church and Celtic ruins of Santa Luzia, Municipal museum - Bravães - Lindoso - Braga – Ponte de Lima golf course (18-hole). **Open** All year.

This rural manor house, surrounded by vineyards and close to Ponte de Lima, offers a breathtaking view of the Rio de Lima valley. On this vast property you find, in addition to the manor house, two small villas, the Casa da Eira and the Casa da Oliveira, both equipped to receive families. In the main house, the rooms are a little dark but nicely decorated, and there is a lounge plus an attractive dining room, all in *azulejos*. While more simple, the casitas, all pleasantly furnished in regional style, offer greater facilities for visiting the north of Portugal where the distances involved are never very great.

How to get there *(Map 1): 60km north of Porto towards Valença via A3, exit number 10: Vila Verde, towards Ponte de Lima.*

Paço da Gloria TH

Jolda
4970 Arcos de Valdevez (Viana do Castelo)
Tel. 258-94 71 77 - Fax 258-94 74 97

Rooms 10 with telephone, bath. **Price** double 20,000-25,000Esc; extra bed 3,500Esc. **Meals** Breakfast included. **Restaurant** In Ponte de Lima see pp. 225-226. **Credit cards** Not accepted. **Pets** Dogs not allowed. **Facilities** Swimming pool, parking. **Nearby** Ponte de Lima (Church and Museum of São Francisco); market (Mon every 2 weeks) - Viana do Castelo: Church and Celtic ruins of Santa Luzia, Municipal museum - Bravães - Lindoso - Braga — Ponte de Lima golf course (18-hole). **Open** All year.

The region around Ponte de Lima offers numerous possibilities for visitors to find lodging with the local inhabitants. These places are invariably of top quality and where the reception you receive is particularly cordial. The Paço da Gloria is truly a jewel in the crown of the Turismo d'Habitação. Once you embark on the road going to Jolda, you experience what the owner calls "the dance with the trees" which comes to an end only when you arrive at the château. Here you find Romanticism pushed to its limit as greenery climbs along the building's superb exterior adorned with towers, loggias, porches bearing coats of arms, battlements and red roofs, all singing a hymn to the beauty of stone. The garden is a delightful collection of staircases, fountains, trimmed boxwoods plus century-old pines and oaks. The two rooms in the paço are altogether on a par with the garden which is immense, as are the bathrooms which are lighted through glass-brick walls. The others, in what were once the stables, are equally comfortable. There is nothing more to be said; you simply have to visit this place.

How to get there (Map 1): *7km northwest of Ponte de Lima towards Arcos de Valdeves.*

Pousada do São Teotónio *

4930 Valença do Minho (Viana do Castelo)
Tel. 251-82 42 42 - Fax 251-82 43 97

Rooms 16 with air-conditioning, telephone, bath, WC, TV, minibar. **Price** Single 12,500-21,000Esc, double 14,300-22,500Esc; extra bed +30%. **Meals** Breakfast included, served 8:00-10:00. **Restaurant** With air-conditioning. Service 12:30PM-3:00PM, 7:30PM-10:00PM – à la carte 3,650Esc. Specialties: Fish - Salmón - Bacalhao da pousada. **Credit cards** All major. **Pets** Dogs not allowed. **Nearby** Fortress of Valença do Minho - Monte do Faro - Minho valley from Valença to S. Gregorio via N101. **Open** All year.

Opposite the Spanish town of Tuy, Valença do Minho is a very touristy village dominating the left bank of the Minho River. This fortified town, made up of two strongholds linked by a sole bridge, has been invaded by restaurants and boutiques. The Pousada do São Teotónio is inside the fortified sector, and from the lounge and dining room one can see the other bank of the Minho River and the Galician town. The rooms, even though a little dated in their decor, are very comfortable. Rooms 1, 2, 3, 7, 9 and 11 all have terraces or balconies overlooking the gardens and ramparts. The family cuisine is good and the ambiance friendly.

How to get there (Map 1): 122km north of Porto via N13; opposite the Spanish border.

156

Casa de Rodas ^{TH*}

4950 Monção (Viana do Castelo)
Tel. 251-65 21 05
Sra Maria Luisa Távora

Rooms 9 and 1 apartment (2 pers.) with bath. **Price** Single 11,600Esc, double and apart. 14,000Esc; extra bed 3,000Esc. **Meals** Breakfast included. **Credit cards** Not accepted. **Pets** Dogs not allowed. **Facilities** Swimming pool. **Nearby** Fortress of Valença do Minho - Monte do Faro - Minho valley from Valença to S. Gregorio via N101 - Viana do Castelo. **Open** All year.

The road that follows the winding course of the Minhoia River is lined with eucalyptus, pines, and trellised vines–producing the famous *vinho verde*–and passes through large wine-making villages such as Monção. The Casa de Rodas is a beautiful manorhouse attached to the vineyard that produces the "Avantinho" wine, one of the major wines of this region. The entrance to the house is sheltered by two enormous magnolias. The lounges and bedrooms display family souvenirs and antique furniture accumulated over many generations. Breakfast is served in the kitchen, which has preserved its immense open fireplace. You can enjoy walks in the garden bordered by box hedges, or in the woods surrounding the property.

How to get there *(Map 1): 120km north of Porto via N13, 69km of Viano do Castelo.*

Quinta da Boa Viagem ᴬᵀ*

Além do Rio 4900-036 Areosa
Tel. 258-83 58 35 - Fax 258-83 68 36
Sr Teixeira de Queiroz

Apartments 3 with kitchenette, 1 bedroom, bath; 2 apart. with kitchenette, 2 bedrooms, bath; 1 apart. with kitchenette, 3 bedrooms, bath. **Price** apart. 2 pers. 14,000Esc, apart. 4 pers. 22,400Esc, apart. 6 pers. 28,800Esc. **Meals** Breakfast included, served 8:00-10:00. **Restaurant** In Valença do Minho see p. 226. **Credit cards** Not accepted. **Pets** Dogs not allowed. **Facilities** Swimming pool, parking. **Nearby** Ponte de Lima (Church and Museum of São Francisco) - Viana do Castelo: Church and Celtic ruins of Santa Luzia, Municipal museum - Bravães - Lindoso - Beaches — Ponte de Lima golf course (18-hole). **Open** All year.

Built in the 16th century on a hill facing the sea, Boa Viagem has long been a spot venerated by fishermen. This is a very pretty "quinta" with saffron-colored walls and red shutters. The apartments for guests are in the former farm buildings which have been tastefully decorated with canopied beds, and regional fabrics and prints; all have a lounge and open fireplace. On the ground floor they open straight out onto the side of a hill, with a marvelous park filled with fountains, ponds, and pretty white-stone seating, from which walkers may admire the enchanting view of the sea stretching away to the horizon. One can enjoy the same view from the swimming pool, situated near a garden. José Teixeira de Queiroz and his wife, a French teacher, will make your stay a very special one.

How to get there *(Map 1): 75km north of Porto via N13, in Viana do Castelo towards Valença road for 3km; then turn right at the sign "Turismo do habitação."*

Pousada Monte de Santa Luzia *

4900 Viana do Castelo
Monte Santa Luzia
Tel. 258-82 88 89 - Fax 258-82 88 92

Rooms 47 and 1 suite with air-conditioning, telephone, bath, WC, satellite TV, minibar; elevator. **Price** Single 14,800-25,000Esc, double 16,300-26,500Esc, suite 24,300-39,300Esc; extra bed +30%. **Meals** Breakfast included, served 8:00-10:00. **Restaurant** Service 12:30PM-3:00PM, 7:30PM-10:00PM – à la carte 3,650Esc. **Credit cards** All major. **Pets** Dogs not allowed. **Facilities** Swimming pool, tennis, parking. **Nearby** Ponte de Lima (Church and Museum of São Francisco) - Viana do Castelo: Church and Celtic ruins of Santa Luzia, Municipal museum - Bravães - Lindoso – Povoa de Varzim golf course (9-hole). **Open** All year.

This hotel is found on the hill of Santa Luzia, reached by funicular or by car via a pretty paved road that climbs with hairpin turns up through the pine trees, eucalyptus, and mimosas. From the hotel's windows and beautiful terrace are magnificent panoramic views over the town, the estuary of the Lima River, and long ocean beaches. The interior surprises with its contemporary decor, which is a great success. The furniture was designed a specially for the hotel and is perfectly adapted to such vast interior spaces. The bedrooms are very comfortable, the service impeccable and the cuisine and wine cellar excellent.

How to get there (Map 1): 70km north of Porto via N13 to Viana do Castelo, then take the road to Santa Luzia.

Casa Grande de Bandeira ^{TH*}

4900 Viana do Castelo
Largo das Carmelitas, 488
Tel. 258-82 31 69
Sra Calado Majer de Faria

Rooms 3 with 2 communal bath. **Price** Single 11,600Esc, double 14,000Esc; extra bed 3,200Esc.
Meals Breakfast included. **Restaurant** See p. 225. **Credit cards** Not accepted. **Pets** Dogs not allowed.
Nearby Ponte de Lima (Church and Museum of São Francisco) - Viana do Castelo: Church and Celtic
ruins of Santa Luzia, Municipal museum - Bravães - Lindoso – Povoa de Varzim golf course (9-hole).
Open All year.

Very well situated on a little square in the historical quarter of Viana do Castelo, this old house has belonged to the same family for many generations. You will be warmly welcomed by Maria Teresa, who will show you a round the house and garden, where she grows magnificent camellias and black bamboo from China. The furniture, family objects, and souvenirs all add to the charm of this traditional house. Three rooms reserved for guests are not very large but have a lovely view over the garden. This is a place that will attract those preferring not to stay in a hotel, providing that sharing the bathroom is not a problem.

How to get there (Map 1): 70km north of Porto via N13.

Casa de Esteiró TH

4910 Caminha (Viana do Castelo)
Tel. 258-72 13 33 - Fax 258-92 13 56
Maria do Patrocínio Villas-Boas

Rooms 3, 1 apart. (2 pers.), 1 apart. (4 pers.) with bath, TV in apart.; wheelchair access in apart. **Price** Double 16,000Esc, apart (2 pers.) 11,000-12,500Esc, apart (4 pers.) 19,000-20,000Esc. **Meals** Breakfast included, served 9:00-11:00. **Restaurant** See p. 226. **Credit cards** Not accepted. **Pets** Dogs not allowed. **Facilities** Swimming pool, parking. **Nearby** Caminha - On th side of Minho de Caminha in Valença do Minho - Viana do Castelo - Bravães - Lindoso - Ponte de Lima — Povoa de Varzim golf course (9-hole). **Open** All year.

Caminha is a charming town on the estuary of the River Minho which long had to protect itself from the heights of its fortified promontory from invasion by the neighboring Galicians. The historic center has preserved some fine remains like the collegiate church and the houses with coats of arms of rua dereita. This former 18th-century hunting lodge is on the edge of a rather noisy road, but in a garden of century-old box trees and many other species: oaks and chestnuts cohabit with palm trees and orange trees, hortensias with camellias and holly. Until recently, the house passed down the female line, the present owner being a man without a sister. This is the source of a number of anecdotes: so it was here in 1915 that the first international tennis tournament took place, the grand-father, whose large portrait is in the drawing-room, founded the Bank of Portugal and the oratory preserves the field altar that was brought back here with the remains of the great-grandfather, who died in battle. The interior is also full of souvenirs, giving the place something of the atmosphere of a museum. The rooms are luxuriously furnished. The garden house with two comfortable, independent apartments is simpler. Elegant service.

How to get there (Map 1): 1km south of Caminha.

Paço d'Anha [TH]

Paço d'Anha 4900 Viana do Castelo
Tel. 258-32 24 59 - Fax 258-32 39 04
Sr A. J. Agorreta d'Alpuim

Apartments 4 with 2 bedrooms, living room and kitchenette, telephone, WC, bath, TV. **Price** 2 pers. 18,000Esc, 4 pers. 25,500Esc, 5 pers. 31,500Esc (cleaned included). **Meals** Breakfast included. **Restaurant** See p. 225. **Credit card** Amex. **Pets** Dogs allowed. **Facilities** Tennis, parking. **Nearby** Lindoso - Church of São Salvador in Bravães - Viana do Castelo - National park of Peneda-Gerês (Rio Cavado in Leonte, Serra do Gerês, Fraga negra Belvedere) - Beaches (3km). **Open** All year.

"**P**aço" means that this place has had the privilege of receiving the king: the visit dates back to 1580 when he was hiding from the Spaniards. The property's extensive acreage stretches over the slopes of a hill, and includes a vineyard producing the famous *vinho verde* wine bottled on the estate, a farm, and a charming park with a narrow, winding path. In the distance is the sea. The apartments are set in the former distillery, the stables, and the wine pressroom; all are on the ground floor, and have direct access to the surrounding nature. The host is very friendly and speaks perfect French and English, and he will make you share his love of his estate and his region.

How to get there (Map 1): 60km north of Porto by IC 1; 15 km before Viana do Castelo, take the Braga-Barcelos exit; at the roundabout, take the north turning towards the industrial zone; after Shell, turn left and follow the blue signs showing Turismo d'Habitacão, then Paço d'Anha.

Estalagem da Boega

4920 Vila Nova da Cerveira - Gondarém (Viana do Castelo)
Quinta do Outeiral
Tel. 251-590 05 00 - Fax 251-590 05 09
Sr Amorim

Category ★★★ **Rooms** 30 and 4 suites with telephone, bath, WC, satellite TV. **Price** Double 9,500-16,500Esc, suite 11,000-18,000Esc. **Meals** Breakfast included, served 8:00-10:30. **Restaurant** Service 1:30PM and 8:30PM - closed Sun evening – mealtime specials 2,850Esc – Specialties: Vitela assada - Bacalhao a Boega. **Credit cards** Amex, Visa, Eurocard, MasterCard. **Pets** Dogs not allowed. **Facilities** Swimming pool, tennis, parking. **Nearby** Lindoso - Church of São Salvador in Bravães - Viana do Castelo - National park of Peneda-Gerês (Rio Cavado in Leonte, Serra do Gerês, Fraga negra Belvedere). **Open** All year.

The Estalagem da Boega numbers among the many old rural properties that have been converted into small family hotels. Its traditional-style architecture blends well with the surrounding countryside. Here you'll find comfortable, well-equipped rooms, a TV- and video-room, and a superb swimming pool in a garden. Charming details abound, including fireplaces decorated with *azulejos* tiles, wooden ceilings, terraces (Rooms 12 and 13), and the romantic "nuptial chamber." The rooms in the annex are less attractive. After dinner on Saturday evenings the hotel organizes fado singing.

How to get there (Map 1): 100km north of Porto via N13.

Pousada Dom Dinis *

4920-296 Vila Nova de Cerveira (Viana do Castelo)
Praça da Liberdade
Tel. 251-79 56 01 - Fax 279 56 04
António Neiva

Rooms 26 and 3 suites with air-conditioning, telephone, bath, WC, satellite TV, minibar. **Price** Single 12,300-21,000Esc, double 14,300-23,000Esc, suite 19,800-28,800Esc; extra bed +30%. **Meals** Breakfast included, served 8:00-10:30. **Restaurant** Service 12:30PM-3:00PM, 7:30PM-10:00PM – à la carte 3,650Esc – Portuguese cooking. **Credit cards** All major. **Pets** Dogs allowed on request. **Nearby** Lindoso - Church of São Salvador in Bravães - Viana do Castelo - National park of Peneda-Gerês (Rio Cavado in Leonte, Serra do Gerês, Fraga negra Belvedere). **Open** All year.

On the banks of the Minho River, the Pousada was built like a small village inside the ramparts and towers of the medieval château of Vila Nova de Cerveira. Absolute quiet reigns in this enclosed and protected place, and in all the rooms one finds clear signs of good taste. The bedrooms are spacious and well furnished, with good amenities; thirteen have a terrace and suite number 6 even has a small garden. One can walk around the sentries' path on the ramparts, with its beautiful view over the river (ferry 200 m from the hotel), countryside, and town.

How to get there (Map 1): 100km north of Porto via N13.

Casa da Azinhaga ^{TR}

Azinhaga 2150 Golegã (Santarém)
Tel. 249-957 146 - Fax 249-957 182
Sr Joao Vicente Oliveirax Sousa

Rooms 5 and 1 suite (for 4 pers. with air-conditioning) with bath, WC. **Price** Double 14,000-16,000Esc, suite 28,000-32,000Esc. **Meals** Breakfast included, served 8:00-10:00. **Evening meals** On request. **Credit cards** Not accepted. **Pets** Dogs not allowed. **Facilities** Swimming pool, riding, parking. **Nearby** Tomar: Convento do Christo, old town (synagogue) - Barrage of Castelo de Bode - Abrantes -Fátima - Santarém - Castelo de Almourol. **Open** All year.

Coming from Lisbon, you leave the highway at Torres Nova and start inland through wheat fields and olive trees before you arrive at the village of Azinhaga. The casa is on the main street and, with its ivy-covered façade, it is impossible to miss. Once through the gate, you discover a courtyard surrounded by stables that once housed horses and carriages as well as the house whose architecture may be discerned through yet more flourishing ivy. The rooms are in an independent wing, all comfortably furnished including the suite which is more like an apartment with a private entrance and lounge. The only room to avoid is the one on the street, more for the view - or lack of it - than for the noise. The large living room is at your disposal; it is very nicely furnished and has imposing cowhide details which figure prominently in the region's traditional decoration. Behind the large courtyard is an attractive swimming pool, a splendid place to cool off during the summer months. It is here that your breakfast is served. This is an excellent hotel, one offering exceptional landscapes.

How to get there (*Map 3*): *128km north of Lisboa via motorway, exit Torres Novas, then Golegã and Azinhaga.*

Quinta de Santo André (São Jorge) ᵀᴿ

2600 Vila Franca de Xira (Lisboa)
Estrada Monte Gordo, Apt 132
Tel. 263-272 143 - Fax 263-272 776 - Sra Brumm

Rooms 5 with bath, WC. **Price** Single 6,000Esc, double 12,000Esc, suite 15,000Esc. **Meals** Breakfast included, served from 9:00. **Restaurant** See p. 226. **Credit cards** Not accepted. **Pets** Dogs allowed. **Facilities** Swimming pool, garage. **Nearby** Monte Gordo Belvedere - Lisboa – Estoril golf course (9- and 18-hole). **Closed** Nov 1 - 15.

Lost in the greenery of the countryside, this beautiful house has a fuchsia-color roughcast finish, and the façade of the upper floor is clad with ocre-color tiles. The area offers very good riding country and the owners will advise you of the nearest stables. For those who are not tempted by horseriding, the swimming pool will provide many a pleasant afternoon. You dine at a large communal guests' table among friends, then meet again beside the open fireplace. The bedrooms are all charming and comfortable. Only thirty kilometers from Lisbon Vila Franca de Xira provides a glimpse of the Portuguese countryside without having to drive too far.

How to get there *(Map 3): 30km northeast of Lisboa towards Estrada Monte Gordo; follow sign or ask for "la Quinta dos Alemanes."*

Quinta do Alto

2600 Vila Franca de Xira (Lisboa)
Estrada Monte Gordo
Tel. 263-276 850 - 21-317 32 99 - Fax 263-276 027
Sr Manuel Ricardo

Rooms 10 with telephone, bath, WC, satellite TV. **Price** Single 16,000-18,000Esc, double 18,500-20,500Esc. **Meals** Breakfast included, served 8:00-10:30. **Evening meals** On request. **Credit cards** All major. **Pets** Dogs allowed. **Facilities** Swimming pool, tennis, squash, sauna, riding, parking. **Nearby** Monte Gordo Belvedere - Lisboa – Estoril golf course (9- and 18-hole). **Open** All year.

Not far from the two guest houses that typify Portuguese charm, the Quinta do Alto is quite original in that it offers traditional hotel facilities and highly professional service in the setting of an agricultural property. The old house where the owners live overlooks the Tagus River and its newly-added wing offers ten rooms. All of them are large, comfortable and nicely equipped and each has an individual shaded terrace. The decoration is somewhat impersonal but never in bad taste. There are plenty of leisure-time activities in the hotel itself, and here is an excellent place for a refreshing vacation.

How to get there *(Map 3): 30km northeast of Lisboa towards Estrada do Miradouro de Monte Gordo.*

Quinta das Covas TR

Cachoeiras 2600 Vila Franca de Xira (Lisboa)
Tel. 263-28 30 31 - Fax 263-28 45 43
Suzanna and Andreas Murschenhofer

Rooms 9 with bath or shower. **Price** Single and double 8,000-20,000Esc. **Meals** Breakfast included, served 6:00-11:30. **Restaurant** By reservation. **Credit cards** All major. **Pets** Dogs allowed. **Facilities** Parking. **Nearby** Monte Gordo Belvedere - Lisboa – Estoril golf course (9- and 18-hole). **Open** All year.

Twenty kilometers from Lisbon on the hills of Vila Franca is the small hamlet of Cachoeiras with its white houses outlined in bright colors. This is truly rural and authentic Portugal. The owners receive you in a noble residence on a three-hectare property dating from the 18th century. The principal building bypasses the rules of classical architecture in the decoration of the façades; they are painted yellow with white trim and enjoy the refreshing shade that magnolias and laurels always provide. You can choose either one of its three rooms (that share two bathrooms) which may be rented together for families or a room in one of the smaller buildings. The most attractive as well as the most spacious and the most expensive offers a large terrace with a fine view of the quinta's fruit trees. You mustn't miss having breakfast in the manor house where the dining room is handsomely decorated with *azulejos*. What was once a horse-pond fed by spring water has been transformed into a swimming pool and there is a nearby pergola, almost invisible among the walnut and orange trees.

How to get there (Map 3): 25km northeast of Lisboa, by N1, exit Vila Franca de Xira and Cachoeiras. At Cachoeiras, the first and second street on the right lead to the quinta.

Quinta Vale de Lobos ᵀᴴ

Azoia de Baixo 2000 Santarém
Tel. 243-42 92 64 - Fax 243-42 93 13
Veronica and Joachim Santos Lima

Rooms 4 and 2 cottages with bath. **Price** Single 13,000Esc, double 15,000Esc, cottage (2 pers. and 2 children) 18,000Esc; extra bed 3,000Esc. **Meals** Breakfast included for bedrooms, 8:00-11:00. **Restaurant** Lunch at the swimming pool by reservation. **Credit cards** Not accepted. **Pets** Dogs not allowed. **Facilities** Swimming pool, parking. **Nearby** Santarém - Tage valley to Vila franca de Xira (village of Manique do Intende) and to Torres Novas. **Open** All year.

A few kilometers from Santarém, the capital of Ribatejo, which dominates the lower valley of the Tagus, the magnificent estate of Vale de Lobos was for a time occupied by the famous Portugese writer, Alexandre Herculano. His room has been preserved as it was. The house is surrounded by a garden with lots of trees which has the good smell of pine and cedar. The interior has the charm of a house which has kept traces of its past. Breakfast is served in the main drawing room, richly decorated with old furniture. The rooms have plenty of style with their tall curtains giving the measure and height of the ceilings. We prefer the one situated at the end of the corridor with a balcony, over which the property's two-hundred year old tree throws its refreshing shade. The two apartments are situated in an annex; they are well-equipped but still small if you are considering a long stay. A siesta on the lawn by the pool is a delightful moment, especially if Veronica comes to tell you the story of the house.

How to get there (Map 3): 80km northeast of Lisbon; 6km northeast of Santarém towards Torres Novas.

Quinta da Anunciada Velha ^{TR}

Cem Soldos 2300 Tomar (Santarém)
Tel. 249-34 52 18/34 54 69 - Fax 249-34 57 52
Sra Sofia Pinto da França

Rooms 3, 1 suite and 2 apartments with telephone, bath. **Price** 2 pers. 12,000-15,000Esc. **Meals** Breakfast included, served 8:00-10:00. **Evening meals** On request. **Restaurant** See p. 226. **Credit cards** Not accepted. **Pets** Dogs allowed. **Facilities** Swimming pool, parking. **Nearby** Tomar: Convento do Christo, old town (synagogue) - Barrage of Castelo de Bode - Abrantes - Fátima - Santarém. **Closed** Dec, Jan and Feb.

The Convento do Christo is certainly the principal reason for visiting Tomar. It was enlarged during the 12th and 13th centuries, adding churches, cloisters and convent buildings which today are a compendium of the Portuguese architecture of the period. Not to be missed is the "Window of Tomar," a veritable treasure in itself. The Quinta da Anunciada Velha is an excellent place to stay with white buildings and yellow trimming enclosing a large courtyard. The salon offers a fine view of the countryside, its decoration somewhat superior to what is found in the rooms although all are quite spacious and offer similar views. In addition, the Casa da Aida, a small independent house with two rooms and a kitchen, is both attractive and highly typical of the region.

How to get there (Map 3): 3km of Tomar towards Torres Novas.

Quinta de Santa Bárbara

2250-093 Constância (Santarém)
Tel. 249-739 214 - Fax 249-739 373
Sr Manuel Vieiro da Feira

Rooms 8 with bath, WC. **Price** Single 9,000Esc, double 11,500-12,000Esc. **Meals** Breakfast included, served 8:00-10:00. **Restaurant** Service 12:00PM-3:00PM, 7:30PM-10:00PM. **Credit cards** Visa, Eurocard, MasterCard. **Pets** Dogs not allowed. **Facilities** Swimming pool, tennis, parking. **Nearby** Tomar: Convento do Christo, old town (synagogue) - Barrage of Castelo de Bode - Abrantes - Fátima - Santarém. **Open** All year.

When you travel through Portugal, you shouldn't miss staying at the Quinta de Santa Barbara which overlooks the village of Constancia in a heavily wooded valley. It is here that the Rio Zezere joins the Tagus. The quinta is a group of attractive 18th-century buildings constructed by a former governor of the West Indies. Later, they were then lived in by Jesuits before the current owners restored the quinta in 1987. The imposing portal bears the coat of arms of the original builder and beyond it is a large courtyard with palm trees on either side of the entrance. Inside is a series of immense lounges with high ceilings, some of stone and others with ornate frescoes. The impressive furniture dates from the 18th and 19th centuries, and the floors are made of large wooden planks. Each of the rooms has its own charm, and its interesting furniture often suggests some form of religious inspiration. Our favorite is the one you reach via a small gallery above the nave of the small family church. The restaurant is in a large room with a vaulted ceiling of red brick. The food is good, and the swimming pool has been built on several levels, allowing guests to enjoy the panorama.

How to get there (Map 3): 128km north of Lisboa via motorway, exit Torres Novas, then Entrocamento and Constância.

Casa do Foral TH

2250 Rio Maior (Santarém)
Rua da Boavista, 10
Tel. 243-99 26 10 - Fax 243-99 26 11 - Carlos Higgs Madeira
E-mail: moinhoforal@hotmail

Rooms 6 with bath, WC and 1 apart. (2 pers.); wheelchair access. **Price** Single 8,400Esc, double 10,600Esc, apart. 10,600Esc. **Meals** Breakfast included, from 8:00. **Restaurant** See p. 226. **Credit cards** Visa, Eurocard, MasterCard. **Pets** Dogs allowed. **Facilities** Swimming pool. **Nearby** Óbidos - Óbidos lagoon (boating) - Church of Senhor de Pedra - Monastery of Batalha - Monastery of Alcobaça - Caldas da Rainha - Santarém - Lisboa — Golden Eagle golf course. **Open** All year.

Casa do Foral is a simple, rustic and inexpensive place in a little town joined to Lisbon (57km) by the motorway, which allows one to go out on excursions to see the sights of Estremadura. Closer still are the natural park of Serra d'Aire and Candeciros. The façade is covered by a mass of greenery, like the little garden with its many trees and its swimming pool creating a very restful oasis in the center of town. You will also find a pavillion in the garden with a billiard table and other games. The rooms are in the house, well-proportioned, simply decorated but with every comfort, including television (rare in a guest house). In summer, breakfast is served on the patio, while in winter they make use of the magnificent drawing room covered in panels of *azulejos* dating from the end of the 18th Century, decorated with old weapons and hunting trophies. Given the proximity of Satarém and Vila Franca de Xira, the two bull-fighting centers in Portugal, you can watch a tourada (a corrida in which the bull is not put to death, between Easter and October), which causes great excitement, fuelled by the drinking of the local wine, Bucelas.

How to get there (Map 3): 30km between Óbidos and Santarém.

172

Quinta da Cortiçada

Outeiro da Cortiçada
2040 Rio Maior (Santarém)
Tel. 243-47 00 00 - Fax 243-47 00 09

Rooms 6 and 2 suites with air-conditioning, telephone, bath, satellite TV. **Price** Single 12,400-16,500Esc, double 14,400-18,500Esc, suite 17,500-21,600Esc. **Meals** Breakfast included, served 8:00-11:00. **Restaurant** Service 12:00PM-3:00PM, 7:30PM-10:00PM – mealtime specials 4,000Esc. **Credit cards** All major. **Pets** Dogs allowed. **Facilities** Piscine, tennis, parking, garage. **Nearby** Óbidos - Óbidos lagoon (boating) - Church of Senhor de Pedra - Monastery of Batalha - Monastery of Alcobaça - Caldas da Rainha - Santarém - Lisboa – Golden Eagle golf course. **Open** All year.

The road leading to the quinta is magical, passing through timeless villages among forests of pine and eucalyptus. Situated fourteen kilometers from Rio Maior, it is signposted along the whole route. It should be said that this is an estate of 96 hectares which was a very prosperous and very rich farm in the last century. Then it fell into ruins and was bought up and reconstructed in its original form in 1990. Two very long buildings in salmon pink and white lie on either side of the door of the quinta, which is then made up of several buildings linked by paved paths, as in a village. Around it all is a French-style garden with trimmed box hedges, a lake across which impassive swans glide and a swimming pool hidden by large plane trees. The large public rooms on the ground floor enjoy the view of this green enclosure. The rooms are comfortably done up and decorated in the spirit of the region. The suites look out over the lake. Meals are served at the great walnut table in the dining room. Majestic atmosphere, with a slightly operatic side, in which the silence is broken only by the cry of the swans and the clippers of the gardeners trimming the hedge.

How to get there (*Map 3*): *30km west of Santarém, 14km from Rio Maior.*

Quinta da Ferraria

Ribeira de São João 2040 Rio Maior
Tel. 243-94 50 01 - Fax 243-95 56 96
Sra Teresa Nobre

Rooms 11 and 1 suite with air-conditioning, telephone, bath, satellite TV. **Price** Single 11,300-13,400Esc, double 13,200-16,000Esc, suite 14,400-18,500Esc, apart. 19,500-23,700Esc; extra bed 4,800-6,200Esc. **Meals** Breakfast included, served 7:30-10:30. **Restaurant** By reservation – mealtime specials 3,800Esc. **Credit cards** All major. **Pets** Dogs not allowed. **Facilities** Swimming pool, tennis, riding, parking. **Nearby** Óbidos - Óbidos lagoon (boating) - Church of Senhor de Pedra - Monastery of Batalha - Monastery of Alcobaça - Caldas da Rainha - Santarém - Lisboa – Golden Eagle golf course. **Open** All year.

Quinta da Ferraria is some sixty kilometers from Lisbon. It is a huge estate with many associated buildings and a church, which has been restored in the manner of a little village. The little streets have been paved intheold-fashioned way, the houses have been repainted in white and blue, and the roofs have recovered their chimneys which are so typical of Portugese rural architecture. The rooms are near the swimming pool. They are very comfortable with parquet floors, quality rustic furniture and well-chosen fabrics. The best situated are those with a view of the swimming pool and the fields where the estate horses graze. An ecological museum has opened in the former stables illustrating the rural society of the area. A pleasant stop, but one that seems to have been well organized for receptions.

How to get there (Map 3): 100km north of Lisboa; 30km west of Óbidos.

Quinta da Alcaidaria - Mór ᵀᴴ

2490 Ourém (Santarém)
Tel. and Fax 249-54 22 31
Sra Teresa Alvaiázere

Rooms 7 and 2 apartments with bath, WC. **Price** Single 15,000-19,000Esc, double 18,000-23,000Esc; extra bed 6,000Esc. **Meals** Breakfast included, served 8:30-10:30. **Snacks** Available on request. **Credit cards** Not accepted. **Pets** Dogs not allowed. **Facilities** Swimming pool, parking. **Nearby** Castle and Collegiata de Ourém - Fátima - Caves of Mira de Aire, São Mamede, Alvados and Santo Antònio - Tomar. **Open** All year.

A few kilometers from Vila Nova de Ourém on the road leading to Tomar, this ravishing inn is hidden away at the end of a long tree-lined avenue. The small manor house with its modest appearance has belonged to the same family since the 17th century. Despite recent renovation, the buildings have lost none of their charm; the walls are covered with abundant plants and flowers. The rooms are comfortable and refined, and look out on the garden and countryside, or on the small courtyard shaded by plane trees. This peaceful and attractive place also has the advantage of a beautiful swimming pool.

How to get there (Map 3): 28km southeast of Leiria via C113.

Estalagem do Caçador

5340 Macedo de Cavaleiro (Bragança)
Largo Manuel Pinto de Azevedo
Tel. 278-42 63 54 - Fax 278-42 63 81
Sra Manuela

Rooms 25 with telephone, bath, WC, TV; elevator. **Price** Single 11,000-13,200Esc, double 14,300-17,600Esc. **Meals** Breakfast included. **Restaurant** Service 12:30PM-2:00PM, 7:30PM-10:00PM – mealtime specials 2,700-3,500Esc, also à la carte – Specialties: Fish and meat dishes. **Credit cards** All major. **Pets** Dogs allowed except in restaurant. **Facilities** Swimming pool, garage (400Esc). **Nearby** Bragança - Vila Real - Mateus (Manor Solar of Mateus). **Closed** Dec 24 - 25.

This inn, set in the region of Tras-os-Montes ("beyond the mountains"), is near the Spanish-Portuguese frontier in the northeast. The Estalagem do Caçador is found in the lively village square, and a happy holiday ambiance reigns throughout. Rooms here are comfortable, and some have an unusual decor. The swimming pool just beside the hotel is a real treat in the month of August.

How to get there *(Map 2): 40km south of Bragança.*

Solar das Arcas

5340 Arcas (Bragança)
Torre D Chama
Tel. 278-40 14 22 - Fax 278-40 12 33
Maria Francisca Pessanha Lago Montanha

Room 1 with bath, WC, 4 apartments (2 pers.), 2 apartments (4 pers.); wheelchair access in the apart. **Price** Double 18,000Esc, apart. (2 pers.) 10,000Esc, apart. (4 pers.) 20,000Esc. **Meals** Breakfast included in bedroom. **Evening meals** On request. **Credit cards** Not accepted. **Pets** Dogs not allowed. **Facilities** Swimming pool, parking. **Nearby** Bragança - Vila Real - Mateus (Manor Solar of Mateus). **Open** All year.

This magnificent manor house, a fine example of an aristocratic home from the 17th and 18th Centuries, is situated in a distant corner of Portugal and one seldom visited by tourists. It still belongs to the Pessanha family, descendants of Manuel Pessanha, a Genoese who came to Portugal in the reign of D Dinis to teach the sailors of the country the art of navigation. It is common, but still surprising to see such refined architecture in a small village street: its long white façade with its bright blue plinth is divided by a long series of windows surmounted by pediments and finely sculpted granite ornaments. Despite this, the atmosphere of the house is welcoming. Old family furniture graces the drawing rooms and the guest room next to the private chapel. The latter still has its altar with rich woodwork and gilt decorated with paintings. Old and new harmonize in the comfortable, well-decorated apartments. A good place to stop over or for anyone who is not afraid of immersion in the real Portugal for nature or sporting holidays, close to the Park of Montezinho and the Azibo dam.

How to get there (Map 2): 54km south of Bragança.

Casa da Avó TH

5160 Torre de Moncôrvo (Bragança)
Torre D Chama
Tel. 279-25 24 01
Macedo Carvalho Ribeiro

Rooms 5 with air-conditioning, bath, WC. **Price** Single 10,225-11,128Esc, double 12,630-14,034Esc.
Meals Breakfast included. No restaurant. **Credit cards** Not accepted. **Pets** Dogs not allowed. **Nearby**
Vila Real - Vila Nova de Foz Côa - Mirandela. **Closed** Dec and Jan.

If you are crossing this region of Tras-os-Montes in the northeast, which is still more beautiful when the almond and cherry trees are in flower, do not fail to stop over at Torre de Moncôrvo. The village has an interesting architectural past, like this pretty Casa da Avó with its typical façade: *azulejos* and cast-iron balconies. Inside, all the family furniture from the late 19th Century has been preserved. The public rooms with their walls hung with silk and their molded ceilings are decorated with precious furniture and objets d'art. The rooms are no less richly furnished and overlook a peaceful garden where the hundred-year old mandarin tree supplies the fruit for a delicious jam which you may have a breakfast. If you have a choice, ask for the room where presidents Soares and Sanpaio slept when they visited the region. A welcoming spot which will enrich your understanding of the country.

How to get there *(Map 2): 97km south of Bragança on N102.*

Casa das Torres de Oliveira ^{TH*}

Oliveira
5040 Mesão Frio (Vila Real)
Tel. 254-33 67 43/21-840 64 86 - Fax 254-33 61 95/21-846 33 19
Isadora Regüela de Sousa Girão

Rooms 3 and 1 suite with bath or shower. **Price** Double 16,500Esc. **Meals** Breakfast included. No restaurant. **Credit cards** Not accepted. **Pets** Dogs not allowed. **Facilities** Swimming pool. **Nearby** Vila Real - Solar de Mateus - Douro Valley (Peso da Régua: the station and the Casa de Douro) - Amarante - Guimarães. **Open** All year.

After leaving Péso de Regua where, if you have the time, you shouldn't miss visiting the train station and the Winegrowers' Federation at Casa do Douro, you move out of the Douro Valley, going up hills crowned with vineyards. La Casa das Torres is on the outskirts of the town, a remarkable building with white façades and countless windows in gray stone framed by pink tiles. In the interior courtyard, you have numerous fountains as well as a view of the entire valley. The hotel has three rooms, all large and comfortable, as well as a suite. The garden and the swimming pool offer a marvelous view, and in addition to the wine produced by the owner, these are but a few of the reasons to stop here.

How to get there *(Map 1): 36km southeast of Vila Real to Peso da Régua, then on the right towards Oliveira. 10km of Mesão Frio.*

Casa d'Alem [TR]

Oliveira
5040 Solo Mesão Frio (Vila Real)
Tel. and Fax 254-32 19 91
Sr Paulo José Ferreira de Sousa Dias Pinheiro

Rooms 4 with bath or shower. **Price** Double 10,800Esc. **Meals** Breakfast included. No restaurant.
Credit cards Not accepted. **Pets** Dogs not allowed. **Facilities** Swimming pool, garage (400Esc).
Nearby Vila Real - Mateus (Manor Solar of Mateus) - Douro Valley (Peso da Régua). **Open** All year.

When crossing the Douro Valley, particularly beautiful during the grape harvest, to go to Porto or the ocean, you cannot help but be enchanted by the countryside and the villages where time appears to have stood still. This is especially so when you walk along the streets of Oliveira and finally discover the delightful Casa d'Alem, a house belonging to a land owner and now run by his granddaughter. The narrow façade gives no indication that behind it are numerous buildings along with a garden giving onto the valley. There are four rooms, one of which is particularly attractive with a large lounge and a lovely view; the others are rather ordinary. In addition, you will find terraces, shady bowers and a swimming pool, all allowing you to truly enjoy the natural surroundings and the soft golden light that illuminates the vineyards in the evening.

How to get there (Map 1): 36km southeast of Vila Real to Peso da Régua, then on the right towards Oliveira. 10km of Mesão Frio.

Casa Agricola da Levada ^{TH*}

Timpeira 5000 Vila Real
Tel. 259-32 21 90 - Fax 259-34 69 55
Sr Paganini da Costa Lobo
E-mail: casa-agricola-levada@netc.pt

Rooms 4 with telephone, bath, WC, TV. **Price** Double 12,500Esc, extra bed 3,000Esc. **Meals** Breakfast included, served 8:30-10:00. **Evening meals** On request – mealtime specials 4,000Esc. **Credit cards** Not accepted. **Pets** Dogs not allowed. **Facilities** Swimming pool, parking. **Nearby** Mateus: Manor Solar of Mateus - Serra do Marão - Estrada (road) from Vila Real to Amarante - Estrada from Vila Real to Mondim de Basto. **Open** All year on request.

Built in 1922 by a governor of Mozambique, this building in the Portuguese Art Deco-style is attributed to the famous architect Raul Liria. Opened a few years ago, the hotel offers four rooms. As with all such guesthouses, one is assured of a certain degree of refinement, but one enjoys a few more amenities. The well-kept garden is covered with roses in summer, and the fish-filled river will delight anglers. The more adventurous can mount donkeys or mules to tour the "quinta." The house cuisine is good and a wide choice of regional wines is offered. The surrounding countryside offers interesting excursions, for example by train along the banks of the Corgo.

How to get there *(Map 2): 95km east of Porto by IP4 (towards Vila Real), exit Norte. Then towards Vila Real, but take a left turn towards Mateus at the BP service station, then the road on the left before crossing the bridge.*

Vidago Palace Hotel

Vidago 5425 (Vila Real)
Parque de Vidago
Tel. 276-90 73 56 - Fax 276-90 73 59
Sr Jaime Alves

Category ★★★★ **Rooms** 82 and 89 suites with air-conditioning, telephone, bath, satellite TV, minibar; elevator. **Price** Single 11,000-18,000Esc, double 13,000-21,000Esc, suite 22,000-32,000Esc. **Meals** Breakfast included, served 7:30-10:00. **Restaurant** Service 12:30PM-3:00PM, 7:30PM-10:30PM – à la carte – Regional dishes and fish. **Credit cards** All major. **Pets** Dogs not allowed. **Facilities** Swimming pool. **Nearby** Vidago Park - Mateus: Manor Solar of Mateus - Santo Tirso - Guimarães. **Open** All year.

An impressive building emerges from the pine and eucalyptus forests so common in northern Portugal. Its façade runs a full one hundred meters and rises to three stories with a number of large windows rimmed with white stone which sets off very nicely the rust-colored walls. The Vidago Palace recalls the era when a certain society traveled throughout Europe stopping at one "grand hotel" after another. After mounting the monumental staircase, you enter the lobby with, on one side, the restaurant with its seven-meter-high ceilings and surrounding gallery. You reach the equally ornate bar from the other side. The central lobby with its immense and impressive glass ceiling has two staircases leading to the rooms. The rooms can hardly match the impression created by the lobby, the restaurant and the bar, but they are elegant despite the furniture which is functional. All of the rooms look out on the Palace's magnificent garden. The hotel is very well equipped to provide personal all the comforts and quiet enjoyment. This is a unique place, an old and elegant palace in the midst of a wild and natural setting.

How to get there (Map 2): 140km east of Porto.

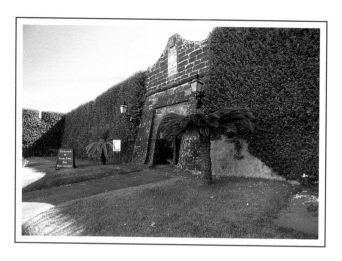

Estalagem de Santa Cruz

Faial Island
9900 Horta
Rua Vasco da Gama
Tel. 292-293 021/22 - Fax 292-293 906 - Sra Manuela Lacerda

Category ★★★★ **Rooms** 25 with air-conditioning, with telephone, bath, TV, 11 with minibar. **Price** Single 11,900-18,300Esc, double 13,700-20,100Esc; extra bed 3,300-4,500Esc. **Meals** Breakfast included, served 7:00-10:00 – half board +2,600Esc, full board +4,700Esc (per pers.). **Restaurant** Service 12:30PM-2:30PM, 7:30PM-10:00PM – mealtime specials 2,200Esc, also à la carte. **Credit cards** Amex, Visa, Eurocard, MasterCard. **Pets** Dogs not allowed. **Nearby** Horta: Church of São Francisco, Nossa Senhora do Carmo (azulejos, view) - Cadera - Caves of Costa de Feteira. **Open** All year.

Faial is the island in the Azores where it's all happening. Yachts flying international flags lie in the harbor and world-famous skippers hang out at the Café Sport, better known as Peter's Friends as it has been run by the same Irish family for over fifty years. It is also here on the port that you will find the Santa Cruz, built inside a fort dating from the 16th century. The side facing the street offers ramparts covered with climbing greenery, and there is a delightful lawn spread out in front of the side facing the sea. The rooms look out over the port with balconies allowing you to watch the boats come and go. This is surely the most charming of the hotels in the center of town.

How to get there (*Map 7*): *On the port.*

Hotel Faial

Faial Island
9900 Horta
Rua Consul Dabney
Tel. 292-292 181/7 - Fax 292-292 081 - Sr Jose de Sousa

Category ★★★★ **Rooms** 119 and 4 suites with telephone, bath, TV, minibar in the suites. **Price** Single 11,500-16,570Esc, double 12,500-17,700Esc, suite 15,200-20,500Esc; extra bed 3,500-4,950Esc. **Meals** Breakfast included, served 7:30-10:00 - half board +2,700Esc, full board +5,400Esc (per pers.). **Restaurant** Service 12:30PM-2:30PM, 7:45PM-10:00PM — mealtime specials 2,700Esc, also à la carte. **Credit cards** Visa, Eurocard, MasterCard. **Pets** Dogs not allowed. **Facilities** Swimming pool, tennis. **Nearby** Horta: Church of São Francisco, Nossa Senhora do Carmo (azulejos, view) - Cadera - Caves of Costa de Feteira. **Open** All year.

The beech trees - "faia" - covering the slopes of this volcanic cone of the Caldeira have given their name to this island, also know as The Blue Island because of the profusion of hydrangea found here. The Faial, located in the midst of the city's greenery, is delightfully quiet and looks out on the sea and the volcano on Pico Island. It is built along international lines with boutiques, conference rooms and a hair-dressing salon, but given the limited number of tourists it attracts, you can enjoy these things without being trampled by vacationers. There is also a nearby sailing club. It is decorated in the style of the 70s and has not quite been brought up to date. A good hotel for a lengthy stay.

How to get there (Map 7): *In the center of the town.*

Residential Infante

Faial Island
9900 Horta
Tel. 292-292 837

Rooms 21 with telephone (15 with bath). **Price** Single 6,000-7,000Esc, double 8,000-12,000Esc.
Meals Breakfast included, served 7:30-10:00. **Restaurant** See p. 226. **Credit cards** Not accepted.
Pets Dogs not allowed. **Nearby** Horta: Church of São Francisco, Nossa Senhora do Carmo (azulejos,
view) - Cadera - Caves of Costa de Feteira. **Open** All year.

A friendly place offering room and board in one of the most beautiful of the
buildings that line the port. It has a delightful view of the boats in the
harbor and Pico Island. By no means a "grand hotel", it has preserved the
slightly out-of-date charm of the 30s. The rooms vary in quality and of them,
the best are on the third floor looking out over the docks and with private
bathrooms. The prices are altogether reasonable, particularly since you could
never find a better location.

How to get there (*Map 7*): On the port.

Quinta das Buganvílias ^{TR}

Faial Island
Castelo Branco 9900 Horta - Jogo, 60
Tel. 292-943 255/943 740 - Fax 292-943 743
Sr Manuel Joachim da Silva Brums

Rooms 8 (7 with bath, some with kitchen). **Price** Single 11,000Esc, double 13,200Esc. **Meals** Breakfast included, served 7:30-10:00. **Restaurant** In Hotrta see p. 226. **Credit cards** All major. **Pets** Dogs allowed. **Nearby** Horta: Church of São Francisco, Nossa Senhora do Carmo (azulejos, view) - Cadera - Caves of Costa de de Feteira. **Open** All year.

A few kilometers from the center of Horta, the Quinta das Buganvilias is the best hotel on the island. This can scarcely come as a surprise once you see its various buildings submerged under a tidal wave of bougainvillae. It should be said that the growing of fruits and flowers is the specialty of the Quinta. The white house, the oldest, is occupied by the owners and offers four rooms. The second, built of gray volcanic stone, is close to the sea and houses the reception area with a bar installed in an old mill. The last little villa has two rooms on both its floors plus a kitchen that may to used to turn it all into an apartment if needed. Everything here has been nicely decorated and is designed for your comfort; a vast marble bathroom is but one example. A delightful garden offers the colors of hydrangea, roses and bougainvillae plus the fragrance of the lemon trees.

How to get there *(Map 7): 10km west of Horta.*

Hôtel São Pedro

São Miguel Island - 9500 Ponta Delgada
Largo Almirante Dunn
Tel. 296-282 223/4/5 - Fax 296-62 93 19 - Luis Cogumbreiro
E-mail: h.atlantico@mail.telepac.pt - Web: www.bensaude.pt

Category ★★★★ **Rooms** 20 and 6 suites with telephone, bath or shower, WC. **Price** Single 16,200-18,900Esc, double 17,300-19,500Esc, suite 27,100-30,600Esc; extra bed 3,150-3,600Esc. **Meals** Breakfast included, served 7:30-10:00. No restaurant but possibility Hotel Açores Atlantico. **Credit cards** Visa, Eurocard, MasterCard. **Pets** Dogs not allowed. **Facilities** Swimming pool, sauna in Hotel Açores Atlantico (50m). **Nearby** Ponta Delgada: Botanical garden, Museum of Carlos Machado, Church of Matriz - Lake of Sete Citades - Lagao do Fogo - Botanical garden of Terra Nostra - Nossa Senhora de Ribeira Grande. **Open** All year.

São Miguel, sixty-five kilometers long and sixteen kilometers wide, is the largest island in the Azores. While residing in the outskirts to enjoy the garden-like quality of its surrounding communities may seem preferable, Ponta Delgada, in the true style of a capital city, is the place to enjoy streets paved with black and white mosaics plus botanical gardens and baroque churches. Formerly the residence of an American consul and close to two hundred years old, this is the best hotel in Ponta Delgada. Its inland façade, trimmed with gray lava, faces the small square where the San Pedro church stands. On the side facing the sea, a terraced lawn slopes down to the port. The vast entrance and reception area as well as the smallest lounge are decorated in Colonial Georgian style with walls and floors covered with various types of exotic wood, evidence that São Miguel was once a major port for ships returning from India and Brazil. A truly comfortable place with an excellent restaurant that allows you to savor the hotel's pleasantly nostalgic atmosphere.

How to get there (Map 7): Near the port.

Convento de S. Francisco

São Miguel Island
9680 Vila Franca do Campo
Tel. 296-583 532 - Fax 296-583 534
Sra Manuela Guerreiro

Category ★★★★ **Rooms** 12 with telephone, bath, WC, TV. **Price** Double 22,000Esc. **Meals** Breakfast included, served 7:30-10:00. No restaurant. **Credit cards** Not accepted. **Pets** Dogs not allowed. **Facilities** Swimming pool, squash, parking. **Nearby** Ponta Delgada: Botanical garden, Museum of Carlos Machado, Church of Matriz - Lake of Sete Citades - Lagao do Fogo - Botanical garden of Terra Nostra - Nossa Senhora de Ribeira Grande. **Open** All year.

It is only a few well-informed tourists who come here and see how an aging volcano has been transformed into a huge park where the roads are lined with hydrangea and the forests are aglow with azelea. Seemingly lost in the middle of the Atlantic, the Convento de San Francisco with its austere refinement may seem to you virtually sophisticated. And what a beauty it is! With a sobriety almost devoid of decoration, the place gives priority to the purity of its lines and the nobility of the material used in its construction. There are very attractive floors made from exotic wood, bathrooms of volcanic rock, and a series of simple glass windows offering different views of São Miguel's lush countryside. Each room is decorated in its own unique style and you will find wood furnishings inlaid with gold, a fur bedspread, wrought-iron objects as well as paintings, both religious and contemporary, all reflecting what is plainly a kind of baroque simplicity which adds up to unquestionable elegance. The terraces provide a fine view of the sea and the mountain so typical of the landscape in the Azores. Close to a beach, a golf course and paths for hiking, the Convento is an excellent place to get away from it all.

How to get there (*Map 7): 30km east of Ponta Delgada.*

Hotel Vinha da Areia

São Miguel Island
9500 Vila Franca do Campo
Tel. 296-58 31 33/4/5 - Fax 296-58 25 01

Category ★★★ **Rooms** 50 and 2 suites with air-conditioning, telephone, bath, satellite TV. **Price** Single 13,000Esc, double 15,000Esc, suite 20,000Esc. **Meals** Breakfast included, served 7:30-10:00. No restaurant. **Credit cards** Not accepted. **Pets** Dogs not allowed. **Facilities** Swimming pool, tennis, beach. **Nearby** Ponta Delgada: Botanical garden, Museum of Carlos Machado, Church of Matriz - Lake of Sete Citades - Lagao do Fogo - Botanical garden of Terra Nostra - Nossa Senhora de Ribeira Grande. **Open** Jul - Sept.

The Vinha da Areia is an attractive hotel right at the water's edge. The buildings, all in Mediterranean style, open onto the sea, giving every room a particularly beautiful view. The regional decoration provides a great deal of warmth to the hotel, with a large colored awning covering the lounge's ceiling, attractive *azulejos* in the bar and a dining room done in granite. What gives the place its charm is its location, nicely situated between two streams with banks of dark sand. Nearby are a swimming pool and tennis courts. A large terrace allows you to commune with the sea. Certain renovations are to be undertaken and it is advisable to inquire about them.

How to get there (Map 7): 10km east of Ponta Delgada.

Casa Nossa Senhora do Carmo ™

São Miguel Island
9500-614 Livramento
Rua do Pópulo de Cima, 220
Tel. 296-64 20 48 - Fax 296-64 20 38 - E-mail : carmo@virtualazores.com

Rooms 5 (4 with bath, 1 with shower). **Price** Single 13,000-15,000Esc, double 14,000-17,000Esc; extra bed 4,000Esc. **Meals** Breakfast included, served 7:30-10:00. **Evening meal** By reservation - dinner 4,200Esc. **Credit cards** Not accepted. **Pets** Dogs not allowed. **Facilities** Parking. **Nearby** Ponta Delgada: Botanical garden, Museum of Carlos Machado, Church of Matriz - Lake of Sete Citades - Lagao do Fogo - Botanical garden of Terra Nostra - Nossa Senhora de Ribeira Grande - Vila Franca. **Closed** Dec.

A few kilometers from Porta Dorada, Livramento is the kind of small village you often find just inland from the coast. The Senhora do Carmo is now a lovely residence. The entrance is unusual, with angels, Virgins Marys and several small altars. Inside, you discover the kitchen-dining room adjoining the salon with its floor covered by a fur rug. Here, too, is a pleasant terrace where coffee is served. The owners have furnished a number of rooms for guests that give onto the garden. A rustic, quite typical décor gives charm to the house. The garden has numerous shady little nooks, and if you go through the small entrance way you find yourself in the owner's banana grove. Maria is a superb hostess who will be glad to show you her cellar, a veritable little museum, where the priests formerly made their wine for Communion.

How to get there (Map 7): 10km east of Ponta Delgada.

Quinta da Terça TH

São Miguel Island
9500 Livramento
Rua Pópulo de Cima
Tel. 296-63 69 37 - Fax 296-64 21 95 - Sra Maria Manuela Soares

Rooms 3 with bath. **Price** Single 12,000-14,000Esc, double 14,500-17,500Esc. **Meals** Breakfast included, served 8:30-10:00. **Evening meal** By reservation - dinner 4,200Esc. **Credit cards** Not accepted. **Pets** Dogs not allowed. **Facilities** Bicycle, riding, parking. **Nearby** Ponta Delgada: Botanical garden, Museum of Carlos Machado, Church of Matriz - Lake of Sete Citades - Lagao do Fogo - Botanical garden of Terra Nostra - Nossa Senhora de Ribeira Grande. **Open** All year.

Not far from the Casa Senhora do Carmo, the Quinta da Terça offers very pleasant lodging. A shaded alleyway leads to the farmhouse which stands beside a very impressive rubber tree. The owner takes particular pride in the stables which have been converted into a lounge. It is, however, more than that, being essentially a museum dedicated to horsemanship. It is important to know that her entire family is utterly devoted to the equestrian art. Her guests of the same persuasion can enjoy interminable discussions on anything dealing with horses, and you shouldn't be surprised if you were to see superb thoroughbreds galloping in nearby fields. The two rooms here are small but comfortable. The service is very attentive and friendly, and you can order breakfast served in your room or a cup of tea at bedtime.

How to get there *(Map 7): 12km east of Ponta Delgada.*

Hotel Terra Nostra

São Miguel Island
9675 Furnas
Tel. 296-584 706 - Fax 296-584 304
Sr José Pimentel

Category ★★★ **Rooms** 79 and 2 suites with telephone, bath, TV; elevator. **Price** Single 11,750-17,300Esc, double 13,000-19,000Esc. **Meals** Breakfast included, served 7:30-10:00. **Restaurant** Service 12:00PM-2:30PM, 7:00PM-9:30PM – mealtime specials 2,700Esc, also à la carte. **Credit cards** All major. **Pets** Dogs not allowed. **Facilities** Swimming pools, parking. **Nearby** Botanical garden of Terra Nostra, therms Jul 1 - Sept 30 - Ponta Delgada: Botanical garden, Museum of Carlos Machado, Church of Matriz - Lake of Sete Citades - Lagao do Fogo - Nossa Senhora de Ribeira Grande. **Open** All year.

Furnas is on the eastern edge of the island and it was the American Thomas Hickling who was responsible for the existence of its well-known botanical garden. He planted the palm grove and the jacarandas, along with countless other forms of exuberant tropical trees and plants. The Terra Nostra is a very pleasant place to stay, but for utmost satisfaction, you should reserve in the delightful old villa, the Casa do Parque, which offers the most luxurious rooms with lovely old-time decor as well as a large living room giving onto the park and a naturally-heated swimming pool. We should point out that most of the remaining accommodation is located in a modern building of no architectural interest. Nonetheless, the interior is both well taken care of and very comfortable. The restaurant here enjoys an excellent reputation for local specialties. From the Terra Nostra, you can visit the romantic lake of the Vale das Furnas and make the inevitable trip to the top of Pico da Vara - 1,080 meters - where you have a view that is nothing less than extraordinary.

How to get there (Map 7): 40km east of Ponta Delgada.

Solar de Lalém ᵀᴴ

São Miguel Island - 9625-391 Maia - Estrada de S. Pedro
Tel. 296-44 20 04 - Fax 296 44 21 64
Gerd and Gabriele Hochleitner
E-mail: solar.de.lalem@mail.telepac.pt – Web: www.azoresnet.com/solardelalem

Rooms 10 with bath or shower. **Price** Single 11,500-14,500Esc, double 13,000-16,000Esc. **Meals** Breakfast included, served 8:00-10:00. **Evening meals** On request - mealtime specials 3,800Esc. **Credit cards** Not accepted. **Pets** Dogs not allowed. **Facilities** Swimming pool, parking. **Nearby** Porto Formoso beaches (7km) - Gorreana (3km) - Ponta Delgada: Botanical garden, Museum of Carlos Machado, Igreja Matriz - Botanical garden of Terra Nostra, therms Jul 1 - Sept 30 - Lake of Sete Citades - Lagao do Fogo - Nossa Senhora de Ribeira Grande – Furnas golf course (8km). **Closed** Dec, Jan, Feb.

If you travel to Maia from Furnas, you will take a very pleasant route through hills and dales, the last traces of volcanic action in the Azores. The slopes are gloriously green, and fences, resplendent with hydrangea, surround peaceful herds of cows, clearly on hand to give milk if the presence of countless mules carrying milk cans is any indication. It is here that you can visit tea plantations and what is known as "the only tea manufacturing plant in Europe" which is located in Gorreana. Solar de Lalém is an aristocratic manor house which has been skillfully remodeled with an eye to tourism, with in particular a swimming pool occupying part of the subtropical garden. As for meals, they may be taken either at the convivial table in the kitchen itself, a colorful place with its old stove and copper utensils, or in the dining room. The rooms are located in both the main house which is more comfortable and have a fine view, and in the annex where rooms open onto the garden. Beaches, especially the Praia dos Moinhos, are not far away, there are trails for hiking and the owners are very friendly indeed.

How to get there *(Map 7): 35km north of Ponta Delgada.*

Casa das Calhetas TH

São Miguel Island
Calhetas 9600 Ribeira Grande - Rua da Boa Viagem
Tel. 296-49 81 20 - Fax 296 49 81 99 - Sr Carlos D. Gonzalez
E-mail: e.regogonzalez@mail.telepac.pt
Web: virtualazores.com/turismo/casacalhetas

Rooms 3 with bath or shower. **Price** Single 12,000Esc, double 14,000Esc. **Meals** Breakfast included, served 9:30-10:00. **Evening meals** On request. **Credit card** Amex. **Pets** Dogs allowed. **Facilities** Parking. **Nearby** Ponta Delgada: Botanical garden, Museum of Carlos Machado, Church of Matriz - Lake of Sete Citades - Lagao do Fogo - Botanical garden of Terra Nostra, therms Jul 1 - Sept 30 - Nossa Senhora de Ribeira Grande. **Open** All year.

Located on the northern end of the island, the Casa das Calhetas is remarkable in a number of ways: it takes great pride in having the tallest tree in the village, a useful landmark, leading you to this superb residence with stunning white façades trimmed with black lava and richly ornamented with coats of arms. We later learned that the Casa is classed as part of the "regional architectural patrimony." Beyond this, we only know that the rooms are built on a loggia surrounding a lovely interior courtyard. Three apartments were to be opened during the year 2000, for guests wanting more independence. Reservation is an absolute must.

How to get there *(Map 7): 15km north of Ponta Delgada; before reaching Ponta Delgada, turn left towards Calhetas.*

Solar do Conde

São Miguel Island
9545 Capelas
Rua do Rosário, 36
Tel. 296-298 887/8/9 - Fax 296-298 623 - Sr Carlos D. Gonzalez

Bungalows 27 with telephone, bath or shower, TV, kitchenette. **Price** Single 10,000-15,000Esc, double 13,000-17,500Esc; extra bed 4,000-4,500Esc. **Meals** Breakfast included in low season, 750Esc, in high season, served 7:30-10:00. **Restaurant** Service 12:30PM-2:30PM, 7:45PM-10:00PM – à la carte 2,500-4,000Esc – Regional cooking. **Credit cards** All major. **Pets** Dogs not allowed. **Facilities** Swimming pool, laundry service, parking. **Nearby** Ponta Delgada: Botanical garden, Museum of Carlos Machado, Church of Matriz - Lake of Sete Cidades - Lagao do Fogo - Botanical garden of Terra Nostra, therms Jul 1 - Sept 30 - Nossa Senhora de Ribeira Grande. **Open** All year.

The small seaside town of Capelas is a scant fifteen kilometers from Ponta Delgada, and the Solar do Conde offers a number of small villas for two people with a bedroom, bath or shower plus a living room that includes a small kitchen. Each one gives out onto the garden and enjoys a small private patch of lawn with a grove of tree-like ferns. For the socially-minded, there is a restaurant and a bar, and for the children a swimming pool that they will thoroughly appreciate.

How to get there (*Map 7*): *15km north of Ponta Delgada.*

Casa do Monte TH

São Miguel Island
Santo António 9545 Capelas
Tel. 296-98 93 44 - Fax 296-98 93 447
Sra Jorgina Franco

Rooms 5 with bath. **Price** Single 8,400-10,800Esc, double 10,500-12,800Esc. **Meals** Breakfast included, served 7:30-10:00. **Evening meals** On request. **Restaurant** In Ponta Delgada see p. 226. **Credit cards** Not accepted. **Pets** Dogs not allowed. **Facilities** Parking. **Nearby** Ponta Delgada: Botanical garden, Museum of Carlos Machado, Church of Matriz - Lake of Sete Citades - Lagao do Fogo - Botanical garden of Terra Nostra, therms Jul 1 - Sept 30 - Nossa Senhora de Ribeira Grande. **Closed** Dec – Feb.

The Casa do Monte has a unique atmosphere, one unchanged by time as the same family has owned it for the past three centuries. It is an authentic farm with chickens, ducks, horses, an old kitchen where breakfast is served, bathrooms with large porcelain sinks plus antique water pitchers which have been preserved despite the presence of running water. The ocean and the limpid waters of Capelas Bay are nearby, and you can also enjoy the mountains and the numerous possibilities for strolling, especially around the Sete Citades lake, named for the seven priests who, fleeing the Moors, took refuge on the island and created seven "cities." The place is superb, and the lake, taking the form of the symbol for Infinity, is made up of two bodies of water, one blue, the other green.

How to get there (Map 7): 15km north of Ponta Delgada.

Quinta da Nasce-Agua ᵀᴴ

Terceira Island
Vinha Brava 9700 Angra do Heroismo
Tel. 295-62 85 01 - Fax 295-62 85 02

Rooms 5 with air-conditioning, telephone, bath, TV. **Price** Single 18,500-19,000Esc, double 20,000-20,500Esc. **Meals** Breakfast included, served 7:30-10:00. **Evening meals** On request. **Restaurant** In Angra see p. 227. **Credit cards** Not accepted. **Pets** Dogs allowed. **Nearby** Angra: cathedral, Monastery of São Francisco (museum) - Bullfight (summer) - Algar do Carvão caves - Lake of Negro, Lake of Ginjal. **Open** All year.

This is among the most elegant hotels on the island of Terceira, located on one the country roads surrounding Angra. There is a golf course very nearby, and for this reason the owners of the hotel have built practice facilities for their guests who also enjoy free access to the golf course. This 19th-century house is in the center of a large and well-designed park which offers a certain privacy as there are shady pathways leading to the pond, an ideal place to catch up on your reading. Not far from there is a swimming pool surrounded by vast lawns which are perfect for sunbathing. The lounge is a friendly place where you can always order a drink. The rooms are large and well situated, offering all the comfort expected in a very fine hotel. Guests are made to feel immediately welcome, and there are car rentals available.

How to get there (Map 7): 4km of Angra do Heroismo.

Quinta do Barcelos ^{TR}

Terceira Island
Terra do Pão, 2-S. Mateus 9700 Angra do Heroismo
Tel. 295-642 684 - Fax 295-642 683
Sr Adelino Barcelos

Rooms 6 with air-conditioning, telephone, bath, satellite TV. **Price** Single 10,000Esc, double 12,000Esc. **Meals** Breakfast included, served 7:30-10:00. **Evening meals** On request. **Restaurant** In Angra see p. 227. **Credit cards** Not accepted. **Pets** Dogs not allowed. **Facilities** Parking. **Nearby** Angra: cathedral, Monastery of São Francisco (museum) - Bullfight (summer) - Algar do Carvão caves - Lake of Negro, Lake of Ginjal. **Open** All year.

It is advisable when visiting the island of Terceira to choose one of the quintas that will allow you to best take advantage of the atmosphere of this island which is exclusively rural. The Quinta do Barcelos is one of the farms offering sojourns focusing on the island's particular natural attractions. Still, you find air-conditioning here plus all the comfort you could ask for, along with rides on horse-drawn carts as well as the availability of rented cars. And by making the necessary reservation, you can enjoy a meal made up entirely of regional specialties in the acega, the local name for a traditional tavern. The charming owner will take the best possible care of you throughout your stay.

How to get there *(Map 7): 5km of Angra do Heroismo.*

Quinta do Martelo ᵀᴿ

Terceira Island
Cantinho - S. Mateus 9700 Angra do Heroismo
Canada do Martelo, 24
Tel. 295-64 28 42 - Fax 295-64 28 41 - Sra Lisa Vieira

Rooms 10 with telephone, bath, TV. **Price** Single 18,000Esc, double 20,000Esc. **Meals** Breakfast included, served 7:30-10:00. **Restaurant** Service 12:30PM-2:30PM, 7:45PM-10:00PM – à la carte. **Credit cards** Not accepted. **Pets** Dogs allowed. **Facilities** Swimming pool, tennis, exercise room, sauna, minigolf, rent car included, parking. **Nearby** Angra: cathedral, Monastery of São Francisco (museum) - Bullfight (summer) - Algar do Carvão caves - Lake of Negro, Lake of Ginjal. **Open** All year.

Is the Quinta do Martelo a farm or a guest house? It is far from easy to describe a place whose self-professed aim is to be a center of ethnography and gastronomy, offering its guests the best of the culture of the Azores. Here you see corn drying in the entrance, an indication that regional agriculture has remained resolutely unchanged and possibly, at least to our eyes, archaic. It is true that the topography of the island is hardly conducive to mechanization, something that has led to the preservation of the traditional gestures and rhythms of everyday life that seem to be dying out elsewhere. Everything here is genuinely rustic, but your comfort has not been sacrificed as evidenced by the large and attractive bathrooms. There are sports facilities, a car will await you at the airport, and you enjoy service very close to that of a classic hotel plus a good restaurant. A very pleasant place to stay.

How to get there (Map 7): 5km of Angra do Heroismo.

Albergaria Penha da Franca

Madeira Island
9000 Funchal
Rua da Penha Franca, 2
Tel. 291-22 90 87 - Fax 291-22 92 61 - Sr Jose Antonio Ribeiro

Category ★★★★ **Rooms** 76 with telephone, bath or shower. **Price** Double 16,500-21,500Esc. **Meals** Breakfast included, served 8:00-10:00. **Bar-Restaurant** At the hotel. **Credit cards** All major. **Pets** Dogs not allowed. **Facilities** Heated swimming pool, parking. **Nearby** Funchal: cathedral, Sacred Art Museum, Quinta de Nazaré (azulejos), botanical garden - Miradouro do Pínaculo - Monte - Eira do Serrada - Pico Ruivo – Palheiro golf course (18-hole) - Santo da Serra golf course (18-hole). **Open** All year.

The Penha da Franca is one of the rare hotels whose charm can rival that of the quintas of Madeira, a genuine oasis among the concrete blockhouses which have sprung up in Funchal. The property, surrounded by trees and delightful lawns and flower beds, is comprised of a number of small, two- and three-story houses in Madeiran style with red tile roofs and green shutters. The rooms are large, each in a different color and with different decoration and view. This explains the large range of prices. Still, they are all very attractive, some with airy terraces. Recently, it has been enlarged. Though it has more modern amenities, the new building is devoid of charm but nonetheless respects the tradition of service and comfort of the original Penha. You are certain to enjoy going to the albergeria's seawater swimming pool or having a drink or dinner at Joe's Bar, a watering hole much appreciated by its clientele.

How to get there *(Map 7): In the center.*

Reids' Palace

Madeira Island
9000 Funchal
Estrada Monumental, 139
Tel. 291-71 71 71 - Fax 291-71 71 77

Category ★★★★★ **Rooms** 162 with air-conditioning, telephone, bath, satellite TV, safe, minibar; elevator. **Price** Single 34,500-55,000Esc, double 48,500-76,000Esc, junior-suite 102,000-144,000Esc, suite deluxe 139,000-320,000Esc; extra bed 9,500-19,500Esc. **Meals** Breakfast included, served 7:00-10:30. **Restaurant** "Garden" (lunch) à la carte: 3,750-4,700Esc; "Villa Cliff" (Italian specialties) à la carte 4,000-4,800Esc; "Les Faunes" (by reservation, closed Sun) à la carte 6,800Esc. **Credit cards** All major. **Pets** Dogs allowed except in restaurants. **Facilities** Heated swimming pool, tennis, swimming sports, parking. **Nearby** Funchal: cathedral, Sacred Art Museum, Quinta de Nazaré (azulejos), botanical garden - Miradouro do Pínaculo - Monte - Eira do Serrada - Pico Ruivo – Palheiro golf course (18-hole) - Santo da Serra golf course (18-hole). **Open** All year.

R eid's enjoys a worldwide reputation. Its exceptional location on a majestic cape overlooking the Bay of Funchal, along with a garden which includes many ex- ceptional sub-tropical species, climbing vines, geraniums and hibiscus, leave an unforgettable impression. Truly a "grand hotel," it offers luxurious and spacious rooms, comfortable and elegant bathrooms, along with the pleasure of having breakfast on a terrace surrounded by pine trees. In addition, there are numerous restaurants and swimming pools, a wide range of water sports plus a pass for the golf clubs in Funchal. All this, of course, has not escaped the notice of the international jet set.

How to get there (Map 7): In the center.

Quinta da Bella Vista

Madeira Island
9000 Funchal
Caminho do Avista Navios, 4
Tel. 291-76 41 44 - Fax 291-76 41 43

Category ★★★★ Rooms 62 and 5 suites with air-conditioning, telephone, bath, satellite TV. **Price** Single 22,500-29,900Esc, double 30,000-37,400Esc, junior-suite 58,000Esc. **Meals** Breakfast included, served 8:00-10:00. **Restaurant** On request. **Credit cards** All major. **Pets** Dogs not allowed. **Facilities** Swimming pools, tennis (750Esc), sauna (750Esc), billiard, parking. **Nearby** Funchal: cathedral, Sacred Art Museum, Quinta de Nazaré (azulejos), botanical garden - Miradouro do Pínaculo - Monte - Eira do Serrada - Pico Ruivo – Palheiro golf course (18-hole) - Santo da Serra golf course (18-hole). **Open** All year.

At the beginning of the century, a number of quintas were built on the land overlooking Funchal to provide wealthy foreigners attractive country homes surrounded by hydrangea, amaryllis, jacarandas and bougainvillae, the flowers that have truly made this island's reputation. The Quinta da Bella Vista today is a fine hotel run family-style with deft professionalism and unfailing courtesy. The fifteen-hectare garden has a beautiful view of the mountains and the sea. The rooms are located in different buildings, the luxury suites in the private house where the library and lounge are at your disposal. The antique furniture and mementos seen here make it the most intimate part of the hotel. The rooms in the other two villas offer more privacy, and our preference goes to those giving onto the lawns where the ferns will soon be as tall as the palm trees. A lounge on each floor is available to the guests and there is an excellent restaurant.

How to get there *(Map 7): On the hills of the town.*

Estalagem Quinta Perestrello

Madeira Island
9000 Funchal
Rua do Dr. Pita, 3
Tel. 291-76 23 33/37 20 - Fax 291-76 37 77

Category ★★★★ **Rooms** 30 with telephone, bath, TV. **Price** Double 20,000Esc, with terrace 22,000Esc. **Meals** Breakfast included, served 8:00-10:00 - full board +4,250Esc. **Restaurant** Service 7:30PM-8:30PM – mealtime specials 4,250Esc. **Credit cards** Visa, Eurocard, MasterCard. **Pets** Dogs not allowed. **Facilities** Swimming pool, parking. **Nearby** Funchal: cathedral, Sacred Art Museum, Quinta de Nazaré (azulejos), botanical garden - Miradouro do Pínaculo - Monte - Eira do Serrada - Pico Ruivo – Palheiro golf course (18-hole) - Santo da Serra golf course (18-hole). **Open** All year.

This quinta overlooks a large garden from which the sea is plainly visible. A terrace extends off the main house and there you can enjoy both breakfast and the surrounding countryside which is always covered with a slight haze. Below is an annex next to a swimming pool with several rooms which are the most attractive, each with a private terrace. Those in the main house, however, are equally comfortable. The reception area is tastefully decorated with antiques in classic style and the fragrance of fresh flowers fills the corridors. The only drawback is a traffic circle not far away that produces a little bit of noise at the height of the season.

How to get there (Map 7): On the hills of the town.

Quinta da Fonte [TH]

Madeira Island - 9050-209 Funchal
Estrada dos Marmeleiros, 89
Tel. 291-23 53 97 - Fax 291-23 53 97
Sr António Gomes Mendonça Estevinho - E-mail: estevinho@mail.telepac.pt

Rooms 5 with bath. **Price** Double 14,000Esc. **Meals** Breakfast included, served 8:00-10:00.
Restaurant See p. 227. **Credit cards** Not accepted. **Pets** Dogs not allowed. **Facilities** Parking. **Nearby**
Funchal: cathedral, Sacred Art Museum, Quinta de Nazaré (azulejos), botanical garden - Miradouro
do Pínaculo - Monte - Eira do Serrada - Pico Ruivo – Palheiro golf course (18-hole) - Santo da Serra
golf course (18-hole). **Open** All year.

This is one of the finest hotels in the Madeiran capital. From here you have
the best view of the city as you look down on a succession of little houses
with red tile roofs. The quinta itself is made up of a series of terraces and
connected buildings that surround a small garden and courtyard with a family
chapel. The interior decoration has all the charm of the Portuguese baroque
period with dark and impressive 18th- and 19th-century wood panelling as well
as religious paintings and sculptures. The beds have canopies that create a
pleasant atmosphere. The reception you receive here is nothing short of
delightful, and Antonio's wife will soon have you sharing her passion for the
liqueurs - twenty-nine varieties - which are all made here on the premises from
plants grown on the island. If you choose to visit the interior, you will enjoy
staying at the Quinta da Capela which also belongs to the Gomes family.

How to get there (Map 7): On the hills of the town.

Quinta da Portada Branca [TH]

Madeira Island
9100 Casais d'Além-Camacha (Santa Cruz)
Tel. and Fax 291-92 21 19
Sr Ricardo Silva

Rooms 5 with bath. **Price** Single 8,500Esc, double 13,000Esc. **Meals** Breakfast included, served 8:00-10:00. No restaurant. **Credit cards** Not accepted. **Pets** Dogs not allowed. **Facilities** Parking. **Nearby** Funchal - Miradouro do Pínaculo -Caniço - Church of Madre de Deus - Gaula - Santa Cruz: Church of São Salvador, Paço do Concelho, Câmara municipal. **Open** All year.

After your visit to Funchal, you can go around the island visiting the *quintas* which will allow you to discover entirely different landscapes and appreciate the respect the people of the region have for their traditions. An inland road leads to Camacha, a town renowned for its basket makers who can be seen at work on their doorsteps as well as its traditional folklore celebrations where the women of the town don traditional costumes. You can get to the hotel via a long road with pine trees and eucalyptus on either side or by another that goes through the forest. Nestled in a valley, this hotel is beautifully done up in the traditional colors of the region, green and scarlet. Here is a place that is cool and peaceful, giving you every reason to spend time here even if we have been unable to visit the interior.

How to get there (Map 7): 20km east of Funchall towards Camacha.

Quinta da Capela [TH]

Madeira Island
9225 Sitio do Folhadal - Porto da Cruz (Machico)
Tel. 291-23 53 97 - Fax 291-23 53 97
Sr António Gomes Mendonça Estevinho
E-mail: estevinho@mail.telepac.pt

Rooms 4 and 1 suite with bath or shower. **Price** Double 13,000Esc. **Meals** Breakfast included, served 8:00-10:00. No restaurant. **Credit cards** Not accepted. **Pets** Dogs not allowed. **Facilities** Parking. **Nearby** Machico - Miradouro de Portela - Quinta da Junta - Camacha - Natural swimming pool 2km away - Sea (3km) – Santo da Serra golf course (18-hole). **Open** All year.

After passing under the landing field of the Santa Catarina airport, you can make a detour and enjoy the lookout at Augua de Pena before stopping at Machico, a delightful little village which a river nicely divides into two distinct districts, one the Old Town with its small streets with pink and turquoise houses, the other with the port and the fortress where Zarco, the Portuguese explorer who discovered the island, is believed to have landed. To get to the Quinta da Capela, you head in the direction of Portela - where you absolutely must enjoy the view from the *miradoura* - and Porto da Cruz. The route is particularly pleasant as it takes you through vineyards, banana groves, eucalyptus forests and delightful *palheiros,* shepherds' dwellings with traditional thatched roofs. A small road leads to the *quinta* which winds along a hillside covered with mauve jacarandas. The hotel was once a 17th-century chapel as its steeple so well points out. Here you find comfortable rooms along with a suite with a private lounge and where you can spend a few days in a most cordial atmosphere and take long country walks and have a look at the region's artisanal products.

How to get there *(Map 7): Between Porto da Cruz and Portela.*

Casa da Dona Clementina ᵀᴴ

Madeira Island
Achada Simão Alves 9800 Santana
Tel. and Fax 291-57 41 44 - Fax 291-22 75 26
Sr Ricardo Jorge Machado Almada Nascimento

Rooms 8 with bath or shower. **Price** Double 13,000Esc. **Meals** Breakfast included, served 8:00-10:00.
No restaurant. **Credit cards** Not accepted. **Pets** Dogs not allowed **Facilities** Parking. **Nearby**
Miradouro de Faial - Santana - hiking in Queimada Park - São Jorge (church). **Open** All year.

The Casa da Dona Clementina is unquestionably a favorite of hikers. The
Queimadas Park offers trails to Pico Ruivo, Pico das Pedras and, for the
more experienced, Caldeirão Verde. You should not miss the Faial's miradouro
and its surroundings which give a greater appreciation of the different
landscapes present on Madeira. A few kilometers from the picturesque village
of Santana, known for its brightly-painted houses, you discover "the House of
Aunt Clementine," where a small garden of roses and hydrangea offers a view
of the sea. The large and solidly-built living room is attractively furnished and
is an excellent setting for breakfast - or a place simply to relax after a hard day's
hike.

How to get there *(Map 7): 39km northeast of Funchal.*

Casa da Piedade TH

Madeira Island
Sitio do Laranjal 9240 São Vicente
Tel. 291-84 60 42 - Fax 291-84 60 44
Sra Conceição Pereira

Rooms 7 with air-conditioning, telephone, bath, TV. **Price** Single 6,500Esc, double 8,000Esc; extra bed 1,500Esc. **Meals** Breakfast included, served 8:00-10:00. No restaurant. **Credit cards** Not accepted. **Pets** Dogs not allowed. **Facilities** Parking. **Nearby** Seixal - Porto Moniz - Ribeira da Janela - Santa. **Open** All year.

This beautiful baronial residence three kilometers from the port of São Vicente is exceptionally well located; its white façade harbors numerous windows that allow guests to fully appreciate the island's vivid topography. In front is a large lawn equipped with comfortable chairs, while to the rear, you encounter vegetation both dense and colorful. The staircase leading to the lounge is of wicker construction, made from locally-grown water-willow. The rooms are upstairs, each well furnished and with a lovely view.

How to get there *(Map 7): 55km north of Funchal.*

Casa do Lanço TH

Madeira Island
Sitio do Lanço 9240 São Vicente
Tel. 291-84 60 73 - Fax 291-74 24 12
Sra Filomena

Apartments 4 with bath. **Price** Single 8,660Esc, double 11,550Esc, apart. 13,200Esc for 2 pers., extra pers. +3,950Esc; extra bed 750Esc. **Meals** Breakfast included, served 8:00-10:00. No restaurant. **Credit cards** Not accepted. **Pets** Dogs not allowed. **Facilities** Parking. **Nearby** Seixal - Porto Moniz - Ribeira da Janela - Santa. **Open** All year.

The countryside surrounding Ponta Delgada is covered with vineyards and groves of citrus trees and produces an excellent Malvoisie, a delightful Greek-style wine. A few kilometers away is the seaside town of São Vicente. Not far from the water is the Casa do Lanço whose entrance and terrace stand at the foot of a rocky peak rising above the river valley leading to the sea. Here, you have the choice between sprightly-decorated rooms with engravings of birds and fruit in the main house or comfortably furnished apartments for three or four people in the adjoining annexes. There is also a small pavilion with a private garden suitable for families. A good place to know when traveling along the northwest coast towards Porto Moniz.

How to get there (Map 7): 55km north of Funchal.

Casa das Videiras TH

Madeira Island
Sitio da Serra d'Agua - Seixal 9270 (Porto Moniz)
Tel. 291-85 40 20 - Fax 291-85 40 21
Sr José Alberto Ascensaõ dos Reis
E-mail: johnny@madeira-island.com - Web: www.casa-das-videiras.com

Rooms 4 with shower. **Price** Double 9,200-12,500Esc (2 nights min.). **Meals** Breakfast included, served 8:00-10:00. **Evening meals** On request. **Credit cards** Not accepted. **Pets** Dogs not allowed. **Facilities** Parking. **Nearby** Porto Moniz - Ribeira da Janela. **Open** All year.

The northern region of Madeira offers numerous and varied landscapes. You notice when you leave São Vicente that the cultivated fields grow increasingly scarce and that waterfalls are suddenly visible at every bend in the road. At Seixal, a small road leads to the sea where shoulder-to-shoulder villas do nothing to improve the view but at the same time do nothing to detract from the peace and calm of the Casa das Videiras. It is immediately clear that here, conviviality reigns in an atmosphere owing much to its charming owner who will not hesitate to go into his kitchen to prepare a meal for you or light the charcoal if you prefer a barbecue in the garden. The rooms are on the second floor and all are reserved for adults. The dining room gives onto a terrace with an ideal view of the surroundings.

How to get there (*Map 7*): *40km north of Funchal.*

Pau Branco ᵀᴴ

Madeira Island
Sitio de Pau Branco - Chão da Ribeira 9270 (Porto Moniz)
Tel. 291-85 43 89 - Fax 291-85 28 60
Sr Edgar Valter Castro Correia

Villa With 2 bedrooms, sitting room, kitchen, bath. **Price** 15,000Esc/day, 12,000Esc/day for 1 week. **Credit cards** Not accepted. **Pets** Dogs not allowed. **Facilities** Parking. **Nearby** Seixal (beach, surf) - Hiking in Madera National Park - Porto Moniz - Seixal. **Open** All year.

Yes, it was love at first sight! Such was our reaction when we discovered Pau Branco. To understand this, you need to enjoy nature to the fullest and also enjoy being in a place that might appear to some as being at the end of the earth. Leaving Seixal, you head inland on a road that features ever-tightening hairpin turns, an ever-increasing density of vegetation plus an imposing mountain that comes ever closer. Finally, you arrive at Pau Branco. It is genuinely magnificent! What was once a shed that housed a flock of sheep is now practically the only dwelling on a site protected by the Natural Park Authority of Madeira, and it offers every feature you could ask for. On the ground floor are two guest rooms as well as a cozy living room furnished in flawless taste with a fireplace which is particularly welcome when the evening fog leaves a slight chill in the air. A terrace leads to the kitchen and on to a very comfortable bathroom. The garden is well tended with a tidy lawn and attractive flower beds surrounding this small house. Your nearest neighbor, a mountain-style restaurant, is not too far away and is always ready to provide whatever is necessary should you suddenly feel too isolated.

How to get there (Map 7): 50km north of Funchal.

Pousada dos Vinháticos

Madeira Island
Vinháticos 9350 Serra da Agua (Ribeira Brava)
Tel. 291-95 23 44 - Fax 291-95 25 40 - Reservation 291-76 56 58
Sr Edgar Valter Castro Correia

Rooms 15 with telephone, bath or shower, TV. **Price** Double 12,000Esc. **Meals** Breakfast included, served 8:00-10:00. **Restaurant** Mealtime specials 4,000Esc. **Credit cards** Not accepted. **Pets** Dogs allowed. **Facilities** Parking. **Nearby** Serra da Agua - Boca Encumeada - Miradouro de Balcões - Pico de Ariero. **Open** All year.

A magnificent landscape lies below the Pousada dos Vinhàticos, a word meaning "red laurels." Close by is Serra da Agua, a town that produces the wicker items you find at the market in Funchal. The countryside offers constant change as vineyards give way to the osier beds that the wicker industry depends on, and as poplars and willows grow side by side with fig trees and eucalyptus groves. The pousada is simply designed but the rooms are cheerfully decorated with flowery fabrics and engravings depicting local flora and fauna, and are exceptionally well looked after. The restaurant extends onto a large panoramic terrace where the view is superb. The rocks surrounding the pousada have skillfully been turned into outposts that allow you to survey the countryside from different angles. If you enjoy vacations with the accent on nature, you will never forget coming to the Pousada dos Vinhàticos.

How to get there (Map 7): 40km north of Funchal to Serra de Agua; 2km towards São Vicente.

RESTAURANTS

EVORA

– **Cozinha de St Humberto**, rua da Moeda 39, Tel. 266-24 251 - Closed in November. Charming restaurant hidden in a little lane near the Praça do Giraldo. Esc 3,500. – **Cozinha Alentejana**, rua 5 de Outubro, 51, Tel. 266-227 72 - Closed in November. Esc 3,000. – **Fialho**, travessa das Mascarenhas, Tel. 266-23 079 - Closed October 1-22, Christmas and New Year. Esc 2,500-5,000. Portuguese taverna, traditional cuisine. – **O Antão**, rua João de Deus 5, Tel. 266-264 59 - Closed June 22 - July 6. Esc 2,000-3,000. Excellent relation of quality to price. – **Guião**, rua da República, Tel. 266-224 27 - Closed in December. One of the good restaurants of the town, Portuguese decor. Esc 3,270-3,700. – **Garfo**, rua de Santa Caterina 17, Tel. 266-292 56. Rustic ambiance. Specialties: pork. – **Jardìm do Paço**, rua Augusto Filipe Simões 2 - You can eat in the gardens of the Palacio near the convent dos Loios.

ESTREMOZ

– **Águias d'Ouro**, Rossio Marquès de Pombal 27, Tel. 268-33 33 26 - Esc 3,000-4,000 - Classical and refined.
– **Adega do Isaias**, rua do Almeida 23, Tel. 268-223 18. Very pleasant bistrot. Specialties: pork.
– **Café Central**, Rossio de Marquès de Pombal. The most popular café in the city.

REDONDO

– **Convento de São Paulo**, Aldeia da Serra, 10 km, Tel. 266-99 91 00 - Hotel-restaurant in a former convent. Esc 3,700-5,400.

BEJA

– **Melius**, Avenida Fialho de Almeida 68, Tel. 284-32 98 69. Esc 2,500-3,700.
– **Os Infantes**, rua dos Infantes 14, Tel. 284-227 89.
– **Luis da Rocha**, rua Capitão João Francisco de Sousa - Very lively café where you can eat very well. Delicious regional pastry. Specilaties: *queijadas* and *porquinhos doces*.

LAGOS

– **Alpendre**, rua de 25 de Abril, Tel. 282-76 27 05 - Much appreciated. Better to reserve but one can wait in the pleasant bar till a table is free. – **Dom Sebástião**, rua de 25 de Abril 20, Tel. 282-76 27 95 - Closed November 22 to December 26. Setting is a rustic taverna, local clientele comes for the house specialties: fish and rock lobsters. Esc 2,000-3,000. – **O Galeão**, rua de Laranjeira 1, Tel. 282-76 39 09 - Closed Sundays, November 27 to December 27. Esc 2,000-3,000. – **A Lagosteira**, rua 1 de Maio, Tel. 282-76 24 86 - Closed Saturday and Sunday midday, January 10 to February 10. Sample the traditional Algarve fish soup. Simple decor. Esc 1,700-3,700. – **O Trovador**, largo do Convento da Senhora de Gloria, Tel. 282-76 31 52 - International cuisine with pleasant and friendly service.

PORTIMÃO

– **A Lanterna**, Estrada 125, Tel. 282-2414 429. Closed Sunday and November 27 to Decembre 28. Esc 3,000-4,000. Specialty: *caldo de peixe*. – **The Old Tavern**, rua Júdice Fialho, Tel. 282-233 25 - One of the oldest Algarve restaurants, which has kept its atmosphere despite renovations. Sample the local specialty: cataplana of rock lobsters. – **Mr Bojangles Bistro Bar**, rua da Hortinha 1, Tel. 282-230 42 - Closed Mondays. Very charming bistro. – **Alfredo's**, rua Pe da Cruz, Tel. 282-229 54 - Specialties: fish, grills. – **Lucio's**, Tenente Morais Sorães 10, Tel. 282-242 92 - The best fish specialties. – **O O Bicho**, largo Gil Eanes, Tel. 282-229 77 - For the most authentic cataplana, palourdes, pork stewed with tomatos and white wine.

PRAIA DA ROCHA

(3km from Portimão)

– **Bar of the Hotel Bela Vista** - To take a glass in this old Moorish-style house. – **Titanic**, Edificio Colúmbia, rua Engenheiro Francisco Bivar, Tel. 282-223 71 - Closed in December. Good cuisine, international specialties, elegant. Esc 2,300-3,000. – **Falesia**, av. Tomás Cabreira, Tel. 282-235 24. Closed January 8 to February 8. - Pleasant service on the terrace.

PRAIA DOS TRES IRMÃOS

(5km from Portimão)

– **Alfredo**, 5 de Outubro 9, Tel. 289-520 59 - Savory cuisine, house wine. – **O Montinho**, at Montechoro, km 4, Tel. 289-539 59 - Closed Sundays, January 15 to February 15, and November 15 to December 15. In one of those beautiful Portuguese quintas with so much charm. Esc 3,000-5,000. – **O Búzio**, Aldeamento da Prainha, Tel. 282-45 85 61 - Closed November to March. Very popular, reservation advised, nicer for dinner. Esc 4,000-6,000.

BARS

– **Harrys Bar**, on the market place. The unavoidable meeting place of the region. – **Caves do Vinho do Porto**, rua la Liberdade 23. Sampling and purchase of port wine.

TAVIRA

– **Avenida**, av. Dr. Mateus T. de Acevedo, Tel. 281-811 13 - Esc 1,700-2,600.

A QUATRO AGUAS, 2KM – **Portas do Mar**, Tel. 281-812 55 and **4 Aguas** Tel. 32 53 29. Closed in November. Esc 2,000-4,000. Two good addresses for fish and seafood.

FARO

– **Cidade Velha**, rua Domingos Guieiro 19, Tel. 289-271 45 - Closed Sundays and December. Behind the cathedral in a pretty house. Esc 2,500-3,500. – **Dois Irmãos**, largo do Terreiro do BiSão 18 - Portuguese bistro dating from 1925. Fish, depending on catch, and seafood.

SANTA BARBARA DE NEXE

(12km from Faro)

– **La Réserve**, Tel. 289-999 234

- Elegant restaurant of hotel of same name. Refined cuisine, good cellar. Esc 5,500-8,000.

LOULÉ

– **Aux Bons Enfants**, rua Enghero Duarte Pacheco 116, Tel. 289-39 68 40. Closed Sunday and January 20 to February 20 Esc 3,500-4,500. Specialties: French cooking. – **Bica Velha**, rua Martin Moniz 17, Tel. 289-46 33 76. Closed Sunday midday and November 15 to 30. Esc 3,000. Rustic. – **O Avenida**, av. José Costa Mealha 40, Tel. 289-46 21 06 - Closed Sunday and November. Esc 3,500. Decoation with foreign money, and football cups.

BAR-PATISSERIE

– **O Morgadinha**, rua 1 de Dezembro. The welcome is pleasant.

B   E   I   R   A

FUNDHÃO

– **Herminia**, av. da Libedade 123, Tel. 275-525 37. Esc 2,500.

COIMBRA

– **Piscinas**, rua Dom Manuel 2, Tel. 239-71 70 13 - Closed in February. Classical, Portuguese cuisine and local specialties. Evening piano bar. Esc 2,200-3,500. – **Dom Pedro**, avenida Emidio Navarro 58, Tel. 239-

291 08 - Esc 3,000. One of the good addresses of Coimbra. – **Real das Canas**, vila Méndes 7, Tel. 239-817 877 - Closed Wednesday. 2,000-2,500 Esc

CAFÉS

– **Café Santa Cruz**, prata 8 de Mayo - Closed Sundays. The best known café of Coimbra and Northern Portugal, a meeting place for students and university people.

AVEIRO

– **Salpoente**, rua Canal São Roque 83, Tel. 234-38 26 74 Closed Sundays, November 15 to 23. Esc 2,200-3,000. – **Centenário**, prata do Mercado 9, Tel. 234-227 98. House specialty: sopa do mar. Esc 3,000.

GUARDA

– **O Telheiro**, estrada N16 (1.5km), Tel. 271-21 13 56. Esc 3,200-4,000. The most pleasant table in Guarda, terrace and view.

SEIA

– **Monte Neve**, rua A. de Oliveira in San Romao – **O Degrau**, rua Sacadura Casabral 48 in Loriga – **O Marquès de Seia**, av 1 de Maio 22 in Seia. Specialties: cod, haricot beans, pork.. all good.

VISEU

– **Trave Negra**, rua do Loureiros 40, Tel. 232-261 38 – **O Cortiço**, rua Augusto Hilário

43, Tel. 232-423 853 - The Portuguese themselves call this restaurant típico. – **Churrasqueria Santa Eulalia**, bairro de Santa Eulalia (1.5km), Tel. 262 83. Esc 2,000-3,000.

NELAS

– **Os Antónios**, largo Vasco de Gama, Tel. 232-949 515 - Esc 2,500-3,500.

MEALHADA

– **Pedro dos Leitões**, Tel. (031) 220 62 - Closed Monday, 2 weeks in April and September 1 to 15. Esc 2,500-3,000Esc.

D U O R O

AMARANTE

– **Outeiro de Baixo**, rua Antinio Carveiro. A good small restaurant. – **Zé da Caltada**, rua 31 de Janeiro. On the river – **Confeitera do Ponte**, tea room on the river.

PORTO

– **Portucale**, rua de Alegria, Tel. 22-57 07 17 - Two elevators take you to the roof of the Albergaria Miradouro for an intimate and refined dinner with a beautiful view of the town. Esc 5,000-9,000. – **O Escondidinho**, rua de Passos Manuel 144, Tel. 22-200 10 79 - Closed Sundays. Taverne atmosphere, collection of old Portuguese pottery, fish soup and grilled sardines. Esc

4,800-6,500. – **Mesa Antiga**, rua de Santo Ildefonso 208, Tel. 22-200 64 32 - Closed Saturdays, October. The best place for sampling reginal cuisine. Esc 2,500-5,000. – **Taverna do Bebobos**, Cais da Ribeira, Tel. 22-31 35 65 - Closed Sundays and in March. Reserve if you want to have a chance of dining in this very small restaurant beside the river, one of the oldest addresses of Porto. Fish specialties. Esc 1,700-2,000. – **Aleixo**, rua da Estatão 216, Tel. 22-57 04 62. Authentic, family and popular atmosphere – **Mercearia**, Cais de Ribeira 32, Tel. 22-200 43 89.

Foz do Douro – **Portofino**, rua do Padraõ 109, Tel. 22-617 73 39. Closed Saturday lunchtime and August 1 to 15 Esc 2,500-3,700. Pretty façade with azulejos The pretty façade with azulejos is appealing and you won't be disappointed.

At Leça da Palmeira, 8km away. – **O Chanquinhas**, rua de Santana 243, Tel. 22-995 18 84 - Seafood. – **Garrafão**, rua António Nobre, Tel. 22-995 16 60 - Closed Sundays, August 15 to 21. The other good address on the beach. Fish and seafood (from tanks).

At Leça da Palmeira-Matozinhos – **Esplanada Marisqueira Antonio**, Tel. 22-938 06 60. Closed Monday. Fish, seafood, game.

CAFÉS AND WINE CELLARS

– **Solar do Vinho de Porto**, in the manor house sheltering The Romantic Museum of La Quinta da Marcieirinha, at rua de Entre Quintas 220. Sampling of port wine till 22:30 on Saturdays. Closed Sundays. Seafood.

– **Garrafeira do Campo Allegre**, rua do Campo Allegre 1598. **Garrafeira Augusto Leite**, rua do Passeio Alegre.

CAFÉ-PATISSERIE

– **Majestic Café**, rua de Sta Catarina - Freqented by intellectuals, Brazilian coffee naturally, and some food served.
– **Casa de Serralves**, rua de Serralves - Museum of Contemporary Art with a very pleasant tea room in the park of this pretty house 1930.
– **Casa Margaridense**, traversa de Cedofeita 20. Specialies: *marmelada* and *pào de lò*
– **Confeitaria Império**, rua Santa Catarina 231.

SHOPPING

– **A Pérola da Guiné**, rua Costa Cabral 231 and **A Pérola do Bolhão**, rua Formosa 279. Two shops for Brazilian coffee.

– **Casa Oriental**, Campo Mòrtires da Patria. Typical groceries (bacalau), **Bolhão market** and **Ribeira market**.

CRAFT INDUSTRY

– **José Rosas**, rua Eugénio de Castro 282 and **Luis Ferreira & Filhos**, goldsmiths trade.

FADOS

– **Mal Cozinhado**, rua do Outeirinho 13, Tel. 22-38 13 19 - The best *casa de fado*.

POVOA DO VARZIM

(30km from Porto)

– **Casa dos Frangos II**, N13 road towards Viana do Costelo. Closed Mondays. Very popular for its fish stew. – **O Marinheiro**, N13 road for 2km, Tel. 252-68 21 51 - Fish and shellfish in a ships decor. Esc 3,500-5,000.

SANTO TIRSO

– **São Rosendo**, prata do Municipio 6, Tel. 252-853 054. - Esc 2,500-3,000.

LAMEGO

– **O Marquês**, Urb. da Ortigosa, estrada do Peso de Régua. Terrace.
– **O Combadino**, rua da Oleiria 84 - Closed Sunday - Typical tavern. Lamego is the best place to tast Vinho verde in the cellars near the municipal market.

ESTREMADURE

LISBON

GASTRONOMIC RESTAURANTS, THE MOST BEAUTIFUL AND MOST EXPENSIVE

– **Casa de Comida**, travessa de Amoreiras 1, Tel. 21-387 51 32 - Closed Saturday middays and Sundays. The favorite restaurant of gourmets, welcoming atmosphere, charming patio. Reservation needed. Esc 6,100-11,000.
– **Tavares**, rua de Misericórdia 37, Tel. 21-342 11 12 - Closed Saturdays and Sunday midday. Esc 5,500-9,000. Initially Tavares was a café (1784), and it has kept the gilt, the mirrors, the stucco and 18th century spirit. Traditional classic cuisine. Esc 5,500-8,000.

220

– **Conventual**, Prata da Flores 45, Tel. 21-390 91 96. Closed Saturday middays and Sundays. Esc 6,000.

– **Antonio Clara Clube de Empresàrios**, Av. de la Rep·blica 38, Tel. 21-796 63 80 - Closed Sundays. Esc 7,000. Meeting place for those in politics and business.

– **Aviz**, rua Serpa Pinto 12-B, Tel. 21-342 83 91 - Closed Sundays. Esc 6,000-8,000. Azulejoa and gleaming chandeliers for fine, authentic Portuguese cuisine.

– **Tágide**, largo da Academia nacional de Belas Artes 18, Tel. (21)-342 07 20 - Closed Satur-

days and Sundays. Portuguese provincial specialties. Beautiful view over the old town and River Tagus. Esc 6,000-8,000.

TYPICAL CUISINE

– **O Faz Figura**, rua do Parafso 15, Tel. 21-886 89 81 - Closed Sundays. Portuguese cuisine: tipica bacalhau (codfish), the national specialty, and vinho verde (white or sparkling red wine). Ask for a table on the veranda with view on the Tagus. Esc 5,500-6,500. – **O Funil**, avenida Elias Garcfa 82, Tel. 21-796 60 07 - Closed Sunday evenings. Good selection of national specialties, fish and codfish. The house wine will be agreeable as you wait for a table to become free. Esc 2,500-4,500. – **Fidalgo**, rua da Barroca 27 – **A Primavera**, Trav. da Espera; and **O Poleiro**, rua de Entrecampos; are three typical establishments and not expensive. – **O Nobre**, rua das MercFs 71, Tel. 21-363 38 27 - Closed Saturday middays and Sundays. Esc 4,000-6,000. – **Mercado de Sta. Clara**, Campo de Sta. Clara, Tel. 21-87 39 86 - Closed Sunday evenings and August. Difficult to find, ask for advice. Esc 3,000-4,000. – **Floresta do Ginjal**, Ginjal 7, Tel. 21-275 00 87 - Ferryboat from the Praça do Comércio or Cais do Sodré for the Ginjal quay. – **Pap'Açorda**, rua da Atalaia 57, Tel. 21-346 48 11 - Closed Saturdays and Sundays. The fashionable and with it restaurant. Unavoidable, even if only average cuisine.

RESTAURANTS WITH A VIEW

– **Espelho d'Agua**, Av. de Brazilia, Tel. 21-301 73 73 - Closed Sundays. On a small artificial lake. Esc 4,000-6,000.

– **Via Graça**, rua Damasceno Monteiro 9B, Tel. 21-87 08 30 - Closed Saturday lunchtime and Sunday. View of the São Jorge chateau, the town and the River Tagus. Esc 3,000-4,500.

DINNERS AT BELEM

– **São Jerónimo**, rua dos Jerónimos - Stark and Corbusier furniture. Good place for lunch after visiting the monastery. Esc 4,000-5,000.

DINNERS AND FADOS

– **Il Senhor Vinho**, rua Meda Alapa, Tel. 21-397 74 56 - One can dine here, reservation imperative.

– **A Mascotte da Atalaia**, rua de Atalaia 47 - Very authentic, in the Bairro Alto.

– **Parreirenha da Alfama**, Beco do Espfrito Santo 1 - Fados, and nothing but fados. One can dine here.

– **Adega Machado**, rua do Norte 91, Bairro Alto, Tel. 21-342 87 13 - One of the favorite clubs of Portugal. Dinner possible, fados and folk dancing.

– **A Severa**, rua das Gáveas 51, Tel. 21-342 83 14 - In the Bairro Alto. One of the oldest fado houses, which has seen the start of many famous fadista careers.

CAFÉS-RESTAURANTS

– **Versailles**, Av. de la Republica 15-A. You can lunch here in a very beautiful stucco and mirror decoration

– **Alcântara Café**, rua Maria Luisa Holstein 15. A old warehouse decorated by António Pinto.

– **Cervejaria Trindade**, rua Nova de Trindade - The oldest tavern of the Sagres brewers. Beer, naturally, but one can also eat. Beautiful azuleros, garden.

– **Pavilhão Chines**, rua Don Pedro V 89. A must for tea, cocktails or a late-night drink. Unusual poetic décor.

– **O Chapitò**, rua Costa do Castelo 7. Terrace with a view on Alfama. – **Martinho de Arcade**, prata do Comercio, corner rua da Prata - One of the oldest cafés. Weekly literary meetings. – **Brasileira**, rua Garret 102 - Fin de siècle decor. *Una bica paça favor* (small coffee). – **A Ginjinha**, travessa de Saõ Domingo 8. Stop at Rossio, near the Saã Domingo church, for the Lisbon specialty: cherry liqueur. – **Nicola**, prata Dom Pedro IV 26, on the Rossio - The most famous of Lisbon cafés. – **Procòpio**, Alto de São Francisco 21. A lot of atmosphere in this café-salon with an end of the century decor. – **Os Pasteis de Belem**, rua de Belem 84 - Ideal at teatime to sample the famous pasteis of Belem, in the very factory where the recipe is jealously guarded. – **Confeteria Nacional**, prata de Figueria - Old-fashioned patisserie in the Rossio, offering delicious toasted bread sandwiches with salted butter. – **Solar do Vinho do Porto**, rua de São Pedro de Alcantara 45 - Closed Sundays. At the terminus of the Glória funicular. Tasting port wines. Wide choice, the *cálice* (glass) costs Esc 70-700.

NIGHT CLUBS

– **XXIV de Julho**, avenida XXIV de Julho 116. Young, 'in' people. – **Fragil**, rua da Atalaia 126. Since 1974. – **Kapital**, avenida XXIV de Julho 68.

SHOPPING

– **Casa Quintão**, rua Ivens 30 and **Casa de São Vicente**, Azin-

haga das Viegas 1 in Marvila, carpets from Arraiolos. – **Principe Real Enchovais**, rua Escola Polìtecnica 12, fine linen. – **Casa Regional da Illha Verde**, rua Paiva de Andrade 4, linen from the Azores. – **Madeira House**, rua Agusta 131, linen from Madiera.

CASCAIS

– **O Pescador**, rua das Flores, Tel. 21-483 20 54 Considered the best fish restaurant in Cascais. Esc 4,000-5,000. – **Visconde da Luz**, jardim Visconde da Luz, Tel. 21-486 68 48. Esc 5,000-7,000. Excellent. – **Reijos**, rua Frederico Arouca, Tel. 21-483 03 11 - Closed Sundays, Decmber 20 to Januar 19. American and Portuguese specialties. Always lots of people. Esc 2,700-4,400. – **O Batel**, travessa das Flores, Tel. 21-483 02 15 - Opposite the fish market. Reasonable prices. House specialty: lobster Thermidor. Esc 4,100. – **Granda Tasca**, rua Sebastipo José de Carvalho e Melo, Tel. 21-483 11 40 - Success has no secrets: attractive decor, good cuisine, reasonable prices. Also a wine bar.

GINCHO

(4km from Cascais)

– **Porto de Santa Maria**, Guincho road, Tel. 21-487 02 40 - Fish and shellfish. Chic and expensive. Esc 8,000-12,000. –

Mar do Gincho Estalagem, Praia do Guincho - This inn serves a very good cuisine.

ESTORIL

– **Four Seasons**, Hotel Pálacio, Tel. 21-468 04 00 - The chic seaside resort of the Portuguese riviera. Chic and elegant restaurant, and good cuisine as well. – **Tamariz** - The most popular restaurant on the Estoril beach.

QUELUZ

– **Cozinha Velha**, Palácio Nacional de Queluz, Tel. 21-435 02 32 - You lunch or dine in the kitchen of the Queluz Palace, a brilliant example of the Portuguese rococo style. Esc 4,000.

SINTRA

– **Tacho Real**, rua de Ferreria, Tel. 21-923 52 77 - Closed Wenesday. Regional and international cuisine, well prepared fish. Reservation needed. Esc 3,300-5,600. – **A Tiborna**, largo Rainha D. Amelia - Closed Wednesdays. Friendly welcome from Francisco Freitas who also serves a good cuisine of Mediterranean recipes. Esc 2,800-4,300. – **Casa Piriquita**, rua das Padarias 1/3. Specialties: Queijadas.

LOURHINÃ

– **Frutos do mar**, porto das Barcas - Closed Tuesdays. – **Nordsêe**, Porto Dinheiro beach.

Closed Wednesdays. Fish and wonderful view.

CALDAS DA RAINHA

– **Esplanade do Parco**, Dom Carlos park - **Pateo da Rainha**, rua de Cam)es 39. Regional cooking.

SETUBAL

– **Isidro**, rua Pr Augusto Gomes 1, Tel. 265-53 50 99. Esc 4,500 – **O Beco**, largo do Misericórdia 24, Tel. 265-52 46 17 - Closed Tuesdays and September 15 to October 10. Family restaurant, efficient service. Esc 2,000-3,300.

OBIDOS

– **A Ilustre Casa de Ramiro**, rua Porta do Vale, Tel. 262-95 91 94. Closed Thursday and January 5 to February 5. 4,000-5,000Esc. – **Alcaide**, rua Direita, Tel 262-95 92 20. Closed Monday and in November. Esc 3,000-4,000. – **Dom João V**, largo da Igreja Senhor da Pedra - are two small pleasant restaurants and not expensive.

CAFÉS

– **Ibn Errik Rex**, 8 de Maio. The meeting-place of Obidos society where the talk is helped along by numerous rounds of *ginjinha*.

ALCOBACA

– **Trindade**, prata Dom Alfonso Henriquez - Closed Saturdays in winter. The best stopping place after visiting the superb Cistercian monastery.

NAZARÉ

– **Arte Xavega**, Calçada do Sitio, Tel. 262-55 21 36 - Closed in November. Esc 3,000. – **Beira Mar**, avenida da República - Closed from December to February. One of the best restaurants of the port. Esc 2,000. – **Mar-Bravo**, prata Sousa Oliveira 75 - One of the most popular for fish and seafood. Esc 4,500.

FATIMA

– **O Recinto**, av. D. José Alves Correia da Silva, Tel. 249-53 30 55.In the Galeria do Parque, terrace. Esc 2,000-3,000. – **O Truão**, largo da Capela, Tel. 249-52 11 95. Typical décor and cuisine.

M   I   N   H   O

GUIMARPES

– **Vira Bar**, largo 28 de Maio, Tel. (053) 41 41 16 - One of the nicest in town. Esc 3,000-5,000. **Quinta de Castelães**, Castelães, road N 101, Tel. 253-55 70 02 - Closed Sunday evenings and Monday. Esc 4,000.In a former quinta,in the countryside. (4 km).

BRAGA BON JESUS
DO MONTE

– **O Inácio**, Campo das Hortas

4, Tel. 253-61 32 25 - Closed Mondays and first week in October. Rustic decoration and local color. Good cellar and cuisine.

VIANA DO CASTELO

– **Os 3 Potes**, Beco dos Fornos 7, Tel. 258-82 99 28 - Has everything to satisfy the tourist, typical decor and ambiance, dancing on Fridays and Saturdays in summer, but the cuisine is good. – **Alambique**, rua Manuel Espregueira 86, Tel. 258-82 38 94 - Specialties of northern Portugal including the famous *peijuada a transmontana.* – **Pastelaria Zé Natàrio**, rua dos Combatentes da Grande Guerra. Specialties: *manjeriscos de Viana* and *princesas do Lima.*

PONTE DE LIMA

– **Encanada**, av. Marginal, Tel. 258-94 11 89. After going round the market (two Mondays in every month), you can have lunch in this picturesque restaurant. – **Madalena**, Monte de Sta Maria Madalena, Sulestre (3.5km). Tel. 258-94 12 39. Closed Wenesday and November. Esc 2,500-4,000.

BARCELOS

– **Arantes**, Av. de la Liberdade, 33. Tel. 258-81 16 45. Specialties: *papas de sarabuhlo* and *pade de anho.*
– **Confeitaria Salvatão**, rua António Barroso 127. Regional

pastries: *laranjas de doce* and *les belas queijadinhas.*

CAMINHA

– **O Barão**, rua Barão de São Roque 33, Tel. 258-72 11 30 - Closed Monday evenings, Thursday and January 15 to February 15. Esc 2,000-3,000 – **Solar do Pescado**, rua Visconde de Sousa Rego 85, Tel. 258-92 27 94 - Closed Monday from October to May and November. Esc 3,000. Fish and seafood.

VALENCA DO MINHO

– **Fortaleza**, rua Apollinário da Fonseca, 5. Closed Thusday and Januar 15 to Februar 15. Esc 3,000.

TOMAR

– **Bela Vista**, on corner of rua Marques and rua Fonte do Choupo, Tel. 249-31 28 70 - Closed Monday evenings, Tuesdays and in November. Pretty view of the town.

SANTAREM

– **Portas do Sol**, jardim das Portas do Sol, Tel. (043) 295 20 - Closed Sunday evenings and Mondays. One of the best restaurants of Santarém offering a well prepared regional cuisine and a good selection of wines. Beautiful panoramic view from the terrace.

VIAL FRANCA DE XIRA

– **O Redondel**, praça de Touros. Closed Thusday and in August. Esc 3,000-4,000.

RIO MAIOR

– **Adega da Raposa**, travessa da estalagem - Closed Sunday and July. Esc 3,000 – **Cantinho da Serra**, antiga estrada - Closed Monday and July. Two good restaurants, welcoming and authentic.

FAIAL ISLAND

– **Capitolio**, rua Conselheiro Modeiros 23 – **O Lima**, rua Serpa Pinto 9.

CAFÉS

– **Peter's Friends**, the international rendez-vous for sailors landing in Horta.

SÃO MIGUEL ISLAND
PONTA DELGADA

In the center, the restaurants close early.

– **London**, rua Ernesto do Cauto 21 – **Casa Velha**, in Popolo de Cima, Tel. 296-225 00. Closed Sundays. By reservation only. – **Chez Shamin**, in São Roque, Tel. 296-312 51. On the beach. Oriental specialties.

ANGRA DO HEROISMO
– **Beira Mar**, rua de São Jopo 1
– **Marcelino**, rua de São Jopo 47.

M A D E I R A

FUNCHAL

– **Casa Vehla**, rua Imperatriz D. Amelia 69, Tel. 291-22 57 49. The best panoramic restaurant in Funchal. Esc 3,500-5,000 – **Casa dos Reis**, rua Imperatriz D Amelia 101, Tel. 291-22 51 82. Specialties: tuna and veal. Esc 4,000 – **Caravela**, rua dos Comunidades Madeirenses 15, Tel. 291-22 84 64. Esc 2,000-3,500 – **Dona Amelia**, rua Imperatriz D. Amelia 83, Tel. 291-22 57 84. Esc 3,500.

WINE TASTING

– **Madeira Wine Association**, av. de Arriaga 16. Closed Saturdays and Sundays. All the Madeira wines.

SHOPPING

– **Casa do Turista**, rua do Conselheiro; basketries, embroideries.
Flower market, behind the cathedral, every day.

INDEX

C

INDEX HOTELS AND COUNTRY INNS

239

HUNTER RIVAGES
4TH EDITION

HOTELS AND COUNTRY INNS
of Character and Charm
IN ITALY

— • WITH COLOR MAPS AND PHOTOS • —

HUNTER RIVAGES

3RD EDITION

HOTELS AND COUNTRY INNS
of Character and Charm
I N   S P A I N

• WITH COLOR MAPS AND PHOTOS •

HUNTER RIVAGES

4TH EDITION

HOTELS AND COUNTRY INNS
of Character and Charm
IN FRANCE

• WITH COLOR MAPS AND PHOTOS •